A STUDY OF BRITISH GENIUS

The Riverside Press
CAMBRIDGE · MASSACHUSETTS
PRINTED IN THE U.S.A.

PREFACE

FOR many years past material has been growing under my hands bearing on the psychological and anthropological characters of genius, and from time to time I have examined the data, and reached certain, more or less secure, conclusions. At one time indeed I hoped to set forth these conclusions and a summary of the material on which they are founded in a series of volumes. The present volume was published in 1904 as the first of these studies of genius. It would now appear that it is also likely to be the last. I am well content that this should be so. It deals with a subject which can scarcely fail to be of interest to most of us, even apart from the biological questions involved, and, as it stands, it seems to illustrate by a single concrete example of the first magnitude — the genius of Great Britain — many of the special characteristics of genius. At the same time it also illustrates the method of investigation which to me seems desirable, on one hand avoiding the superficial and casual and unsystematic ways current in the past, and, on the other hand, equally avoiding the attempt to introduce elaborate apparatus of precision which, when we bear in mind the nature of the data, would be worse than supererogatory.

In the past the phenomena of genius have mostly

I had purposed to represent the results of this study graphically by means of curves. On consideration, however, it seemed that such a method was unsuited to the nature of the data, and might tend to mislead the reader. In most of the groups of facts here dealt with the data are necessarily incomplete, and although a more thorough sifting of the sources would certainly yield further facts, they would in the end still remain incomplete. It is undesirable to give an air of precision to data which we have, indeed, good reason to consider approximately correct, but which at the same time do not enable us to reach the exact composition of the whole of the groups we are dealing with.

In bringing out this new edition after an interval of more than twenty years I have been seriously concerned as to the degree of revision and enlargement which might be desirable. In looking back at it from this distance of time I see, in the main outlines, no important modifications to make. It was prepared with much care and caution, in part as an essay in the method of studying a genius-group on the basis of the available data, and in part as an attempt to ascertain the special traits of a national group, which might later be compared with other national groups, when such other groups were similarly studied, and I had myself actively begun the study of the German national group, though I was compelled through stress of different work to lay it aside. At every point, so far as I can see, the conclusions remain as sound to-day as when I worked them out.

It has, indeed, sometimes seemed to me that I might fortify and check these conclusions by embodying in them an examination of the results yielded by the supplementary volumes of the *Dictionary of National Biography* containing lives of all the important persons of British genius who have died in the interval since my book was published. But on consideration this has seemed to me unnecessary or even undesirable. The recent group would be too small to carry much weight taken separately, while to amalgamate the recent group with the main group would involve a complete re-calculation of the results, which would not only be unlikely to reveal any significant modification, but also mean a degree of tedious labour hardly worth while to undertake again. The preparation of this book was indeed more laborious than any other work I have ever undertaken. One fails to realise beforehand that even a very crudely statistical study of this nature, with a large number of various units, involves endless possibilities of small errors and confusions, and must be slowly repeated many times to ensure absolute correctness. I still recall weary hours spent on some bench in the Luxembourg Gardens in Paris, near which I chanced then to be living, over these calculations. I am pleased to be able to add that no critic has discovered any errors in the calculations except one (an anthropologist of repute, sad to say, now no more), and his 'discovery' was merely a careless misapprehension of my statements. Moreover, while it might seem that the investigation of recent persons of genius offers special facilities, practically that is not so. Biographers of recent personages may know more, but they tell less, nor is it so easy to estimate the real intellectual stature of our contemporaries as of the men of the past, so that the perspective is likely to be injured. Therefore this study remains, on the whole, much as it was originally prepared.

It is true that in the interval I have been able to change many of the data in small details, to correct some of them and to enlarge others. I have noted a few of these modifications in the text. They could not, however, affect the general conclusions, though they might give them a little more weight. I have also enlarged some of the special discussions and I have referred to the results of various investigations along allied lines made in recent years, for the most part confirming the conclusions I have reached.

It may seem inconsistent if I proceed to say that I have added several new chapters to the volume, and I have in fact only done so with hesitation, almost with reluctance. These additional chapters, four in number, were not written to form part of the book, and therefore, to my eyes, they destroy its symmetry, since, being supplementary chapters, they follow the 'General Conclusions.' I prefer to think of the book without them. But they are all concerned with special aspects of the problem of genius and for the most part British genius. They do also really help to elucidate some of the points treated in the book, and the better because more discursively. I know also that to many readers they are of considerable interest. On these grounds, therefore, I have sought to overcome my own objection to their inclusion in this volume. As some of them were written nearly thirty years ago, it is scarcely necessary to say that they would have been written differently to-day and that more recent authorities would have been quoted. But in the main I still regard their conclusions as sound; and since the changes made necessary by time will be obvious to the instructed reader, I have preferred to leave them as they were written, save for a few minor modifications and omissions.

HAVELOCK ELLIS

CONTENTS

CONTENTS

A STUDY OF BRITISH GENIUS

A STUDY OF
BRITISH GENIUS

I

INTRODUCTORY

The problem to be investigated — The method of investigation
— The *Dictionary of National Biography* — The principles
ruling the selection of names — Cattell's method of selection —
— Reasons for the principles here adopted — Proportion of
eminent women to eminent men — The distribution of intellectual ability in the various centuries — The biological data
with which the present inquiry is chiefly concerned — Fallacies
to be avoided.

UNTIL now it has not been possible to obtain any
comprehensive view of the men and women who
have chiefly built up English civilization. It has
not, therefore, been possible to study their personal characteristics as a group. The sixty-six
volumes of the *Dictionary of National Biography*
(later increased by a second supplement of three
volumes) have for the first time enabled us to con-
struct an authoritative and well-balanced scheme
of the persons of illustrious genius, in every department, who have appeared in the British Isles from
the beginning of history down to the end of the
nineteenth century; and, with a certain amount of
labour, they assist us to sum up their main traits.
It has seemed to me worth while — both for the

sake of ascertaining the composition of those elements of intellectual ability which Great Britain has contributed to the world, and also as a study of the nature of genius generally — to utilize the *Dictionary* to work out these traits. I propose to present here some of the main conclusions which emerge from such a study.

The *Dictionary* contains some record — from a few lines to several dozen pages — of over thirty thousand persons. Now, this is an impracticable and undesirable number to deal with — impracticable because, regarding a large proportion of these persons, very little is here recorded or is even known; undesirable because it must be admitted that the majority, though persons of a certain note in their own day or their own circle, cannot be said to have made any remarkable contribution to civilization or to have displayed any very transcendent degree of native ability. My first task, therefore, was to discover a principle of selection in accordance with which the persons of relatively less distinguished ability and achievement might be eliminated. At the outset one class of individuals, it was fairly obvious, should be omitted altogether in the construction of any group in which the qualities of native intellectual ability are essential: royalty, and members of the royal family, as well as the hereditary nobility. Those eminent persons, the sons of commoners, who have founded noble families, are, of course, not excluded by this rule, according to which any eminent person whose father, at the time of his birth, had attained the rank of baronet or any higher rank, is necessarily excluded from my list. Certainly the son of a king or a peer may possess a high degree of native ability, but it is practically impossible to estimate how far that ability would have carried him had he been the son of an ordinary citizen; it might be maintained that a successful merchant, ship-owner, schoolmaster or tradesman requires as much sagacity and mental alertness as even the most successful sovereign; by eliminating those individuals in whom the accident of birth counts for so much, we put this insoluble question out of court. I am surprised to find how few persons of obviously pre-eminent ability are excluded by this rule, and many whom, at first, one would imagine it excludes, it really allows to pass, especially in the case of sons born before the father was created a peer. In order to avoid any scandalous omissions, I have thought it well to rule in all those sons of peers whose ability has clearly been of a kind which could not be aided by position and influence; thus I have included the third Earl of Shaftesbury, for it cannot be held that the possession of an earldom tends to aid a man in becoming a philosopher. It has, however, very rarely indeed been necessary to accord this privilege; I have always refrained from according it in the case of soldiers and statesmen.

Having eliminated those whose position in the world has clearly been influenced by the accident of birth, it remained to eliminate those whose place in the world, as well as in the *Dictionary*, was comparatively small. After some consideration I decided that, generally speaking, those persons to whom less than three pages were allotted were evidently not regarded by the editors, and could scarcely be generally regarded, as of the first rank of eminence. Accordingly, I excluded all those individuals to whom less than that amount of space was devoted. When this was done, however, I found it necessary to go through the *Dictionary* again, treating this rule in a somewhat more liberal manner. I had so far obtained some seven hundred names, but I had excluded many persons of undoubtedly very eminent ability and achievement; Hutton, the geologist, and Jane Austen, the novelist, for instance, could scarcely be omitted from a study of British genius. It was evident that persons with eventful lives had a better chance of occupying much space than other persons of equal ability with uneventful lives. Moreover, I found that a somewhat rigid adherence to the rule I had laid down had sometimes resulted in groups that were too small and too ill-balanced to be useful for study. In the case of musical composers, for instance, while those of recent times, of whom much is known, bulk largely in the *Dictionary*, the earlier musicians, of whom little is known, though their eminence is much greater, were excluded from my list. On the other hand, a certain number of persons had been included because, though of quite ordinary ability (like Bradshaw, the regicide), they happened by accident to have played a considerable part in history. In going through the *Dictionary* a second time, therefore, I modified my list in accordance with a new rule, to the effect that biographies occupying less than three pages should be included if the writers seemed to consider that their subjects had shown intellectual ability of a high order, and that those occupying more space should be excluded if the writers considered that their subjects displayed no high intellectual ability. In this way I eliminated those persons who rank chiefly as villains (like Titus Oates), and have little claim to the possession of any eminent degree of intellectual ability. I likewise felt compelled to exclude women (like Lady Hamilton) whose fame is not due to intellectual ability, but to beauty and to connection with eminent persons. I also omitted one or two persons for the reason that, although their claim to inclusion was unimpeachable, we are not in possession of a single definite biographical fact concerning them; from the present point of view they would merely cumber the ground.

So far as possible, it will be seen, I have sought to subordinate my own private judgment in making the selection. It has been my object to place the list, so far as possible, on an objective basis. At the same time, it is evident that, while I only reserved to myself a casting vote on doubtful points, there was inevitably a certain proportion of cases where this personal vote had to be given. A purely mechanical method of making selections would necessarily lead to various absurdities, and all that I can claim is that the principles of selection I adopted have involved a minimum of interference on my part. It is certainly true that, even after much consideration and repeated revision, I remain myself still in doubt regarding a certain proportion of people included in my list and a certain proportion omitted. Indeed any reader who finds on going through my list that there are certain omitted names which most certainly ought to have been included, and certain included names which might well be omitted, will have reached precisely the conclusion which I have myself reached. However often I went through the *Dictionary*, I know that I should each time make a few trifling readjustments, and any one else who took the trouble to go over the ground I have traversed would likewise wish to make readjustments. But I am convinced that if my principles of selection are accepted, the margin for such readjustment is narrow.

It will be observed that, by means of a slightly complicated and so far as possible objective method of selection, I have not merely sought to include only individuals of a very high order of intellectual

ability, but have at the same time sought to avoid, so far as possible, the omission of others who may have an equal claim to inclusion on account of their possession of a high degree of intellectual ability. It will at the same time be observed that I do not claim to be absolutely successful either as regards the inclusions or the omissions. I must hasten to add that any failure here very slightly impairs the primary object of this study. It has not been my main object to attain a final list to date of those British men and women who have shown the highest degree of intellectual ability. I wished to ascertain some of the biological characteristics — anthropological and psychological — of persons of the highest intellectual ability produced by Great Britain. For this purpose it was essential that the list should be carefully and impartially obtained; it was not essential that it should be faultless, although that was the ideal I set before myself.

There is some interest in comparing my list with another list, prepared by Professor Cattell, of the 1000 most eminent men that have appeared in the world generally (J. McKeen Cattell: 'A Statistical Study of Eminent Men,' *Popular Science Monthly*, February, 1903). Professor Cattell, in constructing the list, adhered rigidly to the very simple and mechanical method of selection which I had at first proposed to follow, but, as has been above explained, found it desirable in some degree to modify by the adoption of additional rules of selection. He took six biographical dictionaries — Eng-

lish, French, German, and American — and, reducing
space to a common standard, selected the 1000 persons
who were allowed the greatest average space, inclusion
in at least three of the dictionaries being regarded as an
essential condition. The list was thus, so far as Professor
Cattell was concerned, absolutely objective.

Of Professor Cattell's 1000 most eminent persons,
243, or nearly a quarter, appear to be British or to have
flourished in Great Britain. Of these as many as at
least 60 are not found in my list. (As the names in Professor Cattell's list appear without dates, the identifi-
cation is not always quite certain.) Of these 60, 33 were
excluded from my list as royal personages, and 20 as belonging to the hereditary aristocracy. There remain 7
who, since they thus figure among the 1000 most eminent persons who ever lived, ought surely to appear in
my longer list of purely British persons. One, Jeffreys,
was excluded because, although he may not have been
without legal ability, the space which he occupies in the
minds of men is not due to his ability, but to the scandal
which he caused. In a somewhat similar manner, Mac-
pherson, who appears in Professor Cattell's list but n
in mine, was excluded because, although he occupies
important position in literary history, his contribut
to literature have their main value from the tradit
they embody; he is an insignificant character wh
cidently aroused great controversies, and showed l
or no ability in his undoubtedly original literary w
Another, Thomas Brown, is a metaphysician, who,
all events in the *Dictionary*, is regarded as of little i
portance. Another, Robert Hall, was a Baptist preach
who left a reputation for pulpit oratory. The remainin
three — Arbuthnot, Armstrong, and Akenside — are
minor literary men whose productions are now unread,
though it is possible that one, Armstrong, is unde-
servedly neglected. I do not consider that the exclusion
of these seven persons reveals a very serious defect in my

list, even though it may well be that a few individuals have found their way into my list who showed intellectual ability that was of but little higher order.

An examination of Professor Cattell's list suffices to show how extremely difficult it is to obtain a reliable estimate of intellectual eminence on a simple objective basis. A test which places Napoleon III as the eleventh greatest man that ever lived — before Homer, Newton, and Alexander the Great — and includes some unread minor poets, while it excludes Gilbert, 'the father of experimental science,' is scarcely satisfactory. It is certainly better than a subjective method, but its results seem to justify such an attempt as I have made, however imperfectly, to adopt a more complexly objective method of selection.

In the final result my selection yields 975 British men of a high degree of intellectual eminence. The eminent women number 55, being in proportion to the men about 1 to 18.

A slightly lower standard of ability, it would appear, prevails among the women than among the men. On account of the greater rarity of intellectual ability in women, they have often played a large part in the world on the strength of achievements which would not have allowed a man to play a similarly large part. It seemed, again, impossible to exclude various women of powerful and influential personality, though their achievements were not always considerable. I allude to such persons as Hannah More and Mrs. Montagu. Even Mrs. Somerville, the only feminine representative of science in my list, could scarcely be included were

she not a woman, for she was little more than the accomplished popularizer of scientific results. In one department, and one only, the women seem to be little, if at all, inferior to the men in ability, that is in acting.

Professor Cattell finds the proportion of women in his list of the most eminent persons of history generally to be 3.2 per cent, while in my British list it is higher, being 5.3 per cent. This is a difference which might have been anticipated, since my list refers only to post-classical times, includes persons of a lower degree of eminence, and is concerned with a people among whom the conditions have possibly been more than usually favourable to the development of ability in women.

It may be asked how these 1030 persons of pre-eminent intellectual ability have been distributed through the course of English history. I find that from the fourth to the tenth centuries, inclusive, there are only 11 men of sufficient distinction to appear in my lists, nearly half of these belonging to the seventh century. From that date onwards (reckoning by the date of birth) we find that the eleventh century yields 5, the twelfth yields 11, the thirteenth 9, the fourteenth 16, the fifteenth 32, the sixteenth 161, the seventeenth 191, the eighteenth 372, the nineteenth 223. It is probable that the estimate most nearly corresponds to the actual facts as regards the seventeenth and eighteenth centuries. Before that time our information is too scanty, so that many men of notable ability have passed away without record. In the nineteenth

century, on the other hand, the material has been too copious, and the national biographers have probably tended to become unduly appreciative of every faint manifestation of intellectual ability. The extraordinary productiveness of the eighteenth century is very remarkable. In order to realize the significance of the facts, however, a century is too long a period. Distributing our persons of genius into half-century periods, and omitting the scanty early figures, I find that the following groups are formed:

1101–1150	1151–1200	1201–1250	1251–1300	1301–1350
4	7	2	7	6
1351–1400	1401–1450	1451–1500	1501–1550	1551–1600
10	6	26	49	112
1601–1650	1651–1700	1701–1750	1751–1800	1801–1850
112	79	134	238	219

Only four individuals belong to the second half of the nineteenth century. It is scarcely necessary to remark that the record for the first half of the nineteenth century is still incomplete. Taking the experience of the previous century as a basis, it may be estimated that some 35 per cent of the eminent persons belonging to the first half of the

nineteenth century were still alive at the time
when this inquiry terminates. This would raise
that half-century to the first place, but it may be
pointed out that the increase on the previous half-
century would be comparatively small, and also
that the result must be discounted by the inevitable tendency to overestimate the men of recent
times. We have to accept the perspective by which
near things look large and remote things look small,
but we must not be duped by it.

When we bear in mind that the activities of the
individuals in each of these groups really fall, on
the whole, into the succeeding period, certain
interesting points are suggested. We note how
the waves of Humanism and Reformation, when
striking the shores of Britain, have stirred intellectual activity, and have been prolonged and
intensified in the delayed English Renaissance.
We see how this fermentation has been continued
in the political movements of the middle of the
seventeenth century, and we note the influence of
the European upheaval at the end of the eighteenth
century. The extraordinary outburst of intellect
in the second half of that century is accentuated
by the fact that, taking into account all entries in
the *Dictionary*, the gross number of eminent men
of the low standard required for inclusion shows
little increase in the eighteenth century (5789, as
against 5674 in the preceding century, is the editor's estimate); the increase of ability is thus in

quality rather than in quantity. It is curious to note that, throughout these eight centuries, a marked rise in the level of intellectual ability has very frequently, though not invariably, been preceded by a marked fall. It is also noteworthy that in every century, from the eleventh to the eighteenth, with the exception of the seventeenth, the majority of its great men have been born in the latter half. This outburst is very distinct at the beginning of the nineteenth century, and, as we have seen reason to believe, it was probably succeeded by an arrest, if not a decline, in the production of genius.

It is noteworthy that the progress of European ability generally, as illustrated by Professor Cattell's results, has followed very much the same curve as I have found in the case of British genius. 'Following the extraordinary development of the two nations of antiquity,' Professor Cattell writes, summarising his own diagrams, 'we have a decline, not sudden, . . . but the light fails towards the fifth century. The curve shows a rise towards the tenth century, increasing in rapidity as it proceeds. There are three noticeable breaks. Thus in the fourteenth century there was a pause followed by a gradual improvement and an extraordinary fruition at the end of the fifteenth century. . . . There was a pause in progress until a century later. . . . The latter part of the seventeenth century was a sterile period, followed by a revival culminating in the French revolution.' For Europe generally, as for Great Britain, the latter half of the eighteenth century represents the unquestionable climax of genius, 238 individuals belonging to the eighteenth century altogether as against less than one hun-

dred for the previous century. Professor Cattell's curve
also shows the same general tendency for genius to become productive towards the end of each century, with
the same very marked exception in the case of the
seventeenth century, the fall here, Professor Cattell
finds, extending to nearly every department of intellectual ability. In England we might have been tempted
to attribute the fall to the social disturbance caused by
the Civil Wars, but since it was a general European
phenomenon (except in Germany, where the eighteenth-
century expansion began earliest) this is impossible; it
represents a period of rest between the activity of the late
sixteenth and early seventeenth centuries, and the still
greater intellectual energy of the eighteenth century.

When the list of eminent persons had at last been
completed my task had still scarcely begun. It was
my object to obtain as large a mass as possible of
biological data — anthropological and psychological — so that I could deal with these persons of
eminent intellectual ability as a human group and
compare them with other human groups, normal
and abnormal. I had, somewhat too innocently,
assumed that the national biographers would
usually be able to furnish the elementary data I
required, whenever such data were extant. I soon
realised, however, that the biographers were, with
a few notable exceptions, literary men, unfamiliar
with biological methods, and that they had seldom
realised that biography is not a purely literary
recreation, and that it demands something more
than purely literary aptitudes. Method was, for the
most part, conspicuously absent; if, for instance,

one wished to know if an eminent man had or had not been married, it was frequently necessary to read through the whole article to make sure that one had not missed a reference to this point; when found, one was still left frequently in doubt as to whether or not there had been offspring of the marriage, and when no reference to marriage could be found one was left in doubt as to whether this meant that there had been no marriage, or that the point was unknown, or simply that the biographer had forgotten to refer to the matter. This failure of precision in regard to so elementary a biographical fact introduced into the consideration of a very important matter a margin of error which I have had much difficulty in controlling, and it still remains considerable. Again, much trouble has been caused by the persistent vagueness of the biographers in describing the eminent man's position in his father's family. There is distinct interest in knowing the size of the family from which the great man sprang and his precise position in that family; but the biographers, in possibly the majority of cases, use such expressions as 'eldest son,' 'second son,' 'youngest son,' which tell us almost nothing. A brief personal description of the eminent man, once more, is always very instructive for biological purposes, and when the great man lived several centuries ago the biographer is usually careful to reproduce any scrap of information bearing on this point. But no such care is shown in the case of the more modern persons concerning whom the information obtainable is still copious, and even when the biographer has personally known his subject he omits, almost as a rule, to give any information regarding his personal appearance. These and the like imperfections might easily have been avoided, and the value of the *Dictionary* immensely increased, had the editors adopted the fairly obvious device of issuing a few simple instructions to their fellow-workers on the question of method.

The greatest part of my labour has been due to these defects of the *Dictionary of National Biography* in respect of those biological data which necessarily form the central and most essential part of biography. In order to supplement the information furnished by the *Dictionary* I have consulted over three hundred biographies, as well as many other sources of information in memoirs, personal reminiscences, etc. In regard to some of the more recent persons included I have been able to fill in various facts from my own knowledge. As concerns eye and hair colour I have made a systematic examination of several picture galleries, more especially the National Portrait Gallery.

Having thus explained the nature of the data with which we have to deal, and the methods by which it has been obtained, we may now proceed, without further explanations, to investigate it. We have to study the chief biological characteris-

tics — anthropological and psychological — of the
most eminent British men and women of genius,
here using that word merely to signify high intellectual ability.

II

NATIONALITY AND RACE

The determination of place of origin — Birthplaces of grandparents the best available criteria — Relative productiveness
in genius of England, Wales, Scotland, and Ireland — The
group of mixed British origin — The group of mixed British
and foreign origin — Importance of the French element —
Origins of eminent British women — The distribution of
English genius according to counties — The genius of Kent —
The regional distribution of English women of ability — The
probable predominance of Norfolk and Suffolk in relative
amount of ability — The three great foci of English genius —
The East Anglian focus — The apparent poverty of London in
aboriginal genius — The south-western focus — The Welsh
Border — The Anglo-Danish district — The psychological
characteristics of East Anglian genius — The characteristics of
the south-western focus — The characteristics of the Welsh
Border — The significance of the position of Kent — The
distribution of genius in Wales — The distribution of genius in
Scotland — The distribution of genius in Ireland — The
regional distribution of various kinds of ability — The distribution of scientific ability — The regional variations of scientific
aptitude — The distribution of eminent soldiers — The distribution of eminent sailors — The distribution of artists —
The distribution of dramatic ability — The possible modification of racial factors by environmental conditions.

IT is scarcely necessary to remark that nationality
and race, when used as distinguishing marks of
people who all belong to the British Islands, are
not identical terms and are both vague. The
races — however we may describe them * —
constituting the people of Great Britain are to be
found in all the main divisions of the two islands,

* For summary of the position of this question, see Ripley's
Races of Europe, ch. XII.

and the fact that a man is English or Scotch or Irish tells us nothing positive as to his race. Some indication of race, however, is in many cases furnished if we know the particular district to which a man's ancestors belonged, and this indication is further strengthened if we can ascertain his physical type.

In determining on a large scale the place of origin of men of genius the usual method hitherto has been to adopt the crude plan of noting the birthplace. I have so far as possible discarded this method, for a man's birthplace obviously tells us nothing decisive as to his real place of origin.

It has seemed to me that a man's place of origin can most accurately be determined by considering the districts to which his four grandparents belonged. If we know this we know with considerable certainty in what parts of the country he is really rooted, and in many cases we can thus form an estimate of his probable race. I have expended a very considerable amount of time and trouble over this part of my inquiry; yet so vague, confused, or conflicting is often the available evidence that probably none of my groups of data contain so many slight inaccuracies as this. It is only in a very small proportion of cases (even when the information derived from the *Dictionary* is supplemented) that I have been able to determine the origins of all four grandparents; I have usually considered myself fortunate when I have been able to tell where the father and mother came from, and have often been well content merely to find out where the father came from. Only in a few cases have I admitted the evidence of birthplace.* London as a birthplace has been ignored altogether. When the facts are available it is nearly always found that the parents had migrated to London; we may reasonably assume that this is probably the case when the facts are not available. It very rarely occurs (as in the case of J. Bentham) that even one grandparent belonged to London.

In order to represent the varying values of this evidence, I have adopted a system of marks. If the four grandparents are of known origin, an eminent man is entitled to four marks, these marks being divided among the counties to which he belongs; when the evidence is less explicit the marks are correspondingly diminished. By this method I am able to give due weight to the very numerous cases in which the parents (or grandparents) belonged to different parts of the kingdom.

Every one of the 1030 persons included in this inquiry may be definitely classed, with at all events a fair degree of probability, in one part or another of the British Islands. When this is done we obtain the following results:

* This evidence varies in value; in the case of an eminent person whose father was a farmer it is fairly acceptable; but if the father was a clergyman it has little or no value.

English	659	Mixed British	97
Welsh	28	Mixed British and foreign	46
Scotch	137		
Irish	63		

Omitting for the moment the individuals of mixed ancestry, we find that 74.2 per cent are English, 3.1 Welsh, 15.4 Scotch and 7.1 Irish. If we take the basis of the present population and regard the proportion of eminent persons produced by England as the standard, Wales has produced slightly less than her share of persons of ability, Ireland still less, and Scotland decidedly more than her share.

As regards Wales we have to bear in mind the difficulty of a different language. As regards Scotland we probably have to recognise that intellectual aptitudes are especially marked among the Scotch, and also that the tendency has been fostered by circumstances, since, as is well known, the lowland Scotch are almost identical in racial composition with the northern English, and there are no artificial barriers of language. On the other hand, the Irish have been seriously hampered by geographical and to some extent by linguistic barriers, as well as by unfortunate political circumstances, in contributing their due share to British civilisation.

Mr. A. H. H. Maclean has shown (*Where We Get Our Best Men*, London, 1900) that of some 2500 British persons of ability belonging to the nineteenth century 70 per cent are English, 18 per cent Scotch, 10 per cent

Irish, and 2 per cent Welsh. We thus find that, by taking a much lower standard of ability and confining ourselves to the most recent period, Scotland stands higher than ever, while Ireland benefits very greatly at the expense of both England and Wales. This is probably not altogether an unexpected result. It is on the whole confirmed by an analysis of British *Men of the Time*, made by Dr. (now Sir) Conan Doyle (*Nineteenth Century*, August, 1888).

Both Mr. Maclean and Sir Conan Doyle adopted the crude test of birthplace. The somewhat higher place which they give to the Irish is, however, really confirmed by the analysis of my results. At an earlier stage of my inquiry, when the standard of ability adopted was higher, and the most recent group of eminent persons (those included in the supplement to the *Dictionary of National Biography*) had not been added, I found that the English contribution was larger, and the Irish smaller, than I now find it. It appears evident that possibly with some lowering of the standard of ability, and certainly with the advent of modern times, the Irish contribution tends to reach a larger proportion.

When we turn to consider the 143 persons who are of mixed British, or mixed foreign and British, race, we find that they may be divided as follows:

English and Irish	33
English and Scotch	30
English and Welsh	25
Mixed British, other than above	9
British and foreign	46

In percentages these results are: English and Irish, 23; English and Scotch, 20.9; English and Welsh, 17.4; other British, 6.2; British and foreign, 32.1. We here reach the interesting result that not-

withstanding the extreme frequency of English-
Scotch marriages, and the very high proportion of
ability among the unmixed Scotch, the English-
Irish group stands, even absolutely, above the
English-Scotch group, while the English-Welsh
group is still more largely out of proportion with
the small pure Welsh group, and is not far behind
the English-Scotch group. It would appear that,
so far as ability is concerned, the Irish and the
Welsh are much better adapted for crossing with
the English than are the more closely related
Scotch.

There are forty-six persons in whom one or more
elements of foreign blood are mingled with one or
more British elements. These do not, of course,
include all the foreigners who have played a part
in English civilisation, since no person of purely
foreign blood was taken into account in the preparation of my list. This has, for instance, led to the
omission of numerous early Normans (like Becket)
some later French Huguenots (like Romilly), and
several eminent Jews.

Even though the purely French persons of eminence are omitted, the French elements remain
distinctly the most important. At least seventeen
of our forty-six individuals of partly foreign origin
have had a French parent or grandparent. Some
of these were Huguenots. No account has been
taken of ancestors beyond the grandparents, but
a Huguenot ancestral element seemingly more re-

and indeed the inevitable, basis for this part of the inquiry is the division into counties. It is, however, a very awkward and inconvenient basis. The counties are very unequal in size, usually too small, and in most cases they correspond to no ancient boundaries. They have neither the historical significance of the ancient French provinces, nor the practical convenience of the modern French departments. The ancient English dioceses furnish on the whole a better basis and one that for the most part corresponds to real ancient divisions;* but it was obviously inconvenient and inadvisable to fall back on an extinct division of the country. It was necessary to be content with the county basis and to seek so far as possible to minimise its disadvantages.

In the first place the English counties may be presented in accordance with the absolute number of elements of ability which each possesses, with no attempt to show the significance of the numbers. It will, of course, be remembered (and may be clearly seen by reference to Appendix B) that in consequence of the imperfection of our knowledge these elements are of disparate value, so that while one individual may be counted four times (*i.e.*, once for each of his grandparents), another may only be counted once. Most individuals are counted twice.

---

* See, *e.g.*, G. Hill, *English Dioceses*.

Yorkshire	90	Hampshire	19
Norfolk	67	Buckinghamshire	19
Devon	56	Northamptonshire	18
Kent	51	Hertfordshire	18
Suffolk	50	Herefordshire	17
Lancashire	43	Oxfordshire	16
Lincolnshire	37	Cumberland	16
Somerset	30	Nottinghamshire	16
Cornwall	30	Leicestershire	15
Gloucestershire	28	Cambridgeshire	15
Essex	27	Surrey	14
Warwickshire	26	Westmoreland	11
Shropshire	24	Sussex	10
Staffordshire	24	Durham	8
Wiltshire	24	Bedfordshire	8
Northumberland	20	Berkshire	8
Worcestershire	20	Rutland	6
Derbyshire	19	Middlesex	5
Cheshire	19	Huntingdonshire	5
Dorset	19	Monmouth	3

The significance of these results is not quite obvious to casual inspection. We see that the origins of English ability are to be found all over the country, and we see also, as we should expect, that the large counties have produced much ability and the small counties little. How can we ascertain the real significance of these figures?

There are two methods we may adopt for ascertaining the significance of our figures: we may determine the amount of ability in each county in relation to its area, or we may determine it in relation to its population.

The method of comparison which rests on ascertaining the relative amount of ability per square mile for each county is not so absurd in the case of a country like England as it may possibly seem to Kent; it was the home of Marlowe and Lyly, the two teachers of Shakespeare, as well as of Linacre and Harvey, who represent the English Renaissance on the scientific side; at that period it was prolific in administrators, diplomatists, and soldiers. It was strongly Royalist, and suffered greatly in the cause of Charles I. When Charles fell, Kent fell so far as genius-producing power is concerned,* and however it may continue to flourish in population and general prosperity, it has never regained its power to add largely to English ability. In the sixteenth and seventeenth centuries its contributions to the elements of English ability are represented by the figures 15 and 16 respectively — relatively a very large proportion; but in the eighteenth century, so fertile in ability, Kent is only responsible for the relatively small contribution of eleven elements, and in the nineteenth century its contribution has sunk to four elements, which do not include a single individual who was wholly Kentish. Yet, as we shall see, Kent stands almost, if not quite, at the head of all the English counties in its total contribution to English genius. Although no other county could be found to furnish so remarkable an instance of great intellectual fertility fol-

* It cannot be said that this coincidence adequately explains the phenomenon. Dr. Beddoe suggested to me that the decline of Kent may be largely due to the attraction of London draining away its best stocks, and that we may thus account for the fact that Surrey, Essex, and even Suffolk, stand lower in genius-producing power for the nineteenth century than for the whole period.

lowed by intellectual decadence, without decrease in population and prosperity, this case is enough to show that we can by no means assume that the intellectual fertility of a county in one century is any certain index to its general intellectual fertility.

I now present, side by side, the order of decreasing intellectual fertility into which fall the counties our eminent men belong to when we consider the relative amount of the total ability for the whole period on the basis of area (taken as per 1000 square miles), and also the order into which the elements for the nineteenth century fall on the basis of the population of the counties in 1841. A plus sign after the figures in the first column indicates that as the modern population of the county in question is very decidedly below the average for the country generally, we probably ought to add a few units to the figures given; a minus sign indicates that as the modern population is much above the average for the country generally, we probably ought to subtract a few units to reach a fair estimate; the sign of equality means that the population of the county approximates to the average for the country generally. Those counties which contain a proportion of elements of genius equal to more than 19 to the 1000 square miles, or more than 2 per 100,000 inhabitants, must be considered prolific in genius.

	Amount of ability in ratio per 1000 square miles		Amount of ability during 19th century in ratio per 100,000 inhabitants (1841)
Rutland	40+	Norfolk	5.3
Suffolk	33+	Herefordshire	4.3
Kent	32—	Oxfordshire	4.3
Norfolk	31+	Hertfordshire	3.8
Warwickshire	29—	Worcestershire	3.8
Hertfordshire	28+	Westmoreland	3.6
Worcestershire	27—	Dorsetshire	3.4
Buckinghamshire	25+	Cumberland	3.4
Cornwall	22+	Warwickshire	2.7
Gloucestershire	22=	Cornwall	2.6
Lancashire	22—	Buckinghamshire	2.5
Devonshire	21+	Shropshire	2.5
Oxfordshire	21+	Northumberland	2.4
Herefordshire	20+	Wiltshire	2.3
Staffordshire	20—	Cambridgeshire	2.3
Nottinghamshire	19+	Lincolnshire	2.2
Dorsetshire	19+	Suffolk	2.1
Northamptonshire	18+	Nottinghamshire	2.0
Leicestershire	18+	Berkshire	1.8
Somerset	18+	Devonshire	1.5
Shropshire	18+	Yorkshire	1.5
Cambridgeshire	18+	Derbyshire	1.4
Derbyshire	18=	Cheshire	1.2
Surrey	18—	Gloucestershire	1.2
Cheshire	18—	Hampshire	1.1
Essex	17+	Leicestershire	.9
Wiltshire	17+	Somerset	.9
Bedfordshire	17+	Lancashire	.8
Middlesex	17	Staffordshire	.8
Westmoreland	14+	Essex	.8
Yorkshire	14=	Kent	.7
Huntingdonshire	13+	Sussex	.4
Lincolnshire	13+	Surrey	.3
Berkshire	11+	Durham	.3
Hampshire	11+	Bedfordshire	0
Cumberland	10+	Northamptonshire	0
Northumberland	9+	Huntingdonshire	0
Sussex	7+	Monmouth	0
Durham	7—	Rutland	0
Monmouth	5+	Middlesex, omitted *	

* There are three units to Middlesex, but not having the population for Middlesex in 1841, excluding the metropolis, I have not included this county.

If we consider the eminent women separately we find that eleven English counties have produced more than one unit of ability. The absolute numbers are as follows:

Norfolk	9	Lancashire	2
Suffolk	5	Worcestershire	2
Yorkshire	4	Shropshire	2
Hereford	3	Devonshire	2
Kent	3	Cornwall	2
Northumberland	3		

The numbers are too small to make it worth while to attempt to ascertain the relative value of these figures. It is sufficiently clear that Norfolk stands first and that Suffolk, a much smaller county, follows very closely after.*

Although the estimate of ability on the basis of the area of the counties is obviously only roughly approximate, while the more reliable method of ascertaining the proportion to population during the nineteenth century suffers from the defect that it by no means necessarily indicates the amount of ability in previous centuries, and while both methods are hampered by the very small size of many of the counties, we may still reach certain conclusions by considering the two lists together. The counties that stand high on both lists have probably been highly productive of intellectual

* Conan Doyle in his analysis of *Men of the Time* found that 'Suffolk appears to be pre-eminently the county of famous women.' Macfarlane (*Lady's Realm*, March, 1911) classified all the women in the *Dictionary* according to birthplace, and found that (putting aside London, and Yorkshire for its size) Norfolk comes first, followed by Suffolk and Somerset.

ability; those that stand low in both lists have probably been markedly unproductive. We may probably believe that the counties that have contributed most largely to the making of English men of genius are Norfolk, Suffolk, Hertfordshire, Warwickshire, Worcestershire, Herefordshire, Buckinghamshire, Cornwall, Dorsetshire, Oxfordshire, and Shropshire. To these we must certainly add Kent, since its total output more than compensates for its intellectual decadence during recent centuries; but we are perhaps scarcely justified in including Rutland, which by a curious anomaly appears at the head of the first list, though the smallest and one of the most thinly populated of English counties.

It cannot hastily be assumed that, while these counties rank probably at the head of English counties from the intellectual point of view, there are not others which perhaps on a perfectly sound basis ought not to rank almost on a level with them. This would especially be so if we were to take quality of genius as well as quantity into consideration. It is probable that Somerset, Devonshire, Gloucestershire, Wiltshire and Essex should be included among those of the first rank, although the two associated East Anglian counties of Norfolk and Suffolk have a fairly assured position at the head.

Maclean, who finds that Suffolk is among the six English counties which on the basis of population contributed the largest number of eminent men to the Victorian period, places Ipswich first among the towns (excluding the large cities) which have been prolific in ability. Sir Conan Doyle, investigating *Men of the Time*, finds that Suffolk is among the three English counties that stand first in production of intellectual ability on the basis of population, and remarks that its intellectual productivity is 'quite phenomenal.'

It must be remembered that these inquiries were on the basis of birthplace, and that as East Anglians show a marked tendency to emigrate westwards, and especially to London, in a large number of cases they are credited to other districts.

On the basis of these results, and taking into consideration also the special quality of the individuals (as may be done by studying Appendix B), we come, I believe, to the conclusion that there are two, or, rather, three, great foci of intellectual ability in England: the East Anglian focus, the south-western focus, and the focus of the Welsh Border.

The East Anglian focus may for the present purpose be said to include not only Norfolk and Suffolk, but also the adjoining counties of Essex, Cambridgeshire and Hertfordshire, which, though inferior both in the quantity and the quality of their genius to East Anglia proper, are still high in intellectual ability which is nearly always of distinctively East Anglian type; these five counties form a compact whole. Among the eminent men who, so far as our knowledge, sometimes limited, extends, belong wholly to this region are Bishop

Andrewes, the Bacons, Thomas Cavendish, Chaucer (?), Constable, Cotman, Cowper, Cranmer, Flaxman, John Fletcher, Gainsborough, William Gilbert, Grosseteste, the Lyttons, Nelson, the Newmans, Porson, Pusey, Ray, the Veres, Robert Walpole and Wolsey. Among those who belong in part to this region are Airy, the Arnolds, Barrow, Bradlaugh, Colet, Gresham, Stephen Hales, Charles Lamb, the Martineaus, Sir Thomas More, Pater, Sir Thomas Smith and Walsingham. Ethnologically, it may be remarked, this focus is the most recent of the three. East Anglia is a region very open to invasion; Brythons, Romans, Angles, and Normans all seem to have come here in large numbers; and it differs from every other English district (except to some extent Kent, a county closely allied to it) in continuing to welcome foreigners — Dutch, Flemish, Walloon, French — all through mediæval times, down to the revocation of the Edict of Nantes at the end of the seventeenth century.

Middlesex with London lies on the borders of the East Anglian focus, with which, probably, of all the foci of English genius it is most intimately connected. It can scarcely, however, be included within that focus. The Metropolis itself is excluded from our inquiry, partly because we are not taking the accident of birthplace into account, and partly because it seems impossible to find any eminent person who belongs to London, or even to

Middlesex, through all his grandparents. Middle-sex is poor in aboriginal ability, even for a small county, and if we were to class it psychologically at all I believe it would fall in with the predominantly Saxon group of counties which includes Berkshire, Surrey, Sussex and Hampshire — a group which, as we shall see, constitute a district remarkably poor in aboriginal ability.

The marked prevalence of merely native ability in London, and the marked deficiency of really aboriginal ability, are phenomena alike easy of explanation. Among the crowds who drift into every great metropolis there are always many clever and ambitious people; hence the number of able persons who are merely con-nected with a metropolis by the accident of birth. But a great metropolis swiftly kills those whom it attracts; Cantlie (*Degeneration amongst Londoners*, 1885, p. 19) very properly defined a Londoner as one whose parents and grandparents were born and bred in London; but during the four years in which he investigated this ques-tion he was unable to find a single Londoner in this true and definite sense, and even those who were Londoners back to the grandparents on one side only, were usually stunted or feeble, and unlikely to propagate. Dr. Harry Campbell (*Causation of Disease*, p. 245) among 200 London-born children found two or three whose parents and grandparents were born and bred in London, and these children were very delicate.

The south-western focus of English genius is the largest, and although in proportion to the population ability is here less prevalent than in the East Anglian district, in absolute amount, and perhaps even in importance, this region may perhaps be said to oe the most conspicuous centre of English intellectual energy. I regard it as comprising the counties of Wiltshire, Somerset, Dorset, Devon, and Cornwall. These counties, together with part of Hampshire, make up the whole of the south-western promontory of Great Britain. The population of this region is marked by very much darker hair, and therefore a much higher index of nigrescence, than the population of the counties to east of it. The district is defended by Wansdyke and Bokerley Dyke, one of the most important structures of this kind in Europe, and this fact indicates that the region was once arrayed against the rest of Britain. Pitt-Rivers * has shown that this wall is of Roman or post-Roman date, possibly Saxon. This great focus of British genius is, taken altogether, unquestionably the oldest of the three foci which we may detect in England. We may call it the Goidelic-Iberian centre. It is well known that this region was the last stronghold of the early British power in England; when, finally, its power was broken in war the Saxon invaders had become Christianised and settled peacefully side by side with the aboriginal inhabitants. The people of this region were still described by King Alfred as 'Welsh Kin,' and the predominance of the aboriginal element may still be detected in the characteristics of the genius of this region. Among the more eminent

* *Excavations in Cranborne Chase*, vol. 3.

individuals who seem to belong wholly to this region are Roger Bacon, Blackstone, Robert Blake, Saint Boniface, Clifford, Coleridge, Dampier, Drake, Saint Dunstan, Ford, Grocyn, Hawkins, Hobbes, Hooker, John of Salisbury, Keats, Locke, Pym, Raleigh, Reynolds, Rodney, Alfred Stevens, Sydenham, Trevithick, Thomas Young. Among those who belong to it in part are Matthew Arnold, Bradley, Browning, Byron, the Cannings, Fielding, C. J. Fox, Froude, Huxley, the Kingsleys, and the Pitts.

The third focus, that of the Welsh Border, includes the counties of Gloucestershire, Warwickshire, Worcestershire, Herefordshire, Shropshire, and Cheshire. This selection of counties may possibly seem a little arbitrary, but it will be found not to be so on turning to the anthropological map of the British Islands (as given, for instance, in Ripley's *Races of Europe*), founded on Beddoe's observations of the index of nigrescence. These six counties form a dark-haired borderland in western England against Wales, and the eastern enfolding to Warwickshire cannot be disregarded.* Monmouth is properly excluded; its contribution to English genius is extremely minute; it was not

---

* There is a curious and compact island of very dark-haired peoples in the counties to the north of London, possibly connected with the Warwick enfolding of the Welsh Border; and the Chiltern Hills evidently proved a refuge for the earlier and darker peoples of Britain, like Devon and Cornwall; but any psychological affinity of the inhabitants of these counties with those of the Welsh Border does not seem to be clear, though it is possible.

even nominally English until the time of Henry VIII; it still remains anthropologically Welsh, and the study of its surnames shows, as Guppy states in his *Homes of Family Names*, that it is even more Welsh than Wales. The counties here included in the Welsh Border are all much more thoroughly Anglicised, but Welsh was spoken in most of them until comparatively recent times, even in Gloucestershire, undoubtedly a very mixed county.* The language of Shropshire has been described as 'English spoken as a foreign language.' In Herefordshire Welsh appears to be not quite extinct even yet.† The whole of the district represents the mingling on the one side of Welsh elements, on the other of Saxon and Anglian elements. It is not difficult to account for this mingling; when in the eighth century Offa extended the limits of Mercia westwards, changing the name of the British town of Pengwyrn to Shrewsbury, he adopted the policy of leaving on the land all the Britons who wished to remain; in more recent times there has been a Welsh reflux eastwards, and the result is a fairly thorough assimilation of Welsh and English racial elements. The Welsh elements have been regarded as predominantly Bry-

* 'The Transsabrina is very "aboriginal" and dark-haired,' remarks Dr. Beddoe; 'the Cotswolds are largely Saxon and fair; the Vale lies between in race as in position.'

† Rhys and Brynmor-Jones, *The Welsh People*, p. 526; cf. Southall, *Wales and Her Language*, especially ch. ix, dealing with traces of Welsh in the Marches.

thonic rather than Goidelic, the latter people being mainly confined to the north-west and south-west districts of Wales. It may therefore be said that this Anglo-Brythonic district of the Welsh Border is intermediate in age between the recent East Anglian focus and the ancient south-western focus.

Among the more eminent individuals who belong wholly to the Welsh Border are Alexander of Hales, Samuel Butler, Warren Hastings, Sir Thomas Lawrence, Shakespeare, Purcell, William Tyndale and Wycherley. Among those who belong to it in part are Robert Boyle, John Bright, Sir Thomas Browne, Clive, Charles Darwin, Fielding, Keble, the Herberts, the Kembles, Landor, Macaulay, Map, William Morris, the Penns, Wedgwood, the Wesleys, Wren, Wycherley.

It will be noted that all three of the great foci of English intellect belong mainly to the southern half of the country, the most anciently civilised part, although within recent centuries the least prosperous and the most thinly populated. It must be added that nearly the whole of the northern part of England from Lincolnshire, Nottinghamshire and Derbyshire, through Yorkshire well on into the Lowlands of Scotland, constitutes a large region which, although its intellectual elements are of no great density, presents its own peculiar anthropological characters. It is the predominantly Anglo-Danish part of England, containing the fairest

population of the country.* Its intellectual fertility is greatest in its northern portions, which now
form part of Scotland, and at its southern border,
where it blends with East Anglia. To this last
district belongs Sir Isaac Newton, the supreme
representative of Anglo-Danish genius.†

Apart from exact science and from scholarship,
the Anglo-Danish district, in proportion to its size,
has not produced many men in purely intellectual
fields. Its children have usually been more remarkable for force of character than for force
of intellect. Their stubborn independent temper
involves an aptitude for martyrdom; many religious martyrs come from this region, and the mar-
tyrologist Foxe also. East Anglia is productive of
great statesmen and great ecclesiastics; it is also

* Leicestershire should doubtless be included in the Anglo-
Danish district. On the basis of place-names Taylor finds it to be
the most Danish county in England. Beddoe's map of the index of
nigrescence, however, shows it to be ethnologically darker than the
Anglo-Danish district proper. Psychologically its genius seems to
me rather mixed but certainly in large measure Anglo-Danish.

† I was formerly inclined to think that Lincolnshire and
Nottinghamshire should be affiliated to the East Anglian focus, but
a more careful consideration of the facts leads to the conclusion
that, on the whole, both anthropologically and psychologically
they belong to the Anglo-Danish district. I still think that the
northern portion of Northamptonshire, and still more emphatically
Rutland, are mainly East Anglian in the character of their genius.
The former county, however, seems to present a very special and
vigorous mixture of East Anglian, Anglo-Danish and aboriginal
elements. (At the Norman Conquest, also, Fleming and Picard
elements were introduced here. *Victoria History of Northamptonshire*, vol. I, p. 289.) It is not easy to fix the exact western limits
of the East Anglian district unless we boldly carry it as far as the
Welsh Border counties, Warwickshire and Gloucestershire.

a land of great scholars. At the same time nearly half the British musical composers and more than a third of the painters have come from this same region. It has no aptitude for abstract thinking, for metaphysics, but in concrete thinking, in the art of treating science philosophically, it is easily supreme. Its special characters seem to be its humanity, its patience, its grasp of detail, its deliberate flexibility, combined with a profound love of liberty and independence.* The characteristic English love of compromise is rooted in East Anglia. So typically English a statesman as Walpole, with his sound instincts in practical affairs, belonged to Norfolk, and Wolsey belonged to Suffolk. In spite, however, of the marked sanity and self-possession of the East Anglian, it may be added that while East Anglia has produced many of the best Englishmen it has also produced a considerable proportion of the worst.† Those who figure in English history chiefly by virtue of their villainy do not appear in my list, but it is notable that many of the great men who have come down to us with a somewhat flawed reputation

* It may be noted that the founders of New England, both on the political and the religious side, were largely produced by East Anglia. The Washingtons came from the related county of Northamptonshire; the Emersons were from Suffolk, or Saffron Walden in Essex on the borders of Suffolk; Winthrop, who, it has been said, more than any other man moulded Massachusetts which moulded New England, belonged to Central Suffolk.

† It must be added, at the same time, that the records of criminality, at all events during the nineteenth century, by no means show the East Anglian counties among the worst.

belong here; Bacon is a typical example of the first rank.

When we turn to the south-western focus of English genius we find ourselves among people of different mental texture, but of equal mental distinction. In positive intellectual achievement they compare with the slow and patient people of East Anglia, while as brilliant personalities they are in the very first rank. They are sailors rather than scholars, and courtiers, perhaps, rather than statesmen; they are innovators, daring free-thinkers, pioneers in the physical and intellectual worlds. Raleigh, on both sides a Devonshire man, is the complete type of these people. They are, above all, impressive personalities, aggressive, accomplished, irresistible, breaking rather than bending, without the careful foresight of the laborious and self-distrustful people of the east coast. This district alone has furnished a third of the great sailors of Britain, and the most brilliant group, with Drake and Hawkins and Gilbert as well as Raleigh. The expansive Elizabethan age gave the men of these parts their supreme chance, and they availed themselves of it to the utmost. Great Britain's most eminent soldiers have not usually been English, but one of the most famous of all, Marlborough, belongs to this region. In the arts of peace this south-western focus shows especially well in painting. It cannot, indeed, be compared to the East Anglian focus in this respect, but Reynolds belongs to

Devon, and is a typical representative of the
qualities of this region on the less aggressive side,
just as Raleigh is on the more militant side, both
alike charming and accomplished personalities.
Both in the material and spiritual worlds there is
an imaginative exaltation, an element of dash and
daring, in the men of this south-western district,
which seems to carry them through safely. The
south-western focus is not quite so homogeneous
as the eastern group. Somerset, which is the centre
of the focus, seems to me to present its real and
characteristic kernel, especially on the purely intellectual side. We do not find here the dashing
recklessness, the somewhat piratical tendency, nor
quite the same brilliant personal qualities as at the
western part of the peninsula. The Somerset group
of men are superficially more like those of East
Anglia, but in reality with a very distinct physiog-
nomy of their own. Like the rest of this region,
Somerset is a land of great sailors, but the typical
sailor hero of Somerset is Blake, and the difference
between Blake and Raleigh is significant of the
difference between the men of Somerset and the
men of Devon.* Somerset with Wiltshire has pro-

* I now place William Blake also in this region. The patriotic
advocacy by Mr. Yeats of Dublin as the ancestral home of
William Blake had led me astray; there is no sound basis for this
ancestry. On the contrary (it is stated by A. T. Story in his life
of Blake) the cousins of William Blake at Southampton had a
tradition that the family is descended from the Somerset Blakes
of the Admiral's family, through a branch settled in Wiltshire.
William Blake would thus be brought into the same south-western

duced the philosophers of this region, Roger Bacon, Hobbes, Locke; and in more recent days Bagehot and Huxley have been typical thinkers of the group. Hooker, the 'judicious,' is among the men of Devon. They are not often scholars (notwithstanding the presence of the 'ever-memorable' Hales), being prone to rely much on their own native qualities. One recalls the remark of Hobbes, when charged with an indifference to books: 'If I read as much as other people I should know as little as other people.' While less concrete than the East Anglians, these eminent thinkers have not the abstract metaphysical tendencies of the North British philosophers; they reveal a certain practical sagacity, a determination to see things clearly, a hatred of cant and shams, a 'positive' tendency, which is one of the notes of purely English thought and may be said to have its headquarters here. The representative scientific man of this region is the brilliant and versatile Thomas Young, whose luminous intelligence and marvellous intuition render him a typical example of genius in its purest form.

It is easy to define the nature of the genius of the Welsh Border. It is artistic in the widest sense, and notably poetic; there is a tendency to literary

focus of English genius as Coleridge, Keats, and other great poets, while it may be added that his characteristics are much in harmony with those of the men of Somerset. If Ireland thus probably loses one of the great figures on my list, she probably gains another in Faraday (p. 57) and the balance is maintained.

and oratorical eloquence, frequently tinged with religious or moral emotion, and among those who belong entirely to this district there are no scientific men of the first order. This region has the honour of claiming Shakespeare; and it may be pointed out that it is difficult to account for Shakespeare without assuming in him the presence of a large though not predominant Celtic element.* Landor, one of the greatest of English masters of prose, comes in part within the Welsh Border, as does Fielding, while Purcell, one of the greatest of English composers, also probably belongs to this district. Sir Thomas Browne, though only a Welsh Borderer on his father's side, is very typical, and Macaulay is characteristic of the Celt as historian. The presence of Mrs. Siddons, although the genius of the Kemble family is attributed mainly to their Irish mother, helps to indicate the characteristics of this region, which although it has produced fewer great personalities than the two main foci of English genius, has certainly had its full share in some of the very greatest. The part of the Welsh Border in Darwin was small, but though he was more characteristically a son of the Anglo-Danish and East Anglian regions, it was probably not without its influence.

It has already been made clear that the county of Kent constitutes a remarkable, though small,

For a discussion of the 'Celtic element' in English genius see a later chapter (pp. 213–43).

centre of English genius. I was formerly inclined
to regard this very interesting district as depend-
ent on the important East Anglian focus. I am
convinced, however, that this is a mistake. If we
carefully contemplate the eminent persons produced by Kent it will be seen that they can be
more easily affiliated, on the whole, to the south-
western than to the East Anglian focus. Harvey,
for instance, the greatest of the Kentish men, re-
sembled the south-western people as much in intellectual temperament, as, by his short stature,
dark hair and eyes, choleric constitution, he re-
sembled them anthropologically. This seeming
affinity of the genius of Kent to that of the south-
western promontory, though it cannot be said to
be complete identity, may perhaps be regarded as
one of the numerous facts which tend to invalidate
the belief, widely prevalent a few years ago under
the influence of several eminent historians and
ultimately resting on some rhetorical expressions of
Gildas,* that the Romano-British inhabitants of
Kent were entirely exterminated by the Teutonic
invaders.

Undoubtedly, however, the Teutonic element
is considerable in all this south-eastern part of
England, as far westwards as Wilts. One is indeed

* Professor H. Williams, in his edition of Gildas (*Cymmrodorion
Record Soc.* 1899, Part I), points out that Gildas is not an historian,
but a preacher of righteousness who is simply seeking to show how
divine anger visits sin. Beddoe finds early elements persisting in
the Kentish population.

tempted to ask whether it may serve to explain another psychological phenomenon which is revealed by the distribution of English genius. The Jutes came to Kent; the Saxons occupied the regions to the west of Kent. This district, including (with Kent and Essex) the whole of the light-haired populations of southern England, is occupied by the counties of Sussex, Surrey, Hampshire and Berkshire. Except in so far as Surrey is suburban to London and profits by this proximity, all this region is comparatively bare of aboriginal genius. Mackintosh observed, in his notable study of the psychic characteristics of British peoples, that the unmixed English Saxon, unlike the Angle (and possibly unlike the Jute), is marked by mental mediocrity. One is tempted to ask whether this fact, if it is a fact, may be invoked to explain the result of the present inquiry as regards this region.

I do not propose to consider in detail the distribution of ability in the other parts of the British Islands, for the figures are here too small to yield reliable results. The distribution of ability in Wales, Scotland and Ireland is, however, so definitely confined to certain districts that a mere inspection of the crude figures suffices to give us for each of these countries a fairly close conception of their intellectual geography.

In the case of Wales the elements of ability are distributed as follows:

Glamorganshire	7	Anglesey	3
Denbighshire	7	Cardiganshire	1
Montgomeryshire	6	Pembrokeshire	1
Radnorshire	6	Merionethshire	1
Flintshire	3	Caermarthenshire	0
Carnarvonshire	3		

It is not difficult to understand why a large, fertile and populous district like Glamorganshire — even leaving out of account its commercial and mining activities — should stand high in actual numbers, although it stands lower in proportion to area and very low in relation to population. It is more remarkable that Caermarthenshire, the largest Welsh county, should show no traceable elements of genius. The really productive intellectual region of Wales is comprised in Denbighshire, Montgomeryshire and Radnorshire. This is a fact of some interest when we recall the ethnological history of this region. Wales is a Goidelic country (that is to say, a country inhabited by the earlier Celts mingled with aborigines), which appears to have been subsequently invaded by the Brythonic Ordovices; these formed a wedge in the country reaching to Cardigan Bay, leaving the Goidels in the north-western district and (as we may still observe in the map founded on the index of nigrescence) in the south-western district. But later still — probably soon after the departure of the Romans — a very vigorous stock led by Cuneda and speaking a tongue very closely allied to Gaulish, came from what is now the south of

Scotland, and established themselves in the centre of the Ordovician region, where their leaders became the acknowledged ancestors of the Gwyned Kings and the best known Welsh saints.* Their land comprised Radnorshire, Montgomeryshire and the south-west of Denbighshire, which is precisely the land which we have found to be the focus of Welsh genius. It is very difficult not to see here one at least, and perhaps the chief, of the factors which have caused this comparatively unimportant and thinly peopled region to be so productive in ability.

In accordance with the comparative poverty of Wales in intellectual achievements during the earlier periods of subjection to England is the statement of Rhys and Brynmor-Jones (*The Welsh People*, p. 471) that 'from the people as a whole hardly a voice comes during the centuries from the Norman Conquest to the middle of the eighteenth century. They tilled their land, attended to their flocks and their herds, married and died in complete obscurity, without being in any great degree touched by the intellectual movements of the sixteenth and seventeenth centuries.' These authors have ably expounded the causes of the intellectual decadence of Wales during this long period.

The absolute figures of the ancestral elements of ability in Scotland are as follows:

Midlothian	28	Fife	15
Aberdeenshire	26	Dumfriesshire	14
Ayrshire	21	Forfarshire	12
Lanarkshire	21	Perthshire	9

* J. Rhys and D. Brynmor-Jones, *The Welsh People*, 1900, p. 21.

Haddingtonshire	9	Inverness-shire	2
Ross-shire and Cromarty-shire	8	Nairnshire	2
		Clackmannanshire	2
Berwickshire	8	Selkirkshire	2
Stirlingshire	6	Wigtonshire	2
Argyleshire	5	Banffshire	2
Elginshire	4	Kinross-shire	1
Roxburghshire	4	Buteshire	1
Renfrewshire	4	Caithness	1
Dumbartonshire	3	Linlithgowshire	1
Sutherland	2	Peeblesshire	0
Orkney and Shetland	2	Kirkcudbrightshire	0
Kincardineshire	2		

It will be seen that the genius of Scotland has
been mainly produced by the tract between the
Cheviots and the Grampians. While, however, the
whole of this district is prolific in ability, a narrow
central belt has proved pre-eminently able to breed
men of intellect. This belt runs from Aberdeen in
a south-westerly direction through Forfar, Fife,
Midlothian, with the surrounding district, and
Lanark (including Glasgow); on reaching Ayr and
Dumfries it widens out, not extending beyond the
English border westward into Galloway. Aberdeen
and Edinburgh have always been the two great
centres of Scotch genius. If, however, we were to
take into consideration the proportions of genius
according to area and population of the various
counties this geographical distribution would appear less decisively marked. The upland counties, whether in or out of the Highlands proper,
appear poor in genius and the Lowland counties
rich. But it must be remembered that the upland counties are also poor in population and the

lowland counties rich. So far as a rough comparison of the total amount of genius with the recent population can be considered as any indication of the true distribution of genius in Scotland it would appear that both Aberdeen and Edinburgh really are very prolific in ability, and that Ayr, Fife, and even Sutherland are little, if at all, inferior in intellectual fertility, while Haddingtonshire, Berwickshire, and Dumfriesshire would appear to stand probably at the head. It would seem that even on a population basis the dark-haired populations show a somewhat less intellectual fertility than the fair-haired populations. This question is obviously complicated by the language question, but it is noteworthy that Sutherland, which is as fair-haired in population as any part of Scotland, would appear to show a fairly high proportion of ability relatively to its population, while Inverness, which is the darkest part of Scotland, stands very low, and Galloway, which is a very dark region, stands very much lower than the border counties, which are very fair. If this tendency prevails in Scotland it is the reverse of the tendency which prevails in England (though not in Wales), where the darker-haired districts seem on the whole to be more prolific in ability than the fair-haired regions. Another point about the distribution of genius in Scotland which may be noted is that the quantity and quality of its ability tend to go together. Knox, Burns and Scott, the three most famous

Scotchmen — it is unnecessary to say the greatest — all belonged to counties which would appear to be among the most prolific in ability.

Turning to Ireland, we find that, as in Scotland, certain regions appear to be rich in genius, others poor, or even absolutely bare. The distribution is as follows:

Dublin	15	Kerry	2
Cork	10	Galway	2
Antrim	9	Mayo	2
Down	8	Donegal	2
Waterford	6	Armagh	2
Londonderry	6	Cavan	1
Kilkenny	5	Carlow	1
Clare	4	Wicklow	1
Westmeath	4	Queen's County	1
Tyrone	4	Longford	1
Wexford	3	Meath, Louth, King's	
Limerick	3	County, Sligo, Roscom-	
Kildare	2	mon, Leitrim, Ferma-	
Tipperary	2	nagh, Monaghan	0

The predominance of Dublin in Ireland, it will be seen, is more decisive than is that of Midlothian in Scotland; it is, however, possible that this is due to a greater ignorance of the ancestry of eminent Irishmen. In any case, however, it will be observed that the region of Ireland chiefly productive in ability is Leinster with the adjoining portion of Munster, and, closely following it, Ulster. Both these districts — for we may consider them as separate though they adjoin, as they are anthropologically distinct, the people of Ulster being much darker — have long been racially mixed. In the first district Goidels and Brythons were both numerous, and various minor foreign immigrations have taken place here since; in comparatively recent times it was chiefly in Waterford and Dublin that the French Huguenots of Ireland settled. Ulster, as is well known, received a large infusion of English and Scotch blood in the seventeenth century, and this admixture has very largely affected the character of the ability it has produced. It is, however, a mistake to suppose that the temperamental, sometimes rather aggressive, energy of Ulstermen is due solely, or even perhaps mainly, to English and Scotch admixtures, influential as these have been. 'There is neither in Alban nor in Ireland,' we read in Lady Gregory's recension of the great Irish saga, 'an army that can put down the men of Ulster when once their weakness is gone and their anger is kindled.' * Giraldus Cambrensis also bears testimony to the vigour of the aboriginal Ulsterman. The 'Saxon' outsider is sometimes tempted to think that in many respects the modern men of Ulster are more Irish than the Irish themselves, and such an opinion finds support in the fact that, as measured by the index of nigrescence, Ulster anthropologically approaches Connaught. There can be no doubt, however, that English and Scotch elements, however largely admixed with aboriginal elements, play a very large part indeed in the manifestations of Irish genius.

It would be of some interest to classify our

* *Cuchulain of Muirthemne*, p. 256.

eminent persons into groups according to their
activities and to note the district in which each
group tends to predominate. Appendix B will enable the reader to examine into this matter for
himself. As might be expected, politicians, divines,
and men of letters abound in all parts of the kingdom. It is curious to note that great lawyers are
also scattered over the whole kingdom with notable
impartiality. While poets are to be found everywhere, they are distinctly more predominant in the
south of England, and to a less extent in Wales and
the Welsh Border counties; but when we consider
the origins of those English poets who are unani-
mously recognised to stand first, we find them
scattered over the whole country as widely apart
as possible, Chaucer in Suffolk, Spenser in Lancashire, Shakespeare in Warwickshire, Milton in
Oxfordshire, Wordsworth in Yorkshire, Shelley in
Sussex, Keats in Devon or Cornwall.

In science Scotland stands very high, Ireland
extremely low. The distribution of scientific men
is as follows:

English	84	Scotch-Irish	2
Welsh	2	English-Irish	1
Scotch	21	English-German	1
Irish	1	English-Dutch	1
Scotch-English	7		

In order to realise the extraordinary preponderance of the Scotch over the Irish contingent, it
must be remembered that until the present century
the population of Ireland has been much larger than

that of Scotland, and it may be noted that the one purely Irish man of science (Tyndall) was of original English origin.*

If we proceed to consider the distribution of English men of science in the four distinct ethnological regions to which reference has already been made, we find that six belong more or less to the East Anglian focus, five to the south-western focus, four to the Welsh Border region, and seven to the large Anglo-Danish district.

It is of interest to compare these results with those obtained by Galton in the case of his modern English men of science (*English Men of Science*, pp. 18, 21). He found that three-fourths were English. Of every ten, there were:

5 Pure English.
1 Anglo-Welsh.
1 Anglo-Irish.
1 Scotch.
1 Included Anglo-Scotch, Scotch-Irish, pure Irish, Welsh, Manx and Channel Islands.
1 Unclassed, including mixture of English, French, German, Creole, Dutch, Swedish, etc.

* I must now add that there is some reason to believe that Faraday was ultimately of Irish origin. His family, which was settled in Yorkshire, had a tradition that they came from Ireland. I disregarded that tradition because I could find no evidence that there are any Faradays in Ireland. Since then two correspondents have furnished me with evidence: Dr. Kiernan of Chicago referred me to Irish pedigree books and stated that 'Faradach' (meaning a dressy man) was an off-shoot of the Irish Kiernans and founder of the Faradays; while from South Wales I was informed that a man, of no education and of undoubted Irish nationality, called Ferriday, was living near Swansea thirty years ago. An Irish origin would certainly help to account for the 'Celtic' quality of Faraday's scientific imagination.

'On an analysis of the scientific status of the men on my list,' he remarks, 'it appeared to me that their ability is higher in proportion to their numbers among those of pure race.'

This may be said to be in agreement with my results, which necessarily deal with men of a higher average order of ability, and which show a very much smaller proportion of individuals of mixed race, though in part this difference may be accounted for by the greater precision of Galton's information in relation to his cases. He further points out that the birthplace of his men of science is usually in towns, away from the coast, and he presents a geographical diagram which shows the distribution. This diagram is of interest, for it shows with great precision the fallacy of birthplace as any true indication of the real distribution of ability. Nearly the whole of both the East Anglian and south-western foci of genius are in this diagram left bare of scientific ability.

'The whole of the Eastern Counties,' Galton remarks, 'and the huge triangle at whose angles Hastings, Worcester, and Exeter, or rather Exmouth, are situated, are very deficient in aboriginal science.' That the deficiency is very far from being 'aboriginal' becomes sufficiently clear when we are careful to ignore the accident of birthplace in determining the origins of men of science.

Psychologically it is not difficult to detect a distinct character in English scientific genius, according as it springs from the Anglo-Danish district or the East Anglian focus or the south-western focus, although I am not aware that this has been pointed out before. The Anglo-Danish district may here be fairly put first, not only on account of the large number of scientific men it has wholly or in part produced, but also on account of the very high eminence of some among them. The Anglo-Dane appears to possess an aptitude for mathematics which is not shared by the native of any other English district as a whole, and it is in the exact sciences that the Anglo-Dane triumphs.* Newton is the supreme figure of Anglo-Danish science; it will be noted that he belongs to the East Anglian border, and by his mother is claimed by Rutland, a little county which, I am inclined to think, really belongs psychologically and perhaps ethnologically to East Anglia. The combination of the Anglo-Dane and the East Anglian seems highly favourable to scientific aptitude; the abstracting tendency of the Anglo-Dane, and the exaggerated independence of his character, with the difficulty he finds in taking any other point of view than his own, are happily tempered by the more cautious and flexible mind of the East Anglian. Darwin (who also belonged to the Welsh Border) belonged in part, like Newton, to the East Anglian border of the Anglo-Danish district, and also (somewhat remotely) to Norfolk, a county which contains many Danish elements. The science of the Anglo-Danish district is not exclusively mathematical, and geology especially owes much to the Anglo-Dane; it will be remembered that geology was one of the first sciences to attract Darwin.

* The mathematical tendencies of Cambridge are due to the fact that Cambridge drains the ability of nearly the whole Anglo-Danish district.

The East Anglian is in scientific matters drawn to the concrete, and shows little or no mathematical aptitude. He is a natural historian in the widest sense. He delights in the patient collection of facts, and seeks to sift, describe, co-ordinate, and classify them. In his hands science becomes almost an art. Gilbert illustrates East Anglian scientific methods in the inorganic world, Ray in the organic, and Francis Bacon, though he cannot himself be classed among men of science, has in the *Novum Organum* and elsewhere presented a picture of scientific method as it most naturally appears to the East Anglian mind.

It is not easy to see anything specific or definitely Brythonic in the scientific activities of the Welsh Border. At most it may be said that there is some tendency for science here to take on a technological character and to become associated with the artistic crafts. The scientific men found here often belong only in part to the district, and many of them seem to possess the psychological characters of the south-western focus.

The scientific characters of the south-western focus are quite clear, and definitely distinct from those of either the Anglo-Danish district or the East Anglian focus. What we find here is the mechanical impulse, and more especially the physiological temper, the instinct to seek out the driving forces of vital phenomena. It is on this account that Harvey, though of Kentish family, may be said

to belong psychologically to this focus, as also
Stephen Hales, though he belonged partly to Kent
and partly to East Anglia. The great scientific
physicians belong here (the surgeons are largely
East Anglian), with Sydenham at the head and
Glisson. Huxley, again, is a typical figure. Inventors are numerous, for the scientific men of this
region have frequently been enamoured of practical
problems, and just as they have been pioneers in
the physical world, so in science they have sought
rather to make discoveries than to formulate laws.
Thus in astronomy we have Adams, and one of the
greatest and most typical scientific men of this
region was Thomas Young.

When we consider the distribution of great
soldiers, we find the following results:

English	22	English-Scotch	4
Welsh	3	English-Irish	2
Irish	4	Scotch-Irish	2
Scotch	13		

Within England seven belong to the Anglo-Danish
district, six to the East Anglian focus, five to the
south-western focus, and four to the Welsh Border.
In England itself, it will be seen, military genius is
relatively less pronounced than in any other part
of the British Islands, and what absolute numerical preponderance the English element possesses
seems to be due exclusively to the earlier periods of
English history; the line of great English generals
apparently ended with Marlborough. The Scotch

stand easily at the head; the Irish would take a much higher place if we considered the nineteenth century separately.

When, however, we turn to the distribution of great sailors, a very different result is shown, and the position of English ability is more than re-asserted. While England has produced as many as 29 great sailors, only two are Scotch, one English-Scotch, one English-Welsh and none Irish. Within England, eleven belong to the south-western focus, ten to the Anglo-Danish district and more especially to its southern border in Lincolnshire, four to the East Anglian focus and four to the Welsh Border.

The distribution of artists (including sculptors and architects as well as painters) is as follows:

English	51	Scotch-Irish	1
Welsh	3	English-French	2
Scotch	10	English-German	2
Irish	5	English-Italian	1
English-Welsh	1	English-Russian	1
English-Scotch	2		

Within England we find that eighteen are scattered over the large Anglo-Danish district, more than a third of these, however, belonging to the small county of Nottinghamshire, twelve are East Anglian, eight belong to the south-west, six to the Welsh Border.

The fertility of Nottinghamshire — a county not otherwise notably productive of genius — in artists is a phenomenon of some interest in view of the fact that Nottinghamshire was a great art-centre in the fourteenth

century, when its 'alabasterers' sent re-tables, screens
and figure-panels to all parts of Western Europe.
(*Architectural Review*, April, 1903, p. 143.) It would be
idle to see here the influences of tradition; we cannot
suppose that there was any continuity of this kind
between the fourteenth-century alabasterers and nineteenth-century painters, the possibility of such continuity having been absolutely destroyed by the Reformation. The reasonable supposition is that we see here a
native bent to art showing itself at one time in one form,
at another time in another form.

In a subsequent chapter (p. 266) I have discussed
some points in the distribution of British artists, and
have shown how the painters of the east coast differ
from those of the west.

A very definite case of special distribution of
ability, differing markedly from the distribution of
ability generally, is furnished by great actors and
actresses. So far as it can be traced this distribution is as follows:

English	23*	English-Irish	6
Welsh	1	English-French	1
Irish	6	Irish-French	1
English-Welsh	1	English-Irish-French-	
English-Scotch	1	Swiss	1
		English-Danish	1

It will be seen that the Scotch virtually do not
appear at all, and that the relative preponderance
of the Irish is enormous. Our knowledge of the
ancestry of actors is peculiarly vague and uncertain, and it is highly probable that if our knowledge

* This number is too high. Thus, following the *Dictionary*, it
includes L. A. Neilson, who (according to Clement Scott) was
really the illegitimate daughter of a Spaniard.

on this point were more precise the preponderance of the Irish element, at the expense of the English element, would be still greater. The distribution of actors within England, so far as we are able to trace it, further illustrates the poverty of the more specifically English districts in dramatic ability of a high order. Four of our great actors and actresses belong more or less to the south-western focus, four to the Welsh Border, three to the East Anglian focus, and only two to the whole Anglo-Danish district.

I do not propose to discuss here the various causes which have led to the special distribution of genius in the British Islands, and to the variations in distribution shown by different kinds of genius. While many of the characters thus revealed are evidently due to racial characteristics, it would be rash to assume that they may all thus be accounted for. We have also to take into account environmental conditions. It is not easy to make an exact comparison on this basis before the nineteenth century. The careful study of the condition of England made by Joseph Fletcher, secretary of the Statistical Society, on the basis of the census of 1841, conveniently enables us to make various comparisons for this period, and we may be fairly certain that the conditions then prevailing had existed during a considerably earlier period.

When, on this basis, we examine the various counties, there would appear to be a tendency to correlation between fertility in genius and (1) amount of real property per head of population; (2) deficiency of persons of independent means; (3) amount of ignorance (Norfolk is among the seven most ignorant counties, while Suffolk and Hertfordshire are also among the ignorant counties); (4) committals for serious offences against the person (Norfolk is at this period the most criminal county in this respect, being in relation to population 80 per cent above average, while Huntingdonshire, with little genius, has the least criminality, being 63 per cent below average); (5) bastardy (the four counties with largest proportion of illegitimate children being Cumberland, Hereford, Norfolk and Nottinghamshire).

On the other hand there appears to be no tendency to correlation between fertility in genius and (1) offences against property (excluding the 'malicious' group which are included in offences against the person); (2) assaults; (3) improvident marriages; (4) pauperism; (5) density of population; (6) crime (general commitments); (7) amount of deposits in savings banks per head of population.

While such comparisons are at various points of much interest and possibly of real significance, it must be remembered that though it is highly probable that there is a real connection between genius and the conditions prevailing in its environment, we must not here too hastily assume such a connection. It may be added that we should also have to take into consideration the conditions prevailing in the birthplaces of men of genius, which are not always the places of their origin.

III

SOCIAL CLASS

Status of parents of British men of genius — Upper class —
Yeomen and farmers — Clergy — Medicine — Law — Army
— Navy — Miscellaneous professions — Commercial classes —
Crafts — Artisans and unskilled — The parentage of artists —
The parentage of actors — How far change has taken place in
the social composition of the genius-producing class — Com-
parison of the genius-producing classes with the ordinary
population.

IN considering to what social classes the 1030
eminent British men and women on our list belong,
we naturally seek to ascertain the position of the
fathers. In 201 cases it has not been easy to
pronounce definitely on this point, and I have,
therefore, omitted these cases as doubtful. The
remainder may be classed with a fair degree of
certainty. I find that they fall into the following
groups:

		Per cent
Upper classes (or 'good family')	154	18.5
Yeomen and farmers	50	6
Church	139	16.7
Law	59	7.1
Army	35	4.2
Navy (and sea generally)	16	1.9
Medicine	30	3.6
Miscellaneous professions	65	7.8
Officials, clerks, etc.	27	3.2
Commercial	156	18.8
Crafts	77	9.2
Artisans and unskilled	21	2.5

In some thirty cases the status of the father is

entered under two heads, but, as a rule, it has seemed sufficient to state what may be presumed to be the father's chief occupation at the time when his eminent child was born.

In the order in which I have placed the groups they may be said to constitute a kind of hierarchy. I place the yeomen and farmers immediately after the upper-class group, although at one end this group includes the peasant-farmer.* Until recent years, the man who lived on the land which had belonged to his family for many centuries, occupied a position not essentially different from that of the more noble families with somewhat larger estates around him. Even at the present day, in remote parts of the country, it is not difficult to meet men who live on the land on farms which have belonged to their ancestors through several centuries. Such aristocrats of the soil, thus belonging to 'old families,' frequently have all the characteristics of fine country gentlemen, and in former days the line of demarcation between them and the 'upper class' must often have been difficult to draw. I have formed my 'upper-class' group in a somewhat exclusive spirit; I have not included in it the very large body of eminent men who are said to

* The yeoman may be defined as an owner-cultivator; the farmer may be only a tenant. The poet Crabbe in 1791 visited his wife's uncle, a Suffolk yeoman, called Tovell, to whom he refers as 'the first-rate yeoman of that period — the yeoman that already began to be styled by courtesy an esquire. Mr. Tovell might possess an estate of some eight hundred pounds per annum, a portion of which he himself cultivated.'

belong to 'old families'; these I have mostly allowed to fall out as 'doubtful,' but there is good reason to believe that a considerable proportion really belong to the class of small country gentlemen on the borderland between the aristocracy in the narrow sense and the yeoman and farmer class. To this class, therefore, must be attributed a very important part in the production of the men who have furnished the characteristics of British civilisation.

The same must be said of the clergy, whom I place next, because they are largely drawn from the same ranks and have on the whole led very similar lives. (With the clergy I have included thirty-two ministers of religion belonging to very various denominations.) The religious movements of the past century have altogether transformed the lives of the clergy, but until recent years the parson was usually simply a country gentleman or farmer somewhat better educated, and more in touch with intellectual tastes and pursuits. The proportion of distinguished men and women contributed from among the families of the clergy can only be described as enormous. In mere number the clergy can seldom have equalled the butchers or bakers in their parishes, yet only two butchers and four bakers are definitely ascertained to have produced eminent children, as against 139 parsons. Even if we compare the Church with the other professions with which it is most usually classed, we find that

the eminent children of the clergy considerably outnumber those of lawyers, doctors and army officers
put together. This preponderance is the more remarkable when we remember that (although I
have certainly included eminent illegitimate children of priests) it is only within the last three and
a half centuries that the clergy have been free to
compete in this field.

It is of interest to note that genius is not the only form
of mental anomaly which is produced more frequently
by the clergy than by any other social class. The clerical
profession, as Langdon Down pointed out many years
ago, also produces more idiots than any other class.

Law, Medicine, and the Army and Navy furnish
contingents which, though very much smaller than
that of the Church, are sufficiently important to
be grouped separately, but all the remaining professions I have thrown into a single group. These
are: artists (painters, sculptors, engravers, architects), 20; actors, etc., 16; musicians, composers,
etc., 9; men of letters, 6; schoolmasters, 7; engi-
neers, surveyors and accountants, 4; men of science, 3. Although so few of the fathers of eminent
men can be described professionally as men of letters or men of science, it must be added that in a
considerable number of cases literary or scientific
aptitudes were present in the parents.

We now reach a group of altogether different
character, Trade. It is a group of great magnitude,
but its size is due to the inevitable inclusion of a

very large number of occupations under a single heading. These occupations range from banking to inn-keeping. The bankers evidently form the aristocracy of the trading class, and a remarkable number, considering the smallness of the class (not less than 12), have been the fathers of eminent sons. Under the rather vague heading of 'merchants' we find 25, and there are at least nine 'manufacturers.' Wine merchants, brewers, vintners, publicans and others connected with the sale or production of alcoholic liquors have yielded as many as 16 distinguished sons, who have often attained a high degree of eminence, from Chaucer to Joule. Tea and coffee are only responsible for one each. There are eight drapers, mercers and hosiers, and six tailors and hatters; grocers and a great number of other shop-keeping trades count at most three or four eminent men each. It is, perhaps, noteworthy that at least four Lord Mayors of London have been the fathers of distinguished sons; only one of them (Gresham) attained fame in business, the others becoming men of letters and scholars. It must be added in regard to this group that in a certain number of cases the particular 'trade' or 'business' of the father is not specified.

The group which I have denominated 'Crafts' is closely related to that of 'Trade,' and in many cases it is difficult or impossible to decide whether an occupation should be entered under one or the other head. But, speaking generally, there is a very clear distinction between the two groups. For success in the essentially commercial occupations is involved, above all, financial ability; the crafts are essentially manual, and success here involves more of the qualities of the artist than of the tradesman. Just as the banker is the typical representative of commercial transactions, so the carpenter stands at the head of the crafts. There seems to be something peculiar in the life or aptitudes of the carpenter especially favourable to the production of intellectual children, for this association has occurred as many as thirteen times, while there are four builders. No other craft approaches the carpenter in this respect; there are five shoemakers, five cloth-workers, five weavers (all belonging to the early phase of industrial development before factories), five goldsmiths and jewellers, four blacksmiths, while many other handicrafts are mentioned once or twice.

Finally, we reach the group of parents engaged in some unskilled work, and, therefore, belonging to the lowest social class. It is the smallest of all the groups, and, though including some notable persons, it can scarcely be said to be a pre-eminently distinguished group. As many as eight of the parents were common soldiers, the rest mostly agricultural labourers.

It may be interesting to inquire whether our eminent men, when grouped according to the

station and occupations of their fathers, show any
marked group-characters; whether, in other words,
the occupation of the father exercises an influence
on the nature and direction of the intellectual
aptitudes of the son. To some extent it does
exercise such an influence. It is true that there are
eminent men of very various kinds in all of these
groups. But there is yet a clearly visible tendency
for certain kinds of ability to fall into certain
groups. It is not surprising that there should be a
tendency for the son to follow the profession of the
father. Nor is it surprising that a great number of
statesmen should be found in the upper-class group.
Men of letters are yielded by every class, perhaps
especially by the clergy, but Shakespeare and, it is
probable, Milton belonged to the families of yeomen. The sons of lawyers, one notes, even to a
greater extent than the eminent men of 'upper-
class' birth, eventually find themselves in the
House of Lords, and not always as lawyers. The
two groups of Army and Medicine are numerically
close together, but in other respects very unlike.
The sons of army men form a very brilliant and
versatile group, and include a large proportion of
great soldiers; the sons of doctors do not show a
single eminent doctor, and if it were not for the
presence of two men of the very first rank —
Darwin and Landor — they would constitute a
comparatively mediocre group.

Painters and sculptors constitute a group which

appears to be of very distinct interest from the point of view of occupational heredity. In social origin, it may be noted, the group differs strikingly in constitution from the general body, in which the upper class is almost or quite predominant. Of 63 painters and sculptors of definitely known origin, only two can be placed in the aristocratic division. Of the remainder 7 are the sons of artists, 22 the sons of craftsmen, leaving only 32 for all other occupations, which are mainly of lower middle class character, and in many cases trades that are very closely allied to crafts. Even, however, when we omit the trades as well as the cases in which the fathers were artists, we find a very notable predominance of craftsmen in the parentage of painters, to such an extent indeed that while craftsmen only constitute 9.2 per cent among the fathers of our eminent persons generally, they constitute nearly 35 per cent among the fathers of the painters and sculptors. It is difficult to avoid the conclusion that there is a real connection between the father's aptitude for craftsmanship and the son's aptitude for art. To suppose that environment adequately accounts for this relationship is an inadmissible theory. The association between the crafts of builder, carpenter, tanner, jeweller, watchmaker, woodcarver, rope-maker, etc., and the painter's art is small at the best, and in most cases non-existent. Nor, on the other hand, is there any reason whatever to conclude that the fathers

have acquired manual dexterity which the sons
have inherited and put to finer use. Without
reverting to the hypothesis of the inheritance of
acquired characteristics, we may well suppose that
among craftsmen there is a natural selection of
individuals possessing special dexterity of hand, and
this tendency to manual skill would tend to be
inherited. Such a supposition would adequately
account for the phenomena which meet us in the
present investigation. That there is physical
selection in occupations we know to be the case, so
that, as Beddoe has shown, butchers tend to be fair
and shoemakers to be dark.

It may be noted that Arréat (*Psychologie du Peintre*,
1892, ch. 11), in investigating the heredity of 200 eminent European painters, reached results that are closely
similar to those I have reached in my smaller purely
British group. He found that very few were of upper-
class social rank, and these not usually among the most
important, while nearly two-thirds of the whole number
were found to be the sons either of painters or of workers
in some art or craft. He refers to the special frequency
of jewellers among the fathers. I may remark that in
my list, working jewellers and watchmakers occurred
twice, a small number, but relatively large considering
that there are only three fathers of this occupation in
the total parentage of British men of ability; Kassel,
also, in his inquiry on an international basis into
heredity (*South Atlantic Quarterly*, April, 1924) found
a significant association between painters and a craft
parentage.

The group of painters and sculptors differs

widely, as we have seen, so far as the social and occupational status of their fathers is concerned, from the general composition of the whole group of eminent persons. The group of actors and actresses, however, reverses altogether the conclusions we reach from contemplating the entire group. While good social class and leisurely cultivated life among the parents would seem on the whole to be of decided advantage for the production of eminent offspring, among actors and actresses low and obscure birth would seem to be a positive advantage. At least three or four were illegitimate children, while in numerous other cases we are led to infer that this was probably the case. Of the thirty whose origin is known, four and probably more — a very large proportion considering the smallness of the unskilled class — can be set down as the children of unskilled labourers or common soldiers, eleven are the children of actors, while the rest mainly belong to miscellaneous and often somewhat unskilled occupations. Only six can be assigned to the whole group of professions (excluding the actor's profession), and only one can be said to belong to the upper class, Booth being the son of an impoverished squire with aristocratic connections. It is not difficult to account for this state of things. The somewhat unbalanced and excessively impressionable nervous system which is apt to result from illegitimate birth, or birth under abnormally Bohemian conditions, the poverty, irregularity, and manifold changes of occupation to which so many great actors and actresses have been subjected in early life, usually among varied and often low social strata, the absence of training and education in formal knowledge and conventional conduct, combined with the abundant opportunity of becoming familiar with the most naturally dramatic section of the community — all these and other characteristics which have tended to mark the early lives of great actors and actresses, would tend to fit them for the histrionic profession and to unfit them for any other field in which natural ability may be shown.

There is some interest in considering separately the eminent persons in my list, 81 in number, who died in the period during which the *Dictionary of National Biography* was being produced, and are therefore included in the Supplement. These may be expected to give us some indication as to the direction in which we may now look for our eminent men. So far as can be judged, however, from so small a group, the social composition remains exactly the same. The aristocratic element is still very large. The most notable difference is that Commerce (represented by 18 individuals) has gained on the Church (which is represented by only 11); the Church has fallen to the proportion of less than 14 per cent, the general proportion of the Church for the whole period being 16.7 per cent;

and Commerce has risen to over 22 per cent as against 18.8. Whether the relative ability-producing powers of the clergy and the commercial classes have changed, or whether, as is possible, the clergy now constitute a smaller and the commercial classes a larger element in the general population, is a question I do not undertake to answer. The quota produced by the medical profession has relatively risen, and that produced by the legal profession fallen (being only represented by one individual). More significant is the fact that the crafts instead of producing over nine per cent have not produced one of this latest group of eminent men, while (unless the reticence of the national biographers is at fault) the artisan and unskilled classes have been equally unproductive. It would appear that the ability-producing powers of the community are becoming narrowed on what is mainly a mixed aristocratic and commercial basis.

In order to realise the significance of our results it is necessary to bear in mind the class constitution of the ordinary population in Great Britain. According to the Anthropological Committee of the British Association, this may be stated as follows:

Professional classes..................	4.46 per cent
Commercial classes..................	10.36
Industrial classes....................	10.90
Artisans.............................	26.82
Labourers...........................	47.46

The comparison with the class of ability-producing

persons is interesting. We have two pyramids, but the base of the one corresponds with the apex of the other, the same inverted relationship existing harmoniously throughout. The aristocratic class which forms the foundation of the ability-producing pyramid (though this fact is slightly disguised by the omission from my list of hereditary peers) forms the fine and invisible apex of the pyramid constituted by the ordinary population. The professional class which (often in close association with the aristocratic class) forms the great bulk of the one pyramid still merely appears as the apex of the other. The commercial class also bulks more largely in the ability-producing pyramid, but to a much less extravagant extent. The industrial class (or craftsmen) which comes in the middle furnishes about the same proportion in each case, while the artisans and labourers who form nearly three-quarters of the general population appear among the ability-producing persons as a vanishing point almost as negligible as the aristocratic class is among the general population.

This is not altogether an unexpected result, though it has not before been shown to hold good for the entire field of the intellectual ability of a country. Maclean's statistical study of the origins of British men of ability during the nineteenth century shows that 26 per cent of those of known origin were sons of 'aristocrats, officials, etc.'; 16 per cent were sons of clergymen; 15 per cent sons of farmers, tradesmen, artisans, etc.; 9 per cent of military and naval officers; 9 per cent of business men; 5 per cent of medical men; 4 per cent of lawyers, etc. The result was almost identical when the 100 men of pre-eminent ability were considered separately. Maclean also finds, as I have, and notes with surprise, that the proportion of men of ability produced by the lower social classes is actually decreasing.

C. H. Cooley (*Annals of American Academy*, May, 1897) investigated the point in regard to a group of distinguished European poets, philosophers, and men of letters, and found that 45 belonged to the upper and upper middle classes, 24 to the lower middle class, and only 2 to the lower class.

Odin, in a laborious though not always very illuminative study of French genius (*Genèse des Grands Hommes*, vol. II, table 31), found that 623 talented people of letters, so far as the position of their parents was known, could be classed as: nobility, 25.5 per cent; magistrature, 30 per cent; liberal professions, 23 per cent; middle class, 11.6 per cent; industrial class, 9.8 per cent.

Galton, among 107 recent English men of science (*English Men of Science*, 1874, p. 22), found, as might be anticipated, that the aristocratic element was smaller, only 8.4 per cent; but the allied professional class (Army, Navy, Civil Service, Church, Medicine, Law, etc.) accounted for as much as 48.5 per cent; while the commercial class furnished nearly all the rest, 40.1.

One is tempted to ask how far the industrial progress of the nineteenth century, the growth of factories, the development of urban life, has altered the conditions affecting the production of eminent men. It seems clear that, taking English history as a whole, the conditions of rural life have, from the present point of view, produced the best stocks.

The minor aristocracy and the clergy — the 'gentlemen' of England — living on the soil in the open air, in a life of independence at once laborious and leisurely, have been able to give their children good opportunities for development, while at the same time they have not been able to dispense them from the necessity of work. Thus, at all events, it has been in the past. How it will be in the future is a question which the data before us in no way help to answer. So far as can be seen, the changing conditions of life have as yet made no change in the conditions required for producing genius. Life in the old towns formerly fertile in intellectual ability — towns like Edinburgh, Norwich, Ipswich and Plymouth — was altogether unlike life in our modern urban centres, and there is yet no sign that the latter will equal the former in genius-producing power. Nor is there any sign that the education of the proletariat will lead to a new development of eminent men; the lowest class in Great Britain, so far as the data before us show, has not exhibited any tendency to a higher yield of genius, and what production it is accountable for remains rural rather than urban.

IV

HEREDITY AND PARENTAGE

The tendency to heredity in intellectual ability — Inheritance of ability equally frequent through father and mother — Mental abnormality in the parents — Size of the families to which persons of eminent ability belong — Normal standards of comparison — Genius-producing families tend to be large — Men of ability tend to be the offspring of predominantly boy-producing parents — Women of ability perhaps tend to belong to girl-producing parents — Position in the family of the child of genius — Tendency of men of ability to be youngest and more especially eldest children — The age of the parents of eminent persons at their birth — Tendency to disparity of age in the parents.

THE heredity of intellectual genius has been very fully discussed, with special reference to eminent persons of British birth, by Francis Galton, especially in his *Hereditary Genius*. With, perhaps, even an excess of zeal — for persons of somewhat minor degrees of ability have sometimes been taken into account — Galton has shown that intellectual ability has frequently tended to run in families.* If this hereditary tendency is by no means omnipresent, the present data prove conclusively that it is a very real factor. Notwithstanding that the effects of hereditary position have

---

* Ability (or 'talent') is more heritable than genius. See, for instance, W. T. J. Gunn (*Eugenics Review*, April, 1924). It may be doubted, indeed, whether genius in the high and narrow sense is ever inherited, although talent may occasionally exist in its ancestry.

been so far as possible excluded, and that our lists
only contain persons of pre-eminent ability, distributed over fifteen centuries, it is yet found that
among these 1030 persons there are 41 groups, of
two or three individuals in each group, who are
closely related. The recognised relationships are
father and son (the Arnolds, Bacon with his two
sons, the Boyles, the Cannings, the Coleridges,
the Copleys, the Grenvilles, the Lyttons, the
Mathewses, the Mills, the Penns, the Pitts, the
Walpoles, the Wilberforces), brother and brother
(the Herberts, the Lawrences, the Napiers, the
Nasmyths, the Newmans, the Scotts, the Veres,
the Wesleys, the Wordsworths), brother and sister (the Arnes, the Carpenters, the Kembles, the
Martineaus, the Rossettis), sister and sister
(the Brontës). The relationship between grand-
children and grandparents, and between uncles
(or aunts) and nephews (or nieces) is best shown
in a table. (See page 83.) It will be observed that
Darwin has the unique distinction of possessing,
within the narrow degrees of relationship here recognised, both a paternal and a maternal ancestor
of the high degree of eminence required for inclusion
in my list.

The table is of considerable interest because it
helps us to answer the question as to the degree in
which genius may be inherited in the female line.
A consideration of direct heredity has no bearing
on this question; a man inherits genius from his

A more probable estimate of the real frequency of heredity may be obtained by considering separately the very recent and better known individuals who appear in the Supplement of the *Dictionary of National Biography*. Of the 81 eminent persons, thus incorporated in my list, who died while the *Dictionary* was in progress, it is found that in the case of 33 the father, the mother, or both are noted as being persons of unusual ability. This is equal to a proportion of about 40 per cent, or the proportion in which, on independent grounds, I have already suggested as representing the probable amount of inherited ability. Even for the modern group, however, we must still suppose the data to be incomplete.

From another point of view the consideration of this modern group is of interest in the light it throws on the question of heredity. I find that among the 38 able parents of the 33 eminent persons who may be supposed to have inherited ability, the sexual division comes out as exactly equal; that is to say, that there are 19 able fathers and 19 able mothers.

This would seem to indicate very clearly that, although that superlative degree of ability which is commonly termed 'genius' is rare in woman, yet a more than average degree of ability in the mother is just as important from the point of view of intellectual heredity as a more than average degree of ability in the father.

Among modern English scientific men Galton (*English Men of Science*, p. 72) has also found that ability is just as likely to be inherited through the female as through the male line. Among 100 scientific men, on the paternal side he found 34 grandfathers and uncles of ability, on the maternal side 37. As in my results, there would seem to be an excess, if any, on the maternal side.

In determining the parents who possessed ability I have taken no note of the cases in which it is merely said that the father or the mother possessed 'poetic tastes,' 'musical tastes,' etc., but only of those cases in which it is clearly stated or implied that there was unusual ability. Such 'ability' in most cases by no means involved recognised 'distinction.' As a matter of fact only one of the 81 had a parent of the same degree of eminence as himself, *i.e.*, sufficiently eminent to be included in my list. So that while the proportion of eminent persons with an 'able' parent approaches one in two, the proportion of eminent persons possessing a parent equally 'distinguished' with themselves is only one in 81. This proportion of eminent parents is shown not to be very far astray by reference to the whole body of individuals on my list, among whom there are fifteen possessing a parent of sufficient eminence to be included in the list, or about one in seventy. If we lowered the standard of distinction demanded in the parents the proportion would of course be raised.

It would be interesting to inquire into the moral
and emotional qualities, the 'character,' of the
parents. This, however, is extremely difficult and
I have not attempted it. In a great many cases the
mother was a woman of marked piety, and we are
frequently led to infer an unusual degree of character, sometimes on the part of the mother, sometimes of the father. Moral qualities are quite as
essential to most kinds of genius as intellectual
qualities, and they are, perhaps, more highly
transmissible. They form the basis on which intellectual development may take place, and they
may be transmitted by a parent in whom such development has never occurred. The very frequent
cases in which men of eminent intellectual ability
have declared that they owed everything to their
mothers * have sometimes been put aside as the
expressions of an amiable weakness. It requires
some credulity, however, to believe that men of
pre-eminent, or even less than pre-eminent, intellectual acuteness are unable to estimate the
character of their own parents. The frequent sense
of indebtedness to their mothers expressed by
eminent men may be taken as largely due to the
feeling that the inheritance of moral or temperamental qualities is an even more massive and
important inheritance than definite intellectual

* A remark of Huxley's in a letter to the present writer —
'Mentally and physically I am a piece of my mother' — may be
taken as typical of such declarations.

aptitudes. Such inheritance coming to intellectual men from their mothers may often be observed where no definite intellectual aptitudes have been transmitted. It is not, however, of a kind which can well be recorded in biographical dictionaries, and I have not, therefore, attempted to estimate its frequency in the group of pre-eminent persons under consideration.

I have, however, attempted to estimate the frequency of one other form of anomaly in the parents besides intellectual ability. The parents of persons of eminent intellectual power may not themselves have been characterised by unusual intellect; but they may have shown mental anomaly by a lack of aptitude for the ordinary social life in which they were placed. In at least fifty-seven cases (or over five per cent) we find that the fathers were extravagant, unsuccessful in business, shiftless, idle, drunken, brutal, or otherwise fell into bad habits and neglected their families. In such cases, we may conclude, the father has transmitted to his eminent child an inaptness to follow the beaten tracks of life, but he has not transmitted any accompanying aptitude to make new individual tracks. This list could easily be enlarged if we included milder degrees of ineffectiveness. A certain degree of inoffensive eccentricity, recalling Parson Adams, seems to be not very uncommon among the fathers of men of eminent ability, and perhaps furnishes a transmissible temperament on which genius may develop. It may be noted that six of the ne'er-do-weel fathers (a very large proportion) belonged to eminent women. This may be simply due to the fact that a ne'er-do-weel father, by forcing the daughter to leave home or to provide for the family, furnishes a special stimulus to her latent ability.

In 403 cases I have been able to ascertain with a fair degree of certainty the size of the families to which these persons of eminent ability belong. A more than fair degree of certainty has not been attainable, owing to the loose and inexact way in which the national biographers frequently state the matter. Sometimes we are only told that the subject of the article is 'the child' or 'the son'; this may mean the *only* child, but it is impossible to accept such a statement as evidence regarding the size of the family, and the number of families with only children may possibly thus have been unduly diminished. Again, the biographers in a very large number of cases ignore the daughters, and from this cause again their statements become valueless.

In estimating the natality of the families producing children of ability I have never knowingly reckoned the offspring of previous or subsequent marriages; so far as possible, we are only concerned with the fecundity of the two parents of the eminent persons. So far as possible, also, I have reckoned the gross fecundity, *i.e.*, the number of children born, not the number of children surviving; in the case of a large number of eminent men this gross fertility is known from the inspection of parish registers; in a certain proportion of cases it is probable, however, that we are only dealing with the surviving children. On the whole, the ascertainable size of the family may almost certainly be said to be under the mark. It is, therefore, the more remarkable that the average size of genius-producing families is found to be larger than that of normal families. The average size of our genius-producing families is 6.5. In order to effect an exact comparison with normal families, I have looked about for some fairly comparable series of figures, and am satisfied that I have found it in the results of an inquiry by Mr. F. Howard Collins concerning 4390 families.* These families furnish an excellent normal standard for comparison; they deal mainly with 'Anglo-Saxon' people (in England and America) of the middle and upper classes; they represent, with probably but very slight errors of record, gross fertility; they are apparently not too recent, and they betray little evidence of the artificial limitation of families. The mean size of Collins's group of fertile families is found by Pearson to be 4.52 children.

* As quoted by Karl Pearson, *The Chances of Death*, vol. I, p. 70. In passing through Mr. Pearson's mathematical hands the 4390 emerge as 4444, and it is on this number that my percentages for normal families are based.

This conclusion as to the abnormally large size of the families from which genius tends to spring may be criticised in two directions. It may be argued that there has been no recognition of the possibly larger size of the normal family in the earlier periods which my list covers. It may be said further that even the size of the modern normal family has been underestimated.

It is unnecessary to speculate concerning the average size of the normal family in former days until definite evidence is brought forward. But I may point out that the large size of genius-producing families holds good even when we only take into account the nineteenth-century persons on my list. If, for instance, we consider separately the 39 individuals from the supplement to the *Dictionary* concerning whom I have definite data, it is found that the average size of the families is 5.7, and nine out of the number belong to families containing from nine to seventeen children. I may add that at an earlier stage in my inquiry (see *Popular Science Monthly*, April, 1901, p. 598) I found that the size of the families from which British men of genius spring was still larger than the present average of 6.5, being nearly 7 (6.96). The reduction in size is due in part, it would seem, to the large number of persons of comparatively minor ability who have since been added, and perhaps in part to a tendency to slightly decreased size among the families from which have sprung the quite recent individuals contained in the *Dictionary of National Biography*.

In regard to the correct estimation of the average size of the normal family, it must be said that while my results for British genius-producing families are, without doubt, distinctly too low on account of the imperfection of the data, yet every estimate of the average size of the normal family, although founded on much more complete data, yields an average decidedly below 6.5. Thus

Ansell found the average size of the family, counting all children born alive, among the English professional classes, to be about 5, or, more precisely, clergy 5.25, legal 5.18, medical 4.82. (C. Ansell, *On the Rate of Mortality and other Statistics of Families*, 1874) Galton found the mean of 204 marriages 4.65 children, Pearson the mean of 378 fertile marriages 4.70 children.

A very interesting table is given in Mrs. Henry Sidgwick's *Health Statistics of Women Students of Cambridge and Oxford and of their Sisters*, 1890. Mrs. Sidgwick found that these students (566 in number) belonged to families of which the average size was as high as 6.8 children. (It must be said that this result is slightly vitiated by the inclusion of 70 half brothers and sisters.) One is inclined to look upon the result as necessarily presenting the normal average for the families of the class from which these students spring. It must, however, be borne in mind that these figures refer largely to the early days of the higher education of women; we may be fairly certain that a considerable proportion of these students were women of unusual intellectual ability, and that in numerous other cases they belonged to families in which the brothers showed high ability. The result therefore represents not the average fertility of the professional and allied classes from which these students spring, but is complicated by the considerable admixture of the special ability-producing group of the population with its high fertility. This interpretation is clearly supported by Mrs. Sidgwick's tables. She has presented separately the results of a large group containing the Honours Students, and we are hereby enabled to discern the notable fact that the Honours Students belong to decidedly larger families than do the students generally. In students generally the 6-children families constitute the largest group; for the Honours division the 8-children group is the largest, while very large

families are relatively much more frequent among the
Honours division than among the division of 'other
students,' so that, for instance, while among Honours
students exactly the same number belong to 11-children
families as to 2-children families, among 'other students'
more than twice as many belong to 2-children families
as to 11-children families. Mrs. Sidgwick's results may,
therefore, be said to confirm the results reached in the
present investigation.

It may be added that the greater fertility which has
been shown to mark the families from which British
persons of ability in general have sprung, has already
been shown by Galton to mark the special group of families from which modern British men of science spring.
Galton found (*English Men of Science*) that the average
number of brothers and sisters (excluding, for the most
part, those who died in infancy) was 6.3. This indicates,
as we should expect, a decidedly higher fertility than in
the families producing the women students, though
probably not higher than would have been shown by
the British ability-producing families generally, had my
data been more complete.

Yoder, in studying the early lives of 50 eminent men
of various nationalities belonging to the eighteenth and
nineteenth centuries (A. H. Yoder, 'Boyhood of Great
Men,' *Pedagogical Seminary*, October, 1894), found
that the average number of children in the families
from which they sprang, excluding half brothers and
sisters, was 6+. This approximates to the result here
reached as regards British eminent men only.

It will be seen that the high fertility which we have
found among ability-producing families stands in opposition to the well-known tendency to small families among
the higher human races and to the universal tendency,
well marked at the present day, for a falling birth-rate
to be associated with a rising level of civilization and

well-being. Within the same nation, also, the families of the poorer classes are larger than those of the richer classes; thus in Holland at the present day, both in town and country, the average number of children per marriage in the poorest class is 5.19, against 4.50 for the rich class.

It would, however, be a mistake to suppose that our results can properly be regarded as unexpected. They are, on the contrary, in harmony with all that we know concerning the fertility of the families producing the nervously abnormal classes, which is on the whole decidedly high. Toulouse (*Causes de la Folie*, 1896, p. 91) has summarised the evidence accumulated by Ball and Régis, as well as by Marandon de Montyel, showing that the size of the families from which the insane spring is decidedly larger than the usual average. Professor Magri ("Le Famiglie dalle quali discendono i Delinquenti," *Arch. di Psichiatria*, 1896, fasc. VI–VII) has further shown that this abnormally great fertility is by no means confined to insanity-producing families, but also characterises the progenitors of numerous other mentally abnormal groups. Thus he found that criminals in the majority of cases spring from large families, and that although the average size of the normal family in Italy is three or four, it was very rarely possible to find a criminal who belonged to a family of only two or three children. Magri also found that hysteria and neurasthenia are notably frequent in large families.

Langdon Down had previously pointed out (*Mental Affections of Childhood*) that imbeciles and weak-minded children tend to belong to large families; he found the average number of living children in the families containing idiots to be as high as 7. In Berlin Cassel (*Was lehrt die Untersuchung der geistig minderwertigen Schulkinder*, 1901) found that the average size of the families from which defective children spring is over 7.

Comparing in more detail the composition of our genius-producing families with the normal average, we obtain the following results:

Size of family	1	2	3	4	5	6	7	8
Normal families...	12.2	14.7	15.3	14.1	11.1	8.6	7.8	6.3
Genius-producing families........	6.9	9.4	10.6	9.4	10.1	10.4	8.9	6.7

Size of family	9	10	11	12	13	14	Over 14
Normal families...	3.9	2.7	1.4	1.0	.5	.2	.1
Genius-producing families........	5.7	4.7	4.9	4.4	2.2	1.9	3.4

Unless, as is scarcely probable, the mental eccentricities of biographers lead to very frequent selection on definite lines, it will be seen that in genius-producing families there is an invariable deficiency of families below the average normal size, and a gradually increasing excess of families above that size. In the largest size group (over 14) the excess becomes extravagantly large; this, however, may be partly accounted for; probably the biographers have here less seldom failed to record the size of the family, so this group may have been more carefully recruited from the families of our 1030 eminent persons. Even on this basis, however, it remains extremely large. Ansell found that in 2000 marriages there was no family of more than 18 children; and in Denmark, it is stated, a family of 22 children only occurs once in 34,000 marriages.*

An interesting point, and one which can scarcely be affected at all by any twist in the biographical mind, is the fact that our men of ability (the women are here excluded) are the offspring of predominantly boy-producing parents. Taking the 180 families in which the number of boys and girls in the family is clearly stated, excluding those (29 in number) which are known to consist only of boys, we find that there are about six boys to five girls, or more exactly 121 boys to 100 girls. The normal proportion of the sexes at birth at the present time in England is about 104 boys to 100 girls. It is in accordance with the predominantly boy-producing tendency of families yielding men of genius that the families yielding women of genius should show a predominantly girl-producing tendency. Here, indeed, our cases are too few to prove much, but the results are definite enough as far as they go. Putting aside the families consisting only

* In our genius-producing group there are four families of more than 19 children. Doddridge was the youngest of 20 children; Popham was the youngest of his mother's 21 children; Colet was the eldest and only surviving child of 22; Dempster was, or stated himself to be, the 24th of 29 children. We cannot be absolutely sure that in every case we are dealing with a single couple. It may be added that much larger families are from time to time recorded as produced by a single couple. I may refer, for instance, to the record (*British Medical Journal*, 12th October, 1901) of a family of 36 children; in such a case there are of course numerous plural births.

of girls, the sexual ratio is almost reversed; there are about six girls to five boys; or, more exactly, the ratio is 79 boys to 100 girls. We find that among the children of parents producing an eminent man there are 55 per cent boys to 45 per cent girls; among the children of parents producing an eminent woman there are only 45 per cent boys to 54 per cent girls. Putting the matter in another way, we may say that, while in every ten families from which men of genius spring, the boys predominate in six families; in the families from which women of genius spring the boys predominate only in about three.

Ansell found in England (as has Geissler in Saxony) that there are normally a larger number of boys in large families than in small families; in families of 1–5 children he found the proportion of males to females 1033 to 1000; in families of 6–10 children, 1075 to 1000; in families of 11 children and over 1083 to 1000. It will be seen, however, that this tendency is by no means sufficiently marked to furnish a sufficing explanation of the large preponderance of boys in the families producing eminent men; nor will it account at all for the apparently large excess of girls — this, however, being based on only a small number of cases — in the families producing eminent women.

I may add that while not an all-sufficing explanation, the tendency pointed out by Ansell is evidently a real factor in this peculiarity among the families producing men of ability. I have found it holds good within the limits of the families producing men of ability. Taking at random 25 families with five or fewer children, I find that the girls are in an absolute and decided majority, while in another series, taken equally at random, of 25 families containing eight or more children, males are to females in the proportion of 130 to 100.

It is possible that some light is thrown on the prevalence of boys in large families by the facts observed among animals. It is believed by many authorities that excess of maternal nourishment tends to produce females, and it has also been found that mares over 14 years of age tend to produce colts (*Veterinarian*, 1st August, 1895). In large families the maternal nourishment would tend to be decreased by much child-bearing. It is noteworthy — although I have not systematically investigated this point — that the interval between the birth of the eminent person and the previous child is often very short.

Yoder, who especially attended to this point, found that in the 26 cases in which the point could be ascertained, the interval was 22.87 months, while the average time in the family, for 30 cases, was 25.36 months. This suggests that it is possible that the maternal exhaustion which tends to produce males also tends to produce children of eminent ability.

It may be said on the whole that this excessive boy-producing tendency of the families which produce men of genius is really the resultant of the combined action of a number of factors, each of which, occurring separately, tends to produce a slighter but still abnormally large excess of boys. Not only would it appear that large families, and families in which the children follow very rapidly, tend to yield a large excess of boys, but observations on man and on other animals indicate that an undue excess of males is also found when the age of the father is unduly advanced (see, *e.g.*, A. J. Wall, *Lancet*, 1887), when the age of the mother is unusually advanced, when the disparity of age between the parents is unusually great, and when the parents live

in the country and are occupied in country pursuits.
All these conditions which favour the production of
boys have also — as we have seen or shall see —
favoured the production of genius in Great Britain.
(For a study of the facts and theories bearing on the
excess of male births, see A. Rauber, *Der Ueberschuss
an Knabengeburten und seine Biologische Bedeutung*, 1900.
See also a more recent study, Hans Günther 'Die
Sexualproportionen,' *Zeitschrift für Sexualwissenschaft*,
October and November, 1925.)

I have made a tentative effort to ascertain what
position in the family the child of genius is most
likely to occupy. In a large number of cases we
are only told his position as a son, not as a child;
these are, of course, excluded. In order to investigate this point I considered the families of at least
eight children (and subsequently those of at least
seven children) and noted where the genius child
came. This showed a very abnormally large proportion of eminent first children, and also abnormally few second and third children. Suspecting
that certain peculiarities of the biographical mind
(needless to enter into here, since we are not investigating the psychology of biographers) may
have somewhat affected this result, I have confined
myself to a simple inquiry less likely to be affected
by any mental tendencies of the biographers. In
families of different sizes, what relation do eldest
genius children and youngest genius children bear
to genius children of intermediate position? The
results are very decisive, and are shown in the
following table:

Size of Family	Position of Eminent Child		
	Eldest	Intermediate	Youngest
2	15	0	12
3	15	6	11
4	10	16	3
5	10	18	7
6	8	20	6
7	15	14	5
8	2	17	4
9	8	7	4
10	5	10	3
11	3	12	2
12	1	10	2
13	1	4	2
14	0	5	2
Over 14	1	9	4

It would appear that there is a special liability for eldest and youngest children to be born with intellectual aptitudes, the liability being greater in the case of the eldest than of the youngest, for there are altogether 94 eldest children to 67 youngest children, the intermediate children numbering 148; or 30 per cent are eldest children, 21 per cent youngest children, and 47 per cent intermediate. It will be seen that while the eldest and youngest children of ability absolutely outnumber those of intermediate position, notwithstanding the large average size of the families producing children of ability, and the consequently much greater number of chances possessed by the intermediate children as a group, the chances of the eldest attaining eminence as compared with the chances of the youngest are not the same throughout. In

the small and medium-sized families it is the eldest
who most frequently achieves fame; in the large
families it is the youngest. It may be added that
if we were to take into consideration the survivors
of a family only (or the net fertility) the youngest
children would occupy a still more conspicuous
position.

This predominance of eldest children and youngest
children among persons of genius accords with the
results reached by Yoder in studying an international
group of 50 eminent men (*American Journal of Psychology*, October, 1894, p. 146); he found that youngest
sons occurred oftener than intermediate sons and eldest
sons oftener than youngest. Galton, in his inquiries as
to recent British men of science, reached the same
result, finding 36 intermediate sons, 15 youngest sons,
and 26 eldest sons. (Galton, *English Men of Science*,
pp. 33–34.)

It must be added that this result is absolutely in accordance with what a consideration of other mentally
abnormal groups would lead us to expect. Sir Arthur
Mitchell appears to have been the first to point out
many years ago (*Edinburgh Medical Journal*, January,
1866) that among idiots the youngest born and especially
the eldest born largely predominate over the intermediate children; he found that among 433 idiots and
imbeciles 31 per cent were first-born children and 20
per cent last-born. It will be seen that the proportion of
eldest and youngest children among Mitchell's idiots
and imbeciles is almost identical with the proportion
found among British persons of genius. Langdon Down
(*Mental Affections of Childhood*) confirmed this conclusion, as regards the tendency of both eldest and
youngest children to be imbecile, and Shuttleworth
(*British Medical Journal*, November 17, 1900, p. 1446)

has confirmed it so far as youngest children are concerned. Criminals have also been found to be in undue proportion first-born children (L. Winter, *States Hospital Bulletin*, 1897, p. 463, as quoted by Näcke), and Dugdale found that the first-born child tends to be a criminal and the last-born a pauper. It would appear (see, *e.g.*, Moll, *Untersuchungen über die Libido Sexualis*. Bd. I, p. 19) that there is some ground for believing that sexual inversion tends especially to appear among eldest and youngest children. It may be added that, according to Sir J. Humphrey, in racing stables opinion is not favourable as regards firstlings.

It is interesting to find that the same points have been brought out as regards normal school children. This question was specially studied in its wider bearings at Professor Starbuck's suggestion by Mr. G. S. Wells, among a large number of children at San José, California. (G. S. Wells, *A Study of the Order of the Birth of Children*, 1901. I am indebted to Professor Starbuck for enabling me to see this study in manuscript.) The children were investigated by trained observers, and their position noted as regards weight, height, weight-discrimination, reaction time, voluntary action, ability, endurance, mental ability, neatness and deportment. In nearly all these respects it was found that eldest children tend to show best, and that youngest children, while inferior to eldest, were superior to intermediate children. Out of numerous curves, fourteen show the first group highest, six the last group highest, only two the intermediate group.

The tendency to nervous abnormality in first-born children would seem to be further indicated by the observations of Miss Carman (*American Journal of Psychology*, April, 1899) that first-born boys are more sensitive, as estimated by the temple algometer, than second or subsequent children. She also found that the first-born boys are strongest with the dynamometer. Macdonald

(*Boston Medical and Surgical Journal*, 1st August, 1901) found that first-born men and women are more sensitive to pain than second-born.

I may remark that I had been impressed twenty-five years ago by the tendency of men of genius to be eldest-born children, although I was not then acquainted with Galton's investigations. It appears to be a popular belief (H. Campbell, *Causation of Disease*, p. 262, combats this belief) that the first-born child is inferior. Shandy said that the eldest son is the blockhead of the family. On the other hand, there are popular beliefs in the other direction. Thus in Northern Iceland (*Zeitschrift für Ethnologie*, 1900, heft 2 and 3, p. 74) it is believed that the first-born child, whether boy or girl, surpasses the others in strength, stature, beauty, wisdom, virtue, and good fortune, and in olden times the eldest child possessed certain privileges not accorded to the others. These conflicting popular beliefs are fully accounted for by the actual facts. The eldest-born represents the point of greatest variation in the family, and the variations thus produced may be in either direction, useful or useless, good or bad.

More recently, the distinguished Italian sociological statistician, Gini, also concludes that the early born children are the most variable (*Revista Italiana di Sociologia*, March–April, 1914), and so also the Editor of the *Journal of Heredity*, September, 1916), who shows that the long-lived tend in a disproportionate number of cases to be the eldest born. W. C. Rivers (*Lancet*, 7th October, 1911), dealing primarily with the excess of deaths from consumption among the first-borns, likewise discusses the multiform abnormality of the first-born, bringing together various facts and references.

Whenever it has been possible, I have noted the age of the father at the birth of his eminent child.

It has been possible to ascertain this in 299 cases, and the data thus obtained may be considered as fairly free from fallacy, so far as the biographical mind is concerned, though we may be sure that the biographers would not neglect to mention the two or three known cases in which that age was extremely youthful or advanced. The range of age is considerable, from sixteen, the age of Napier of Merchiston's father at his son's birth, to seventy-nine, the age of Charles Leslie's father, the period of potency in the case of the fathers of persons of eminent ability thus ranging over sixty-three years. The 299 cases may be grouped in five-year age-periods as follows:

Age of Fathers	Under 20	20–24	25–29	30–34	35–39
Number of fathers.	2	9	45	81	59
Percentages.......	6	3	15	27	19

Age of Fathers	40–44	45–49	50–54	55–59	60 and over
Number of fathers.	44	30	13	8	8
Percentages.......	14	10	4	2	2

It will be seen that the most frequent age of fatherhood is from 30 to 34, but there are two separate years of maximum frequency, 34 and 36,

each with 19 cases. A prevalence of elderly fathers
seems indicated by the fact that the general average falls later than this maximum, being 37.1
years. For one father who begets an eminent
child before the age of maximum paternity —
which is also, we may assume, the age of maximum
general vigour — there are nearly three who beget
an eminent child when that age is past. This result
is the more significant when we remember that we
are chiefly dealing with the upper social classes
(for it is in their cases that these facts are most
easily ascertained), and that we must probably
exclude the recent tendency to retardation of the
age of marriage.

I have thought that it may be of interest to
separate from the main body the one hundred most
recent of the eminent persons on my list (all born
in the nineteenth century) and to consider how the
ages of their fathers are distributed. The result is
as follows:

Age	20—	25—	30—	35—	40—	45—	50—	55—
Number....	1	18	30	18	14	14	4	1

The most frequent age is 34, but the average age
is 37, being almost equal to the average for the
fathers of the whole group, so that this factor in
the biological constitution of the genius group
would appear to be fairly uniform throughout and

independent of social and economic changes, except that the age of the fathers has perhaps tended in the course of time to become slightly lower. Although this decrease in age is very trifling, it appears to be confirmed by the results yielded if we make a separate group of the 71 individuals born before the eighteenth century the age of whose fathers I have been able to determine. The distribution is as follows:

Under 20	20—	25—	30—	35—	40—	45—	50—	55—	60 and over
2	3	13	13	14	10	7	2	4	3

The most frequent age here, taking the years separately, is as low as 25, but on the other hand, the average age is slightly higher than that for the general group, being 37.2. It is possible that this slightly higher age — very trifling as it is — indicates a real tendency. The further we go back the higher becomes the intellectual average of the individuals we are dealing with, and there is some reason to suppose that with such high average intellectual level, the average age of the fathers is also higher, and the range of variation is greater. Such trifling fluctuations would be negligible if they did not all point in one direction.

I may refer to another indication which helps to confirm the conclusion that when we are dealing with a group of men of very high intellectual eminence the average age of their fathers is slightly higher than when we are dealing with a group of lower eminence. On separating into a distinct group all those eminent men on my list who are also included in the first three hundred (*i.e.*, the most eminent section) of Professor Cattell's one thousand most eminent persons in history (see *ante*, p. 8), we obtain a group of 37 individuals who are without doubt of a higher level of intellectual ability than the general average of the British group. The age of the fathers of the pre-eminent men in this special group is as high as 37.7 years.

The ages of the fathers of Galton's recent British men of science in 100 cases were distributed as follows:

20—	25—	30—	35—	40—	45—	50—
1	15	34	22	17	7	4

The average was 36. These results as regards this group may very fairly be compared with the results reached concerning the contemporaneous group of 100 from my list which has been separately calculated. It will be seen that in the more mixed and more eminent British group, as might be anticipated, the variations are greater; there are a larger proportion alike of younger and of elderly fathers. In Yoder's group of 39 fathers of men of various nationalities whose average eminence was of higher degree than mine and much higher than Galton's, the numbers are too small to bear much weight; they were distributed as follows, with an average age of 37.78 years:

20—	25—	30—	35—	40—	45—	50—	55—	60—
1	2	10	13	7	3	2	0	1

The most notable point here, as compared with either Galton's results or mine, is the marked deficiency of fathers under 30. It will be noticed that the average age of the fathers in Galton's, mine, and Yoder's groups rises progressively (36, 37.1, 37.78) with the intellectual eminence of the group. It may well be that this is not a casual coincidence. The tendency for the fathers of men of genius to be elderly had, as Yoder points out, already been noted by Lombroso (*Man of Genius*, p. 149).

According to Ansell (*On the Rate of Mortality*, etc., 1874), the average age of fathers of the professional and allied classes (estimated as the length of a generation, *i.e.*, the difference between the age of father and son) is 36.6. An average tells us nothing concerning the range of variation, but it may be observed that this normal average approximates to that obtained in the most nearly normal of the groups of ability we are here able to compare. I have no other data concerning the normal ages of the fathers of the professional and upper classes in modern England, and in any case we could not be sure how far such data could be comparable with that presented by our group of eminent persons which is spread over many centuries. The influence of the age of the fathers in various normal and abnormal groups of the population has been most carefully and elaborately studied by Marro in North Italy (in his *Caratteri dei Delinquenti*, and more recently in *La Pubertà*). Marro regards fathers below the age of twenty-six as belonging to the period of immaturity; the period of maturity is from twenty-six to forty, and the period of decadence from forty-one onwards. He found, among the normal population, that 9 per cent fathers belonged to the first period, 66 per cent to the second, and 25 per cent to the third. Among the fathers of criminals there was an increase both of immature and of decadent fathers at the expense of the mature, while among the insane fathers there was a similar but more marked increase of immature and decadent fathers. In studying the age of the fathers of school children, Marro found that while children of good intelligence are mostly the offspring of young fathers, those of the highest grade of intelligence are mostly the children of middle-aged and elderly fathers. He found also that the highest proportion of very defectively intelligent children belonged to elderly fathers. Aristotle had long before said that the children of very young or very old people are imperfect in mind or body. We may slightly modify that ancient dictum by saying that the children of such people tend to be abnormal.

I have been able to ascertain the age of the mother in only 86 instances. In these cases it is distributed as follows:

Age of Mother	Under 20	20–24	25–29	30–34	35–39	40–44	45–49	50
Number of cases......	1	14	22	23	13	11	1	1
Per cent.....	1.1	16	25	26	15	12	1.1	1.1

The average age of the mothers is 31.2 years. Taking the years separately we find that there are only three mothers at the age of 25 and only two

at 26, when there is a sudden rise to ten at the age
of 27, representing the chief maximum; there is,
however, a secondary maximum (of eight cases) at
30, and again (also of eight cases) at 33. On the
whole, it will be seen, the ages of the mothers
exhibit the same tendency to late parenthood
which marks the fathers. Instead of falling earlier,
as we should expect, the age of maximum frequency for the mothers falls within the same five
years as for the fathers, and the number of mothers
who have reached the sexually advanced age of 40
is nearly as large as the number of those below the
age of 25. This is the more remarkable since the
predominant tendency of our men of ability to be
first-born children would lead us to expect a corresponding predominance of young women among
their mothers.

In Galton's 100 cases of mothers of modern British
men of science the average age was thirty, and the distribution was as follows:

Under 20	20—	25—	30—	35—	40—	45—
2	20	26	34	12	5	1

It will be seen that in my list of mothers of British persons of ability, the intellectual eminence being greater
than in Galton's, there is a comparative deficiency of
young mothers (indeed, for all ages under 35), and a
very marked excess of elderly mothers, while the average age also is higher than in Galton's. Yoder found

the average age of the mothers in his group to be 29.8, but he is only able to bring forward twenty cases. Vaerting (*Nue Generation*, September and November, 1914) finds that in the parentage of genius the mothers tend to be elderly, in one third of the ascertainable cases older than the father.

Marro in his study of the ages of the mothers of North Italian criminals, insane, school children, etc., found that the relations that existed between the different groups were very much the same as in the cases of the fathers.

The influence of the age of the parents on the children as regards various kinds of mental and nervous ability has been investigated in California by Mr. R. S. Holway, and I am indebted to Professor Starbuck for enabling me to see Mr. Holway's study in manuscript (*The Age of Parents: Its Effects upon Children*, a thesis presented to the Department of Education, Leland Stanford Junior University, 1901). It was found that, while in most physical qualities the children of mature parents tend to come out best, in mental ability the children of young parents show best at an early age, but rapidly lose their precocity; the elder children who show best tend to be the parents of mature and old parents; the exceptionally brilliant children show a tendency to be the offspring of old parents; the children of elderly mothers show a tendency to superiority throughout.

Ansell found that the normal age of mothers in British professional and allied class (estimated as length of a generation) is as high as 32.3 years, but in the absence of information as to distribution we cannot determine the significance of this result. Among the general population of poor class, Collins (*Practical Treatise of Midwifery*) found that the most frequent age of maternity in Ireland (where early marriages are common) was between 25 and 29, the average age being 27. In Edinburgh and Glasgow, however, Matthews Duncan (*Fecundity, Fertility, Sterility, and Allied Topics*, 2nd ed., 1871) found the average age in a similar class of the population to be above 29, the distribution being as follows:

Age	Below 20	20—	25—	30—	35—	40—	45—	50—
Per cent	2.30	22.62	30.89	23.61	14.76	5.15	.58	.03

It will be seen that this distribution closely corresponds with that of the mothers of Galton's men of science, but shows much fewer cases at the higher ages than does my group.

The conclusion that among the parents of our men of genius there is an abnormally large proportion of elderly mothers is confirmed by the normal data furnished by Roberton (J. Roberton, *Essays and Notes on the Physiology and Diseases of Women*, 1851, p. 183). He found that among 10,000 pregnant women in Manchester, only 4.3 per cent were over 40, *i.e.*, were at least in their forty-first year.

From a consideration of these various groups of data, among the mothers of highly intellectual children there would certainly appear to be some deficiency of very young mothers, and there is a decided excess of elderly mothers. If, as we may conclude from the marked prevalence of first-born children among our British people of ability, this tendency to a somewhat advanced age of the parents is associated with late marriages, we perhaps have here one of the factors in the prevalence of an excess of boys in the families producing eminent men, since, as Ahlfeld has shown (*Arch. f. Gynäk*, 1876, Bd. IX, p. 448), there is a gradual though not altogether regular increase with age in the proportion of boys among *primiparæ* between the ages of 28 and 36, so that while at the earlier age there were at Leipzig 110 boys to 100 girls, at the later age there were 190 boys to 100 girls. R. J. Ewart in England also found (*Public Health*, May, 1912) that the older the mother at birth of child the greater the proportion of boys.

It may be noted that in at least 44 cases the mother was a second or third wife. This group is a somewhat distinguished one, including F. Bacon, R. Boyle, Bunyan, Byron, Chaucer, S. T. Coleridge, and Raleigh. The list is certainly very incomplete. In at least nine cases the father was a second husband.

It is instructive to compare the ages of the parents and to ascertain the degree of disparity. I have only been able to do this in 71 cases. There is a marked tendency to disparity which ranges up to 49 years.* In 55 cases the father was older.

The distribution of the various degrees of disparity may be seen in the following table:

Amount of Disparity	None	1–4 yrs.	5–9 yrs.	10–14 yrs.	15–19 yrs.	Over 20 yrs.
Number of cases	4	24	24	13	3	3

The average amount of disparity for the whole of the 71 cases is as high at 7.7 years. It will be seen that the number of cases in which the dis-

* This very exceptional case was that of the father (an eminent bishop) of Charles Leslie, the nonjuring divine. In this case the father was 79, the mother 30.

parity was at least ten years is equal to a proportion of over 26 per cent.

According to Ansell, the mean difference in ages of
husband and wife among the professional classes in
England during the nineteenth century was 4.16 years;
before 1840 it was only 3.89 years, rising to 4.42 years
after 1840. This rise is doubtless connected with the accompanying rise in the age of marriage. It will be seen
that the degree of disparity in the case of the parents of
eminent British persons is nearly double that of the
normal average before 1840, with which only it can be
compared. The distribution of the different degrees of
disparity is not seen from Ansell's tables, but the frequency of high degrees of disparity in age among the
parents of eminent British persons is evidently extreme.
In Buda-Pesth a table given by Körösi (though not
strictly comparable with the present data) shows that
if we take men at ages between 26 and 30, covering the
most frequent normal age of marriage, in only 3 per cent
cases is the discrepancy of age as much as ten years.

A similar tendency to unusual disparity of age in
the parents is found among other nervously abnormal groups. It is so, for instance, among idiots. Many
years ago, the late Dr. Langdon Down, at my suggestion, kindly went through the notes of one thousand
cases of idiots who had been under his care, and found
that in 23 per cent cases there was a disparity of age of
more than ten years in the parents of the idiot child,
the disparity in many cases being more than twenty-
five years.

Disparity of age in the parents is also, as Marro has
found (*La Pubertà*, p. 259), unusually prevalent among
criminals. Among the parents of North Italian school
children he found that the normal proportion of parents
both belonging to the same stage of development (immature, mature, or decadent) is 70 per cent; among the

parents of North Italian criminals it is only 63 per cent.

It has occurred to me as possible that the tendency to disparity of age may be one of the factors in the marked prevalence of boys. As, however, it has only happened that in a comparatively small proportion of cases I have exact data regarding the respective numbers of boys and girls in the families of parents in whom the exact amount of disparity is known, it has not been possible to test this point with any certainty. So far as figures give any indication, they indicate that if disparity is a factor in the sexual proportion of the offspring it can only be so in a very slight degree.

On the whole it would appear, so far as the evidence goes, that the fathers of our eminent persons have been predominantly middle-aged and to a marked extent elderly at the time of the distinguished child's birth; while the mothers have been predominantly at the period of greatest vigour and maturity, and to a somewhat unusual extent elderly. There has been a notable deficiency of young fathers, and, still more notably, of young mothers.

V

CHILDHOOD AND YOUTH

The frequency of constitutional delicacy in infancy and childhood
— Tendency of those who were weak in infancy to become
robust later — The prevalence of precocity — University
education — The frequency of prolonged residence abroad in
early life.

THE first significant fact we encounter in studying
the life-histories of these eminent persons is the
frequency with which they have shown marked
constitutional delicacy in infancy and early life.
A group of at least six — Joanna Baillie, Hobbes,
Keats, Newton, Smart, Charles Wesley, with
perhaps Locke and Sterne — were seven-months
children, or, at all events, notably premature in
birth; it is a group of very varied and pre-eminent
ability (to which among eminent men of later date
Lord Rayleigh must be added). Not including the
above (who were necessarily weakly), at least fourteen are noted as having been very weak at birth,
and not expected to live — even given up as dead;
in several cases they were, on account of supposed
imminent death, baptised on the same day. Altogether as many as 110 are mentioned as being extremely delicate during infancy or childhood, and
the real number is certainly much greater, for this
is a point which must frequently be unknown to
the biographers, or be ignored by them.

In addition to these, we are told of 103 others (10 per cent) of our eminent British persons that their health was delicate throughout life, so that we may reasonably assume that in most cases their feeble constitutions were congenital. Thus at the lowest estimate 213 of the individuals on our list — a very large proportion of those for whom we have data on this question — were congenitally of notably feeble physical constitution.

Professor A. H. Yoder encountered this fact in the course of his interesting study of the early life of a small group of men of genius (*Pedagogical Seminary*, October, 1894), but failed to realise its significance. He put it aside as due to a desire on the part of biographers to magnify the mental at the expense of the physical qualities of their subjects. There is no evidence whatever in support of this assumption.

The significance of such early delicacy has, however, already been recognised by other writers. Thus Sir W. G. Simpson (*Journal of Mental Science*, October, 1893) points out that illness in children is followed by increased mental development.

It may be noted that a tendency to die at birth is also noted among idiots, who often require resuscitation (Matthews Duncan, *Sterility in Women*, p. 61).

Although it may fairly be concluded that this proportion, at least, of our eminent persons showed signs of physical inferiority at the beginning of life, it must not be assumed that in all cases such inferiority was marked throughout life. The reverse of this is notably the case in many instances. This is not indeed absolutely proved by longevity, frequently noted in such cases, for men of genius have sometimes lived to an advanced age though all their lives suffering from feeble health. But there is a large group of cases (probably much larger than actually appears) in which the delicate infant develops into a youth or a man of quite exceptional physical health and vigor. Bruce, the traveller, is a typical example. Very delicate in early life, he developed into a man of huge proportions, athletic power and iron constitution. Jeremy Bentham, very weak and delicate in childhood, became healthy and robust and lived to 84; Burke, weak and always ailing in early life, was tall and vigorous at 27; Constable, not expected to live at birth, became a strong and healthy boy; Dickens, a puny and sickly child, was full of strength and energy at the age of 12; Galt, a delicate and sensitive child, developed Herculean proportions and energy; Hobbes, very weak in early life, went on gaining strength throughout life and died at 81; Lord Stowell, with a very feeble constitution in early life, became robust and died at 91. It would be easy to multiply examples, though the early feebleness of the future man of robust constitution must often have been forgotten or ignored, and it is probable that this course of development is not without significance.

I have noted that in a very large number of cases one or both parents died soon after the birth of their eminent child. One small but eminent group — including Blackstone, Chatterton, Cowley, Newton, Adam Smith, and Swift — had lost their fathers before birth. We may trace here the frequent presence of inherited delicacy of constitution.

The chief feature in the childhood of persons of eminent intellectual ability brought out by the present data is their precocity. This has indeed been emphasized by previous inquirers into the psychology of genius, but its prevalence is very clearly shown by the present investigation. It has certainly to be said that the definition of 'precocity' requires a little more careful consideration than it sometimes receives at the hands of those who have inquired into it, and that when we have carefully defined what we mean by 'precocity' it is its absence rather than its presence which ought to astonish us in men of genius.* Judging from the data before us, there are at least three courses open to a child who is destined eventually to display pre-eminent intellectual ability. He may (1) show extraordinary aptitude for acquiring the ordinary subjects of school study; he may (2), on the other hand, show only average, and even much less than average, aptitude for ordinary school studies, but

---

* For a summary of investigations into the precocity of genius, see A. F. Chamberlain, *The Child*, pp. 42–46. Cf. also an article by Professor Sully on 'Genius and Precocity,' in the *Nineteenth Century*, June, 1886, and another by Professor J. Jastrow (*Journal of Education*, July, 1888) showing that precocity is more marked among persons of transcendent genius than among the merely eminent.

be at the same time engrossed in following up his own preferred lines of study or thinking; he may, once more (3), be marked in early life solely by physical energy, by his activity in games or mischief, or even by his brutality, the physical energy being sooner or later transformed into intellectual energy.

It is those of the first group, those who display an extraordinary aptitude for ordinary school learning, who create most astonishment and are chiefly referred to as proving the 'precocity' of genius. There can be no doubt whatever that even in the very highest genius such extraordinary aptitude at a very early age is not infrequently observed. It must also be said that it occurs in children who, after school or college life is over, or even earlier, display no independent intellectual energy whatever. It is probable that here we really have two classes of cases simulating uniformity. In one class we have an exquisitely organized and sensitive mental mechanism which assimilates whatever is presented to it, and with development ever seeks more complicated problems to grapple with. In the other class we merely have a sponge-like mental receptivity, without any corresponding degree of aptitude for intellectual organization, so that when the period of mental receptivity is over no further development takes place.

The second group, comprising those children who are mostly indifferent to ordinary school learning but are absorbed in their own lines of thought, certainly contains a very large number of individuals destined to attain intellectual eminence. They by no means impress people by their 'precocity'; Scott, occupied in building up romances, was a 'dunce'; Hume, the youthful thinker, was described by his mother as 'uncommon weak-minded.' Yet the individuals of this group are often in reality far more 'precocious,' further advanced along the line of their future activities, than the children of the first group. It is true that they may be divided into two classes, those who from the first have divined the line of their later advance, and those who are only restlessly searching and exploring; but both alike have really entered on the path of their future progress.

The third group, including those children who are only noted for their physical energy, is the smallest. In these cases some powerful external impression — a severe illness, an emotional shock, contact with some person of intellectual eminence — serves to divert the physical energy into mental channels. In those fields of eminence in which moral qualities and force of character count for much, such as statesmanship and generalship, this course of development seems to be a favourable one, but in more purely intellectual fields it scarcely seems to lead very often to the finest results.

On the whole, it is evident that 'precocity' is not a very valuable or precise conception as applied to persons of intellectual eminence. The conception of physical precocity is fairly exact and definite. It indicates an earlier than average attainment of the ultimate growth of maturity. But we are by no means warranted in asserting that the man of intellectual ability reaches his full growth and maturity earlier than the average man. And even when as a child he is compared with other children, his marked superiority along certain lines may be more than balanced by his apparent inferiority along other lines. It is no doubt true that, in a vague use of the word, genius is very often indeed 'precocious'; but it is evident that this statement is almost meaningless unless we use the word 'precocity' in a carefully defined manner. It would be better if we asserted that genius is in a large number of cases mentally abnormal from the first, and if we were to seek to inquire precisely wherein that mental abnormality consisted. With these preliminary remarks we may proceed to note the prevalence among British persons of genius of the undefined conditions commonly termed 'precocity.'

It is certainly very considerable. Although we have to make allowance for ignorance in a large proportion of cases, and for neglect to mention the fact in many more cases, the national biographers note that 292 of the 1030 eminent persons on our list may in one sense or another be termed precocious, and only 44 are mentioned as not precocious. Many of the latter belong to the second group, as defined above — those who are already absorbed in their own lines of mental activity — and are really just as 'precocious' as the others; thus Cardinal Wiseman as a boy was 'dull and stupid, always reading and thinking'; Byron showed no aptitude for school work, but was absorbed in romance, and Landor, though not regarded as precocious, was already preparing for his future literary career. In a small but interesting group of cases, which must be mentioned separately, the mental development is first retarded and then accelerated; thus Chatterton up to the age of six and a half was, said his mother, 'little better than an absolute fool,' then he fell in love with the illuminated capitals of an old folio, at seven was remarkable for brightness, and at ten was writing poems; Goldsmith, again, was a stupid child, but before he could write legibly he was fond of poetry and rhyming, and a little later he was regarded as a clever boy; while Fanny Burney did not know her letters at eight, but at ten was writing stories and poems.

Probably the greatest prodigies of infant precocity among these eminent persons were Cowley, Sir W. R. Hamilton, Wren, and Thomas Young, all of these, it will be seen, being men of a high order of genius. J. Barry, Mill, and Thirlwall were also notable prodigies, and it would be easy to name a large number of others whose youthful proficiency in learning was of extremely unusual character. While, however, this is undoubtedly the case, it scarcely appears that any actual achievements of note date from early youth. It is only in mathematics, and to some extent in poetry, that originality may be attained at an early age, but even then it is very rare (Newton and Keats are examples), and is not notable until adolescence is completed.

The marked prevalence of an early bent towards those lines of achievement in which success is eventually to be won is indicated by the fact that in those fields in which such bent is most easily perceived it is most frequently found. It is marked among the musicians, and would doubtless be still more evident if it were not that our knowledge concerning British composers is very incomplete. It is specially notable in the case of artists. It is reported of not less than 40 out of 64 that in art they were 'precocious'; only four are noted as not being specially precocious.

A certain proportion of the eminent persons on our list have followed the third course of early development as defined above, that is to say, they have been merely noted for physical energy in youth. Sir Joseph Banks was very fond of play till 14, when he was suddenly struck by the beauty of a lane; Isaac Barrow was chiefly noted for fighting at school; Chalmers was full of physical activity, but his intellect awoke late; Thomas Cromwell was a ruffian in youth; Thurlow, even at college, was idle and insubordinate; Murchison was a mischievous boy, full of animal spirits, and was not interested in science till the age of 32; Perkins was reckless and drunken till his conversion. It can scarcely be said that any of these remarkable men, not even Barrow, achieved very great original distinction in purely intellectual fields. In order to go far, it is evidently desirable to start early.

The influence of education on men of genius is an interesting subject for investigation. It is, however, best studied by considering in detail the history of individual cases; generalized statements cannot be expected to throw much light on it. I have made no exact notes concerning the school education of the eminent persons at present under consideration; it is evident that as a rule they received the ordinary school education of children of their class, and very few were, on account of poverty or social class, shut out from school education. A small but notable proportion were educated at home, being debarred from school-life by feeble health; a few, also (like J. S. Mill), were specially educated by an intellectual father or mother.

The fact of university education has been very carefully noted by the national biographers, and it is possible to form a fairly exact notion of the proportion of eminent British men who have enjoyed this advantage. This proportion is decidedly large. The majority (53 per cent) have, in fact, been at some university. Oxford stands easily at the head; 41 per cent of those who have had a university education received it at Oxford, and only 33 per cent at Cambridge. An interesting point is observed here; the respective influences of Oxford and Cambridge are due to geographical considerations; there is a kind of educational watershed between Oxford and Cambridge, running north and south, and so placed that Northamptonshire is on the eastern side. Cambridge drains the east coast, including the important East Anglian district and the greater part of Yorkshire, whilst Oxford drains the whole of the rest of England as well as Wales. This at once accounts both for the greater number of eminent men who have been at Oxford and for the special characteristics of the two universities, due to the districts that have fed them, the more literary character of Oxford, the more scientific character of Cambridge. The Scotch universities are responsible for 14 per cent of our eminent men. Trinity College, Dublin, shows 5 per cent. The remaining 4 per cent have studied at one or more foreign universities. Paris (the Sorbonne) stands at the head of the foreign universities, having attracted as many English students as all the other European universities put together. This is doubtless mainly due to the fact that Paris was the unquestioned intellectual centre of Europe throughout the long period of the Middle Ages, though the intimate relations between England and France may also have had their influence. With the revival of learning Italian universities became attractive, and Padua long retained its pre-eminence as a centre of medical study. During the seventeenth century the Dutch universities, Leyden and Utrecht, began to attract English students, and continued to do so to some extent throughout the greater part of the eighteenth century. It was not until the nineteenth century that English students sought out the German universities. Douai might perhaps have been included in the list as the chief substitute for university education for the eminent English Catholics who have appeared since the Reformation.

Stated somewhat more precisely, it may be said that of our 975 eminent men, 217 were at Oxford (232 if we include those who had also been at some other university); 177 were at Cambridge (191 if we include those who had also been elsewhere); 76 came from Scotch universities (Edinburgh 28, Glasgow 21, St. Andrews 16, Aberdeen 11); from Trinity College, Dublin, have come 27 men; 23 (or 47 if we include those who had previously been at some British university) have been to one or more foreign universities (Paris 23, Leyden 9, Padua 6, Utrecht 3, Louvain 3, Göttingen 2, Bonn 2, Heidelberg 2, etc.).

It may be interesting to compare these results with those obtained by Maclean in his study of nineteenth-century British men of ability. He found that among some 3000 eminent men, 1132, or 37 per cent, are recorded as having had an English, Scotch or Irish university education. Of these 1132, 37 per cent were at Oxford, 33 per cent at Cambridge, 21 per cent at Scotch universities, 7 per cent at Dublin, and the small remainder were scattered among various modern institutions. It will be seen that university education plays a comparatively small part in this group. This may be in part due to the lower standard of eminence, but it may also be due to the wide dissemination of the sources of knowledge. In no previous century would so encyclopædic a thinker as Herbert Spencer have been able to ignore absolutely the advantages of university centres.

In America also, as might be expected, a college education has not been received by the majority of able men. Thus Professor E. Dexter ('High Grade Men in College and Out,' *Popular Science Monthly*, March, 1903) shows that not more than 3237 out of 8602 eminent Americans of the nineteenth century (or 37 per cent, exactly the same proportion as Maclean found in Great Britain) are college graduates; those who reach a high grade of scholarship are, however, more likely to become eminent than those of low grade.

While the fact of university education is easily ascertained, it is less easy to define its precise significance. The majority of our men of pre-eminent intellectual ability have been at a university; but it would be surprising were it otherwise, considering that the majority of these men belong to the class which in ordinary course receives a university education. It would be more to the point if we knew exactly what influence the universities had exerted, but on this our present investigation throws little light. In a considerable number of cases, at least, the university exerted no favourable influence whatever, the eminent man subsequently declaring that the years he spent there were the most unprofitable of his life; this was so even in the case of Gibbon, whose residence at Oxford might have been supposed to be very beneficial, for at the age of 14 he had already been drawn toward the subject of his life task. In a large number of cases, again, the eminent man left the university without a degree, and in not a few cases he was expelled. It is evident, however, on the whole, that university life has not been unfavourable to the development of intellectual ability, and that while our eminent men do not appear to have been usually subjected to any severe educational discipline they have been in a good position to enjoy the best educational advantages of their land and time.

Professor Sully in a study of the influence of education on genius, with special reference to men and women of letters ('The Education of Genius,' *English Illustrated Magazine*, January, 1891), had already reached conclusions in harmony with those here set forth: 'It cannot be said that the boys who afterwards proved themselves to have been the most highly gifted shone with much lustre at school, or found themselves in happy harmony with their school environment. The record of the doings of genius at college is not greatly different. No doubt a number of the ablest men have won university distinctions. In a few cases, indeed, a thoroughly original man has carried everything before him. At the same time it may safely be said that a very small proportion of the men of genius who have visited our universities have presaged their after fame by high academic distinction. Thus it has been computed that, though Cambridge has been rich in poets, only four appear in her honours lists. (See article on 'Senior Wranglers,' *Cornhill Magazine*, vol. 45, p. 225.) . . . In many cases we have too clear signs of a disposition to rebel against the discipline and routine of college life. . . . We find further that more than one distinguished man has expressed in later life his low estimate of university training. The conclusion that seems to be forced on us by the study of the lives of men of letters is that they owe a remarkably small proportion of their learning to the established machinery of instruction.'

If this is not a very decisive result to reach, there is another less recognised method of educational development which occurs so frequently that I am disposed to attach very decided significance to it. I refer to residence in a foreign country during early life. The eminent persons under consideration have indeed spent a very large portion of their whole lives abroad, whether from inclination, duty, or necessity (persecution or exile), and it might be interesting to ascertain the average period of life spent by a British man of genius in his own country. I have not attempted to do this, but I have invariably noted the cases in which a lengthened stay abroad has occurred during the formative years of childhood or youth. I have seldom knowingly included any period of less than a year; in a few cases I have included lengthened stays abroad

which were made about the age of thirty, but in
these cases those periods of foreign residence exerted an unquestionable formative influence. I
have excluded soldiers and sailors altogether (as
well as explorers), for in their case absence from
England at a youthful age has been an almost invariable and inevitable incident in their lives, and
has not always been of a kind conducive to intellectual development. Nor have I included the numerous cases in which transference from one part of
the British Islands to another has sufficed to exert
a stimulating influence of the greatest importance.
With these exceptions, we find that as many as
371 of the eminent persons on our list (nearly as
large a proportion as received a university education), during early life, and in all but a few cases
before the age of thirty, have spent abroad periods
which range from about a year, and in very many
cases have extended over seven years, up to extreme cases, like that of Caxton, who went to
Bruges in early life and stayed there for thirty
years; or Buchanan, who went to France at the
age of fourteen and was abroad for nearly forty
years. It is natural that France should be the
country most frequently mentioned as the place of
residence, but France is closely followed by other
countries, and a familiarity with many lands, including even very remote and scarcely accessible
countries, is often indicated. It may further be
noted that this tendency to an association be-

tween high intellectual ability and early familiarity
with foreign lands is by no means a comparatively
recent tendency. It exists from the first; the earliest personage on our list, Saint Patrick, was kid-
napped in Scotland at the age of sixteen, and con-
veyed over to Ireland; it seems, indeed, that in
the nineteenth century the tendency became less
marked, yielding to the average modern Englishman's hasty and unprofitable method of travelling.
In any case, however, it is evident that there has
been a marked tendency among these men of pre-
eminent ability to familiarise themselves in the
most serious spirit with every aspect of nature and
life. It is equally marked among the men of every
group, among poets and statesmen, artists and
divines. It is not least marked in the case of men of
science from the days of Ray onwards; if it had not
been for the five years on the *Beagle* we should
scarcely have had a Darwin, and Lyell's work was
avowedly founded on his constant foreign tours.
In a notable number of cases this element comes in
at the earliest period of life, the eminent person
having been born abroad and spent his childhood
there.* The presence of so large a number of our
eminent men at a university may be in considerable
measure merely the accident of their social position. The persistence with which men of the first

* It may be noted that at least twelve of our eminent persons
— seemingly a large proportion — belonged on one side or the
other to West Indian families, whether or not they were born in
the West Indies.

order of intellect have sought out and studied unfamiliar aspects of life and nature, or have profited
by such aspects when presented by circumstances,
indicates a more active and personal factor in the
evolution of genius.

VI

MARRIAGE AND FAMILY

Celibacy — Average age at marriage — Tendency to marry late
— Age of eminent women at marriage — Apparently a greater
tendency to celibacy among persons of ability than among the
ordinary population — Fertility of marriage — Fertility and
sterility of eminent persons alike pronounced — Average size of
families — Proportion of children of each sex.

WE have some information concerning the status
as regards marriage of 988 of the eminent persons
on our list. Of these, 79, being Catholic priests or
monks (twelve of them since the Reformation),
were vowed celibates.* Of the others, 177 never
married. We thus find that 25.9 per cent never
married, or, if we exclude the vowed celibates, 19.4
per cent. It must of course be remembered that a
certain though not considerable proportion of the
unmarried were under fifty at death, and some of
these would certainly have married had they survived. It may be added that of the women considered separately, about two-thirds were married,
though several of them (especially actresses) who
were unmarried formed *liaisons* of a more or less
public character and in a few cases had several
children.

It must not be supposed that all these eminent

* One or two priests who belonged to the early centuries before the celibacy of ecclesiastics was firmly established and who
consequently married, are not of course included.

men who lived long lives in celibacy were always so
absorbed in intellectual pursuits that the idea of
matrimony never occurred to them. This was not
the case. Thus we are told of Dalton, that the idea
had crossed his mind, but he put it aside because, he
said, he 'never had time.' In several cases, as in
that of Cowley, the eminent man appears really to
have been in love, but was too shy to avow this
fact to the object of his affections. Reynolds is
supposed only once to have been in love, with
Angelica Kauffmann; the lady waited long and
patiently for a declaration, but none arrived, and
she finally married another; Reynolds does not
appear to have been overmuch distressed, and
they remained good friends. These cases seem to
be fairly typical of a certain group of the celibates
in our list; a passionate devotion to intellectual
pursuits seems often to be associated with a lack of
passion in the ordinary relationships of life, while
excessive shyness really betrays also a feebleness
of the emotional impulse. In the case of many
poets who have adored their mistresses with
passionate fervour in verse it would appear that
there has often been no accompanying fervour in
the love-making of real life. Sir Philip Sidney, even
though he was counted the paragon of his time,
with all his sweet sonnets never shook the virtue of
his Stella (Lady Penelope Rich), who yet eloped
some years later with another man who was not a
poet. Even in many cases in which marriage

occurs, it is easy to see that the relationship was rooted in the man's intellectual passion.

The average age at marriage among the 503 men on the list concerning whom I have information on this point is 31.1 years, the most frequent age being 26 years. The distribution is as follows:

Age	Under 20	20—	25—	30—	35—	40—	45—	50—	55—
No. of cases..	16	88	139	110	66	43	28	9	.4
Per cent.....	3	17	27	22	15	8	5	1.7	7

I have ascertained the ages at marriage of the fathers of the eminent persons on my list (not including the fathers who are themselves of sufficient eminence to be included in the list) in 73 cases; they are distributed as follows:

Under 20	20—	25—	30—	35—	40—	45—	50—
3	7	30	18	9	4	1	1

The most frequent age of marriage of the fathers is 25, but the average is 30 years. It would thus appear that while both British men of genius and their fathers tend to marry at an abnormally late period, the former marry, if anything, even later than their fathers.

If, however, in the 54 cases in which data are

forthcoming we compare the age at marriage of
the individual man of genius with that of his (not
eminent or less eminent) father the results are not
quite concordant. It is found that five married at
the same age as their fathers; while 29 were younger
and only 20 older. The deviations from the paternal example are often very considerable in either
direction, and it can scarcely be said that the data
before us suffice for the conclusion that our British men of genius have married later than their
fathers.

If we compare the distribution of the frequency of
the marriage-age among British men of genius and their
fathers with the general population, the contrast is
very striking. In England generally 57 per cent of the
men who marry before the age of 30 marry between the
ages of 20 and 25, a larger proportion than in any other
European country. The curve for the British men of
genius much more nearly resembles that for the general
population in Sweden or in France, where of all European countries marriage is latest. It is, however, of more
significance to compare British men of genius with the
professional classes of their own land, avoiding also the
fallacy of including second or subsequent marriages.
Ansell found that the average age of marriage for clerical, legal and medical bachelors in the nineteenth century before 1840 was about 28 years. There is thus a
small but distinct delay in the age of marriage among
men of genius, a delay which would be still more marked
if we can assume that the gradual tendency, noted by
Ansell as in progress during the nineteenth century, for
marriage to take place later among the professional
classes, may be pushed back to the previous century. It

would be further marked, if the comparison were made more strictly between professional class men of genius and ordinary professional class men, by omitting from the men of genius those of the aristocratic and plebeian classes, among both of whom I find that marriage has frequently taken place very early.

While not disputing the statement of Ansell that during the nineteenth century there was a progressive tendency among the professional classes for marriage to take place at a later age, I am by no means convinced that we can push this tendency back and assert that in earlier centuries marriage among the same classes took place very early. This seems highly improbable. It is much more likely that while there have been fluctuations from time to time, the age of marriage has not on the whole greatly changed, so far as the professional classes are concerned, for many centuries past. I am confirmed in this opinion by an examination of the age of marriage which prevailed in various branches of my own ancestry (belonging to the middle and upper middle class) during the seventeenth and eighteenth centuries; the general average was 29, and taking the seventeenth-century figures separately (though here the numbers are few) it was decidedly higher. The average age, it will be seen, lies between that which I have found for the fathers of our eminent British persons and that found by Ansell for the British professional classes generally before 1840.

I find in the marriage 'allegations' of the Archdeacon of Essex for the years 1791–97, where the age 'about' is given, that the average for 20 bachelors is 26 years. The exact social class is not, however, obvious.

It remains probable that when we take a sufficiently high standard of intellectual eminence the age of marriage is somewhat later than that of the professional classes generally, but it would scarcely appear that the difference is considerable.

The married women among the British people
of intellectual eminence concerning whom we have
definite information, form but a small group of
26 persons, a group too small to generalise about.
Their average age at marriage was 28 years, and
the most frequent ages of marriage were 22 and
40. The distribution is as follows:

Age	Under 20	20—	25—	30—	35—	40—
Number of persons.....	3	9	4	3	3	4

Although the numbers are so small, it is probably not an accident that the most frequent ages of
marriage should be 22 and 40 years. If we take into
account the ages before 30 only, we note a marked
tendency to early marriage, more marked than
among English women of the professional classes,
more marked even than among the general population. But after the age of 24 there is a sudden and
extraordinary fall, the ages of 26 and 27 are unre-
presented altogether, and, still more remarkable,
the slight rise which eventually takes place is
postponed to the ages of 40 and 41, towards the
end of sexual life.

The interpretation of this curious curve is, however, fairly obvious. The claims of the reproductive
and domestic life are in women too preponderant
and imperious to be easily conciliated with the

claims of a life of intellectual labour. The women who marry at the period of greatest general and sexual activity, between 25 and 30, tend either to have their intellectual activities stifled, or else to be seriously handicapped in attaining eminence. The women, on the other hand, who have either married very early and then escaped from, or found a *modus vivendi* with, domestic and procreative claims, or else have been able to postpone the sexual life and its dominating claims until comparatively late in life, enjoy a very great advantage in attaining intellectual eminence.

Thus it is that among British women of genius very few marriages take place during the period of great reproductive energy; the large majority of such marriages fall outside the period between 23 and 34 years of age. In the majority of cases marriage took place before this period, the relationship, from one reason or another, being very often dissolved not long afterwards; but in a very considerable proportion of cases, marriage never took place until after this period. Thus, Fanny Burney married at 41, Mrs. Browning at 40, Charlotte Brontë at 38, while George Eliot's relationship with Lewes was formed at about the age of 36; these names include the most eminent English women of letters. It would thus appear that there is a tendency for the years of greatest reproductive activity to be reserved for intellectual development, by accelerating or retarding the disturbing emotional and practical influences of real life. This tendency might still be beneficial, even when the best work was not actually accomplished until after a late marriage.

Ansell found the age of marriage of English spinsters belonging to the professional classes, previous to 1840, to be 24.75 years, while after 1840 it was 25.53. Mrs. Sidgwick found the age of marriage of the sisters of Oxford and Cambridge women students, in exact agreement with Ansell, to be 25.53 years, while the age of marriage of the students themselves was 26.70. Among the general population in England the chief age of marriage for women is between 20 and 25. At the end of the eighteenth century the average age ('about') of 19 spinsters in the marriage allegations of the court of the Archdeacon of Essex was 23.5 years.

We have now to consider more minutely the status as regards marriage of our British men and women of eminent intellectual ability. When we eliminate the 79 individuals who had taken vows of celibacy and the 177 others who are definitely known not to have married, we have 774. Of these, 732 are definitely known to have married, while the remaining 42 are doubtful. It is probable that the doubtful may be equally divided between the married and the unmarried. We cannot assume that the same proportion of married and unmarried prevails among them as among the known group, for it would appear that in many cases the omission of the mention of marriage is to be regarded as a tacit statement on the biographer's part that the subject was not married. If this is admitted we must conclude that in the whole body of 1030 persons, including the vowed celibates, 277 never married, that is to say, a proportion of 26.8 per cent. If we omit the vowed celibates, the proportion is reduced to 20 per cent. If we leave out of account alike the vowed celibate group and the small dubious group, and consider only those remaining persons, 909 in number, of whom we have definite knowledge, the percentage of those who never married is found to be 19.4. If we consider separately the most recent group, i.e., those whose names are contained in the Supplement to the *Dictionary of National Biography*, the results are not widely different; the proportion of the unmarried being in the ratio of nearly 18 per cent.

It is natural to ask the question whether the tendency to remain unmarried is greater among our men of ability than among the general population. It is, however, obviously difficult to answer the question with any precision, because we must of course compare the men of ability with normal persons not only of the same class but the same period. A consideration of the results seems to suggest that there is a somewhat greater tendency to celibacy among men belonging to the very highest class of genius than there is among the rank and file of able men, but that so far as the latter are concerned the tendency to celibacy is not notably greater than among the ordinary population of the same social class. We see that the most recent group of our eminent British persons, which probably shows a somewhat lower general level of eminence, also shows a somewhat slighter tendency to celibacy. It is probable that among men of eminent ability the tendency to celibacy has always been slightly, but only slightly, greater than among the general population of the same social class.

This conclusion is confirmed by an inquiry made by Professor E. L. Thorndike ('Marriage among Eminent Men,' *Popular Science Monthly*, August, 1902). He sought to ascertain the proportion of married individuals among the 1000 most eminent men in a biographical compilation of contemporary Americans entitled *Who's Who in America*. The standard of ability here demanded is necessarily very much lower than that of the persons in my list. It was found that of those who had reached the age of 40, 12 per cent were celibate, as against 15 per cent for the most recent group (excluding the women) on my list, nearly all of whom had far passed the age of 40. For the whole male population over the age of 40, in the United States, Professor Thorndike states, the proportion of celibates is from 11 to 7 per cent, decreasing with age.

Of the 753 persons whom we may reasonably suppose to have married, 548 are definitely stated to have had children, 112 are definitely stated to have been childless, the remaining 93 are doubtful. If we assume that two-thirds of this doubtful remainder may be included among the fertile group, we may say that 19 per cent of eminent British men and women who married have remained sterile. If, however, we only take into consideration those cases concerning which we have definite information, we find that the proportion of the sterile is about 17 per cent. This is certainly less than the real proportion for the whole married group, for there can be little doubt that in a large number of cases the biographers have made no mention of children simply because there were no children to mention. In many cases, I have been able to verify this statement that the merely negative absence of information meant a positive absence of children, though this is not invariably the case. We may assume that the real proportion of individuals whose marriages were sterile, for the whole of our married group, is more nearly 19 than 17 per cent.

If we consider the 55 women separately, we find that one was a vowed celibate, and 19 others remained unmarried, while of the 35 who were married, 14 certainly had children and 21 apparently had no children. A few of the actresses occupy an uncertain borderland between the married and the unmarried. They have here, however (according to the same rule as has been adopted with the men), been regarded as unmarried, even though they had a recognised family, whenever they were not generally recognised as married.

The number of sterile persons (like the number of unmarried persons) among our eminent men and women must be regarded as, in all probability, an abnormally large proportion in comparison with the general population of the same period and class. It must be borne in mind that the figures which have been given do not represent the proportion of fertile and sterile marriages, but the proportion of *persons* who have proved fertile and sterile in marriage. As many of our eminent persons entered into two or more marriages during life and frequently only proved fertile in one or in none, it is evident that if we were to consider the ratio of fertile and sterile marriages, instead of the ratio of fertile and sterile persons in marriage, the prevalence of sterility would be much more marked.

Simpson found that the proportion of sterile marriages in two Scotch seafaring and agricultural villages was about 10 per cent, while in the British peerage he found that it was about 16 per cent. (J. Y. Simpson, *Obstetric Works*, vol. 1, pp. 323 *et seq.*)

Professor Karl Pearson, manipulating the data furnished by Howard Collins, has found that during the early part of the past century among the middle and upper classes chiefly of British race, or belonging to the United States — a class fairly comparable to those in the present group — the total sterility was about 12 or 13 per cent, rather less than half of this (*i.e.*, about 6 per cent) being due to what may be termed 'natural sterility,' while the remainder (*i.e.*, 6 or 7 per cent) must be set down to artificial restraints on reproduction. At the present day in the United States sterility has greatly increased, and Dr. Engelmann finds it to exist in 20 per cent of marriages in Saint Louis and Boston in dispensary practice, and in 23 per cent among the higher classes in private practice, although among the foreign elements in the population the proportion is very much lower. In New Zealand also, at the other side of the world, sterility is at the present day very marked. Here the methods of registration enable us to form an approximate estimate of the proportion of childless marriages among a population of somewhat mixed British race with a high standard of living, and the proportion of marriages in which there is no surviving child at the father's death is about 16 per cent; but it must be borne in mind that we have to allow for the early death of the children in some cases, as well as for the early death of the father. We have also to remember that this increase of sterility is a modern phenomenon, and that the artificial restraint of reproduction to which it is in large part, if not mainly, due is of recent development. All the indications point to the conclusion that the sterility of our eminent men is greater than that of their contemporaries of the same social class.

I may add that among the 62 eminent married men on my list who appear in the Supplement to the *Dictionary of National Biography* and therefore constitute the most recent group, the proportion who are sterile appears to be in about the ratio of nearly 20 per cent, which very closely approximates to the general average.

In Galton's group of modern British men of science the proportion of sterile marriages was higher; there were no children in one out of every three cases.

It is somewhat remarkable that, although the number of infertile marriages is so large, the average fertility of those marriages which were not barren is by no means small. We have fairly adequate information in the case of 281 of these eminent men. I have not included those cases in which the biographer is only able to say that there were 'at least' so many children, nor have I knowingly included the offspring of second or subsequent marriages. Whether the number of children represents gross or net fertility, it is, unfortunately, in a very large proportion of instances, quite impossible to say. It is probable that in a certain proportion of cases only the net fertility, *i.e.*, the number of children who survived infancy and childhood, has been recorded. It is therefore probable that the average number of children in these fertile families, which is 4.8, must be considered as slightly below the real gross fertility. The average reached is not far from the normal average, and very decidedly below that of the families from which the men of genius spring.

With regard to the distribution of families of different sizes, the results, as compared with the figures already given, are as follows:

Size of Family	1	2	3	4	5	6	7	8
Normal families........	12.2	14.7	15.3	14.1	11.1	8.6	7.8	6.3
Genius-producing families...............	6.9	9.4	10.6	9.4	10.1	10.4	8.9	6.7
Families of men of genius.............	14.2	16.7	10.3	12	11.3	7.4	8.5	4.6

Size of Family	9	10	11	12	13	14	Over 14
Normal families..........	3.9	2.7	1.4	1.0	.5	.2	.1
Genius-producing families..	5.7	4.7	4.9	4.4	2.2	1.9	3.4
Families of men of genius..	5.3	2.1	2.1	.7	2.1	1.0	1.0

Allowing for certain irregularities due to the insufficient number of cases, the interesting point

that emerges is the return towards the proportions
that prevail in normal families; it will be seen that
in all but a few cases the families of men of genius
differ from genius-producing families by approxi-
mating to normal families. It must be remembered
that in neither of our groups are the data absolutely
perfect, but as they stand they confirm the conclusion already suggested that men of genius belong
to families in which there is a high birth-rate, a
flaring up of procreative activity, which in the men
of genius themselves subsides towards normal proportions. The families of the men of genius seem
to differ chiefly from normal families in showing a
greater tendency to variation; there are more very
small families, there are more very large families.

It will be noticed that the families of sizes ranging between three and six, both inclusive, are unduly few. It might be supposed that this is due to
the artificial limitation of families, more especially
since, in Professor Pearson's opinion, the normal
families themselves show a deficiency in those
groups probably due to this cause. I am, however,
inclined to doubt whether that is so in the case of
families of men of genius, although to a small extent
it may be so. It is possible that from the present
point of view the group may not be homogeneous,
but made up in part of men with feeble vitality
and a tendency to sterility, and in part of men with
a tendency towards unusual fecundity, thus leading to a deficiency of medium-sized families.

The relationship which has been found to exist between our British genius-producing families, and the families which the men of genius themselves produce (*i.e.*, the increased fertility followed in the next generation by diminished fertility), does not represent a novel result. It had already been found by Galton (*English Men of Science*, p. 38) in his group of modern British men of science. Eliminating sterile marriages he found that the average size of the families of the men of science was 4.7 children, almost exactly the same size as we have found for the whole group of British men of genius. Galton, however, only took living children into account.

There would appear to be a considerable resemblance between the fertility of genius families and of insane families. We see that our eminent British persons belong to families of probably more than average fertility, that they themselves produce families of probably not more than average size, and with an abnormal prevalence of sterility. In France, Ball and Régis, confirmed by Marandon de Montyel, appear to have found reason for a similar conclusion regarding the insane. They state that natality is greater among the ascendants of the insane than in normal families, but afterwards it is the same as in normal families, while they also note the prevalence of sterility in the families of the insane. The question, however, needs further investigation (Toulouse, *Causes de la Folie*, p. 91).

In the case of 278 families of our British men of genius it has been possible to ascertain the number of children of each sex. This is found to be over 105 boys to 100 girls, a somewhat higher proportion of boys than has prevailed in Great Britain during the past century, but, in accordance with the results we have reached concerning the size of the families of our men of genius, very much closer to the normal average than are the sexual proportions prevailing among the families from which the men of genius spring. If, however, I am right in supposing that in a certain proportion of our cases the biographers have stated not the gross fertility, but only the net fertility (or the surviving children), we are not entitled to expect so close an approximation to the proportions at birth, since the preponderance of boys begins to vanish immediately after birth. The figures thus suggest that the families of men of genius show the same tendency to excess of boys which we have already seen to be clearly marked in the case of the families producing men of genius. The data are too few to indicate whether there is any corresponding excess of girls in the families of women of genius.

VII

DURATION OF LIFE

The fallacy involved in estimating the longevity of eminent men — The real bearing of the data — Mortality at different ages.

IT has long been a favourite amusement of popular writers on genius to estimate the ages at which famous men have died, to dilate on their tendency to longevity, and to conclude, or assume, that longevity is the natural result of a life devoted to intellectual occupations. The average age for different groups, found by a number of different inquirers, varies between 64 and 71 years. One writer, who finds this latter age for certain groups of eminent men of the nineteenth century, argues that here we have a test from which there is no appeal, proving the pre-eminence of the nineteenth century over previous centuries, and its freedom from 'degeneration.' It did not occur to this inquirer to ask at what age the famous men of earlier centuries died. I have done so in the case of a small group of ten eminent men on my list, dying between the fourth and the end of the thirteenth centuries — including, I believe, nearly all those in my list of whose dates we have fairly definite information during this period — and I find that their average age is exactly 74 years. So that, if this test means anything at all, the freedom of the

nineteenth century from 'degeneration' is by no
means proved.

In reality, however, it means nothing. If genius
were recognisable at birth there would be some
interest in tracing the course of its death-rate. But
it must always be remembered that when we are
dealing with men of genius, we are really dealing
with *famous* men of genius, and that though genius
may be born, fame is made — in most fields very
slowly made. Among poets, it has generally been
found, longevity is less marked than among other
groups of eminent men, and the reason is simple.
The qualities that the poet requires often develop
early; his art is a comparatively easy one to acquire
and exercise, while its products are imperishable
and of so widely appreciated a character that even
a few lines may serve to gain immortality. The case
of the poet is, therefore, somewhat exceptional,
though even among poets only a few attain per-
fection at an early age. In nearly every other
field the man of genius must necessarily take a long
period to acquire the full possession of his powers,
and a still longer period to impress his fellow-
men with the sense of his powers, thus attaining
eminence. In the case of the lawyer, for instance,
the path of success is hemmed in by tradition and
routine, every triumph is only witnessed by a small
number of persons, and passes away without adequate record; only by a long succession of achievements through many years can the lawyer hope to

acquire the fame necessary for supreme eminence, and it is not surprising that of the eminent lawyers on my list only five were under sixty at death. Much the same is true, though in a slightly less marked degree, of statesmen, divines and actors.

It is, therefore, somewhat an idle task to pile up records of the longevity of eminent men of genius. They live a long time for the excellent reason that they must live a long time or they will never become eminent. It is doubtless true that men of genius — mostly belonging to the well-to-do classes, and possessing the energy and usually the opportunities necessary to follow intellectual ends of a comparatively impersonal and disinterested character — are in a far more favourable position for living to an advanced age than the crowds who struggle more or less desperately for the gratification of personal greeds and ambitions, which neither in the pursuit nor the attainment are conducive to peaceful and wholesome living. This may well be believed, but it is hardly demonstrated by the longevity of eminent men.

At the same time it is of some interest to note the ages of the eminent persons on our list at death. Though the facts may have little significance in themselves, they have a bearing on many of the other data here recorded. Excluding women, and including only those men whose dates are considered by the national biographers to be unquestionable, the ages of eminent British men at death range from Chatterton the poet, at seventeen, to Sir A. T. Cotton the man of science, at ninety-six.   They are distributed as follows in five-year age-periods:

Age at death..	under 20	20–24	25–29	30–34	35–39	40–44
Men of genius.	1	2	6	14	15	32

Age at death ..	45–49	50–54	55–59	60–64	65–69	70–74
Men of genius .	50	55	76	90	130	139

Age at death..	75–79	80–84	85–89	90 and over
Men of genius.	100	65	46	20

If we consider the number for each year separately, certain points emerge which are disguised by the five-year age-period, though the irregularities become frequently marked and inexplicable. A certain order, however, seems to be maintained. There is scarcely any rise from 27 to 38, and even at 45 only 3 individuals died; but, on the whole, there is a slow rise after 38, leading to the first climax at 49, when 16 individuals died; this climax is maintained at a lower level to 53, when there follows a fall to a level scarcely higher than that which prevailed ten and more years earlier. This lasts for three years; then there is a sudden rise from 7 deaths at 56, to 25 deaths at 57, and this second climax is again maintained at a somewhat lower level to the age of 67, when the highest climax is attained, with 34 deaths. Thereafter the decline is extremely slow but steady, not becoming accelerated until after 80. Each climax is sudden, and preceded by a fall.

A noteworthy point here seems to be the very low mortality between the ages of 53 and 57. It seems to confirm Galton's conclusion, based on somewhat similar data, that a group of men of genius is in part made up of persons of unusually feeble constitutions and in part of persons of unusually vigorous constitutions. After the first climax at 49 the feeble have mostly died out. The vigorous are then in possession of their best powers and working at full pressure; 57 appears to be a critical age at which exhaustion and collapse are specially liable to occur. The presence of these two classes — the abnormally weak and the abnormally vigorous — would be in harmony with the explanation I have already ventured to offer of the deficiency of medium-sized families left by our men of genius.

The age of the women at death is ascertainable in 51 cases. The average is slightly over 62 years. As among the men, there would seem to be among them a small group tending to die early. The age-distribution arranged in periods of five years is as follows:

Age at death......	30–34	35–39	40–44	45–49	50–54
Women of genius..	2	4	2	2	2

Age at death......	55–59	60–64	65–69	70–74	75–79
Women of genius..	5	4	7	4	4

Age at death......	80–84	85–89	90 and over	
Women of genius..	8	4	3	

VIII

PATHOLOGY

Relative ill-health — Consumption — The psychology of consumptives — Gout — Its extreme frequency in men of ability — The possible reasons for the association between gout and ability — Other allied diseases — Asthma and angina pectoris — Insanity — The question of its significance — Apparent rarity of grave nervous diseases — Frequency of minor nervous disorders — Stammering — Its significance — High-pitched voice — Spasmodic movements — Illegible handwriting — Short sight — Awkwardness of movement.

IT has already been noted (p. 118) that at least 10 per cent of our eminent British persons suffered from a marked degree of ill-health, amounting to more than minor discomfort, during the years of their active lives. It is of some interest to observe how these persons are distributed among the various chief classes of ability. This distribution appears to be as follows:

Soldiers and sailors	3	per cent
Statesmen, etc.	7	" "
Men of science	11	" "
Lawyers	13	" "
Men of letters	15	" "
Artists	16	" "
Poets	16	" "
Divines	17	" "

This marked prevalence of ill-health among divines had already been noted by Galton (*Hereditary Genius*, pp. 255 *et seq.*). He analysed the 196 biographies contained in Middleton's *Biographia Evangelica*, and came to the conclusion that there is 'a frequent correlation between an unusually devout disposition and a weak constitution.' He found that over 13 per cent at least were 'certainly invalids,' while a large number of the others were ailing. He found also that of the 12 or 13 who were alone stated to be decidedly robust, 5 or 6 were irregular in their youth, while on the other hand only 3 or 4 divines are stated to have been irregular in their youth who were not also men of notably robust constitutions.

In a large proportion of cases no reference is made by the national biographers to the diseases from which their subjects suffered, nor to the general state of health. This, however, we could scarcely expect to find, except in those cases in which the state of health had an obvious influence on the life and work of the eminent person. In most of these exceptional cases it is probable that the biographers have duly called attention to the facts, and though the information thus attained is not always precise — in part owing to the imperfection of the knowledge transmitted, in part to the medical ignorance of the biographers,* and in part to the deliberate vagueness of their reference to a 'painful malady,' etc. — it enables us to reach some very instructive conclusions concerning the pathological conditions to which men of genius are most liable.

Putting aside the cases of delicate health in

---

* Thus one of the national biographers informs us that a recent Archbishop of Canterbury had an attack of catalepsy, which is a rare and severe form of hysteria; he probably meant apoplexy.

childhood, with which I have already dealt in a previous section, the national biographers state the cause of death, or mention serious diseased conditions during life, in some 400 cases.

It is natural to find that certain diseased conditions which are very common among the ordinary population are also very common among men of pre-eminent intellectual ability. Thus, a lesion of the vessels in the brain (the condition commonly described as paralysis, apoplexy, effusion on the brain, etc.) is a very common cause of death among the general population, and we also find that it is mentioned 44 times by the national biographers.

Consumption, also so prevalent among the general population, occurred in at least 40 cases. While many of the consumptive men of genius lived to past middle age, or even reached a fairly advanced age, the disease is responsible for the early death of most of the more eminent of those men of genius who died young — of Keats in poetry, of Bonington and Girtin and Beardsley in art, of Purcell (probably) in music. Some appear to have struggled with consumptive tendencies during a fairly long life; these have usually been men of letters, and have sometimes shown a feverish literary activity, their intellectual output being perhaps as remarkable for quantity as for quality, as we may observe in Baxter and in J. A. Symonds. But Sterne in literature, and Black, Priestley, Clifford and other eminent men of science are to be found among the consumptives. It is evident that the disease by no means stands in the way of the highest intellectual attainments, even if it is not indeed actually favourable to mental activity.*

There is, however, a pathological condition which occurs so often, in such extreme forms, and in men of such pre-eminent intellectual ability, that it is impossible not to regard it as having a real association with such ability. I refer to gout. This is by no means a common disease, at all events at the present day. In ordinary English medical practice at the present time, it may safely be said that cases of typical gout seldom form more than one per cent of the chronic disorders met with. Yet gout is of all diseases that most commonly mentioned by the national biographers; it is noted as occurring in 53 cases, often in very severe forms. We have, indeed, to bear in mind that gout has been recognised for a long time, and that it is more- over a disease of good reputation. Yet, even if we assume that it has been noted in every case in which it occurs among our 1030 eminent persons (an altogether absurd assumption to make), we

* The psychology of the consumptive — marked by mental exaltation, hyper-excitability, the tendency to form vast plans and to exert feverish activity in carrying them out, with, at all events in the later stages, egoism, indifference, neurasthenia — has been studied by Maurice Letulle (*Archives Générales de Médecine*, 1901); a summary of his study will be found in the *British Medical Journal*, 4th May, 1901. An interesting symposium on the mental state of the consumptive will also be found in the *Archives de Neurologie*, January, 1903.

should still have to recognise its presence in five per cent cases. Moreover, the eminence of these gouty subjects is as notable as their number. They include Milton, Harvey, Sydenham, Newton, Gibbon, Fielding, Hunter, Johnson, Congreve, the Pitts, J. Wesley, Landor, W. R. Hamilton and C. Darwin, while the Bacons were a gouty family. It would probably be impossible to match the group of gouty men of genius, for varied and pre-eminent intellectual ability, by any combination of non-gouty individuals on our list. It may be added that these gouty men of genius have frequently been eccentric, often very irascible — 'choleric' is the term applied by their contemporaries — and occasionally insane. As a group, they are certainly very unlike the group of eminent consumptives. These latter, with their febrile activities, their restless versatility, their quick sensitiveness to impressions, often appear the very type of genius, but it is a somewhat feminine order of genius. The genius of the gouty group is emphatically masculine, profoundly original; these men show a massive and patient energy which proceeds 'without rest,' it may be, but also 'without haste,' until it has dominated its task and solved its problem.

Sydenham, the greatest of English physicians, who suffered from gout for thirty-four years, and wrote an unsurpassed description of its symptoms, said in his treatise, *De Podagra*, that 'it may be some consolation to those sufferers from the disease who, like myself and others, are only modestly endowed with fortune and intellectual gifts, to know that great kings, princes, generals, admirals, philosophers and many more of like eminence have suffered from the same complaint, and ultimately died of it. In a word, gout, unlike any other disease, kills more rich men than poor, more wise than simple.' And another ancient writer, the Jesuit, Father Balde, who in 1661 wrote a work which he called *Solatium Podagricorum*, called gout *Dominus morborum et morbus dominorum*.

I may remark that a much earlier ancient, Aretæus, indicates the superior intelligence of the gouty in his statement that they are specially skilful in the knowledge of the drugs that suit them. In more recent times a long series of physicians have testified to the intellectual eminence of their gouty patients. Cullen said that gout especially affected 'men of large heads'; Watson stated that gout is 'peculiarly incidental to men of cultivated mind and intellectual distinction.' Sir Spencer Wells believed that, in the absence of hereditary predisposition, gout is not easy to produce except 'in men endowed with a highly organised condition of the nervous system,' and again remarks (*Practical Observations on Gout*, 1856, p. 23), in reference to statesmen, 'those who are known to be subject to gout are among the most distinguished for an ancestry rendered illustrious by "high thoughts and noble deeds," for their own keen intelligence, for the assistance that they have afforded to improvements in arts, science and agriculture, and for the manner in which they have led the spirit of the age. . . . I never met with a real case of gout, in other classes of the community, in a person not remarkable for mental activity, unless the tendency to gout was clearly inherited.'

This association of ability and gout cannot be a fortuitous coincidence. I have elsewhere suggested

(*Popular Science Monthly*, July, 1901) that the secret of the association may possibly to some extent lie in the special pathological peculiarities of gout. It is liable to occur in robust, well-nourished individuals. It acts in such a way that the poison is sometimes in the blood, and sometimes in the joints. Thus not only is the poison itself probably an irritant and stimulant to the nervous system, but even its fluctuations may be mentally beneficial. When it is in the victim's blood his brain becomes abnormally overclouded, if not intoxicated; when it is in his joints his mind becomes abnormally clear and vigorous. There is thus a well-marked mental periodicity; the man liable to attacks of gout is able to view the world from two entirely different points of view; he has, as it were, two brains at his disposal; in the transition from one state to another he is constantly receiving new inspirations, and constantly forced to gloomy and severe self-criticism. His mind thus attains a greater mental vigour and acuteness than the more equable mind of the non-gouty subject, though the latter is doubtless much more useful for the ordinary purposes of life, for the gouty subject is too much the victim of his own constitutional state to be always a reliable guide in the conduct of affairs.

It is, however, possible only to speak tentatively of the nature of the pathological relationship between genius and gout, because the true nature of gout itself is not yet definitely known. Some years ago the theory that gout is caused by uric acid was very vigorously promulgated by Garrod and others, and very widely accepted; this theory, however, no longer receives such wide acceptance, and there is a tendency to regard the uric acid produced in gout as a symptom rather than a cause. According to another view which has been maintained by Woods Hutchinson in a very able discussion of this question ('The Meaning of Uric Acid

and the Urates,' *Lancet,* 31st January, 1903), gout is
certainly a toxæmia, but chiefly of intestinal origin
(the uric acid produced by the disease being comparatively harmless), whence it is that the drugs good
in gout are such as either prevent intestinal fermentation or absorb its products. This theory does not, however, clearly answer the question why it is that some
persons and not others are liable to gout. A theory
which has been upheld by a long series of distinguished
clinical physicians regards gout as primarily and
pre-eminently a neurosis; this was the belief of Stahl,
Cullen, Laycock, Dyce Duckworth (Dyce Duckworth,
'A Plea for the Neurotic Theory of Gout,' *Brain,* April,
1880). I should be going beyond my proper province if
I were to state that the facts here brought forward may
be regarded as an argument in favour of the existence of
a neurotic element in the factors producing gout. That,
however, my data confirm the belief in the prevalence of
gout among men of high intellectual ability can scarcely
be doubted.

I have sometimes found that physicians who readily
accept a special association between intellectual ability
and gout, are inclined to account for it easily by an unduly sedentary life probably associated with excesses in
eating and drinking. This explanation cannot be accepted. Many of the most gouty persons on my list
have been temperate in eating and drinking to an extreme degree, and while it is true that the gouty have
often written much, the general energy, physical and
mental, of the gouty may almost be said to be notorious.
Sir Spencer Wells, in questioning the influence of sedentary habits, referred to the remarkable activity of gouty
statesmen, and Dr. Burney Yeo remarks (*British Medical Journal,* 15th June, 1901): 'The gouty patients that
I have seen have, I should say, in the majority of instances, been extremely active and energetic people,

and it is often difficult to get them to take sufficient rest.' I may note that in a much earlier age Aretæus speaks of a gouty person who, in an interval of the disease, won the race in the Olympic games.

It may be of interest to point out in relation to the connection between genius and gouty conditions, that Marro (*La Pubertà*, p. 256) has observed a very constant relation between advanced age of parents at conception and lithiasis in the child. We have already seen that there is a marked tendency among some of our men of genius for the parents to be of advanced age at the eminent child's conception; and it is possible that the connection between gout and genius may thus be in part due to a tendency of some of the gout-producing influences to be identical with some of the genius-producing influences. If this is so we might probably expect to find that the age of the parents of those of our men of genius who belonged pathologically to the lithiasis group would be higher than the general average. I find that the average age of 19 fathers of eminent gouty men is 37.4, and of seven mothers 33.2 years, while the average age of the fathers of eight eminent men who suffered from stone or gravel is 37.2. These averages are slightly, but very slightly indeed, higher than those for our men of genius generally. It must of course be remembered that the general averages are higher than those for the normal population.

It must not, in any case, be supposed that in thus suggesting a real connection between gout and genius it is thereby assumed that the latter is in any sense a product of the former. It is easy enough to find severe gout in individuals who are neither rich nor wise, but merely hard-working manual labourers of the most ordinary intelligence. It may well be, however, that, given a highly endowed and robust organism, the gouty poison acts as a real stimulus to intellectual energy, and a real aid to intellectual achievement. Gout is thus merely one of perhaps many exciting causes acting on a fundamental predisposition. If the man of genius is all the better for a slight ferment of disease, we must not forget that if he is to accomplish much hard work he also requires a robust constitution.

It may be added that the other diseases usually described as of the uric acid group are common among our men of genius. Rheumatism, indeed, is not mentioned a large number of times (11), considering its prevalence among the ordinary population. But stone, and closely allied conditions, are mentioned 25 times (sometimes in association with gout), and as we may be quite sure that this is a very decided underestimate it is certain that the condition has been remarkably common.

There are two disorders, allied to gout and at the same time distinctly neurotic in character, which are decidedly common among our eminent persons, and we must, I believe, regard them as of considerable significance. I refer to spasmodic asthma and angina pectoris. Asthma is distinctly connected with gouty conditions, and occasionally also it alternates with insanity; it is a disorder common in individuals of high nervous temperament.* I have noted it in 14 cases, often as beginning in early life. Angina occurred in about nine cases, certainly a large proportion considering that

---

* I may refer to the slightly analogous respiratory defect in horses called 'roaring' (due to laryngeal hemiplegia), a neurotic disturbance apt to occur in very highly bred horses.

the disease is one which has only been recognised in quite recent times. It is probable that one or two cases were not true angina but that simulated angina which sometimes occurs in neurotic individuals; on the other hand several of the cases mentioned as heart disease would certainly, had they been more definitely described, be set down as angina.*

One other grave pathological state remains to be noticed in this connection — insanity. To the relationship of insanity with genius great importance has by some writers been attached. That such a relationship is apt to occur cannot be doubted, but it is far from being either so frequent or so significant as is assumed by some writers, who rake together cases of insane men of genius without considering what proportion they bear to sane men of genius, nor what relation their insanity bears to their genius. The interest felt in this question is so general that we may be fairly certain that the national biographers have rarely failed to record the facts bearing on it, although in some cases

---

* The data do not enable us to form any opinion as to the frequency of diabetes, which is, moreover, a disease only recognised clearly toward the end of the seventeenth century. (In 1714 Ford wrote to Swift that Dr. Garth had told him Marlborough was going to Bristol 'to drink the waters for a diabetes.') It is rarely mentioned in the *Dictionary*, but is associated, and seemingly with increasing frequency, with intellectual pursuits. Thus, in France Worms finds (*Bulletin de l'Académie de Médecine*, 23 July, 1895) that in any series of 100 scientists, artists, doctors, lawyers, etc., between the ages of 40 and 60, there will be 10 diabetics.

these facts are dubious and obscure. They may often have passed over gout without mention, but they have seldom failed to mention insanity whenever they knew of its occurrence. It is, therefore, possible to ascertain the prevalence of insanity among the persons on our list with a fair degree of approximation to the truth, as it was known to the eminent man's contemporaries. We thus find that thirteen were, during a considerable portion of their active or early lives, thoroughly and unquestionably insane, in most cases with a clearly morbid heredity which frequently showed itself in early life; in most cases also they died insane. These were J. Barry, Clare, William Collins, Cowper, Denham, Fergusson, Gillray, Lee, Paterson, Pugin, Ritson, Romney, Smart. We further find a second group consisting of individuals who may be said, with a fair degree of certainty, to have been once insane, but whose insanity was either slight, of brief duration, or quickly terminated by death, sometimes by suicide. These were Borrow (?), Chatham (?), Cotman (?), O. Cromwell (?), G. Fox, J. Harrington, Haydon (?), Mrs. Jordan, Kean (?), Lamb, Landseer, Lever, Rodney (?), D. G. Rossetti, Ruskin (?), Tillotson, Sir H. Trollope, Whitbread, Sir C. H. Williams. A third group consists of men who were perfectly sane during the greater part of long lives filled with strenuous intellectual activity, although in two or three cases there was morbid mental heredity or eccentricity

in earlier life, but became insane towards the end
of life. These cases, twelve in number, which may
usually be fairly regarded as senile dementia, are
H. Cavendish, Colman, Marsh, Newton (?), J.
Pearson, Sabine, Southey, Stephen, Swift, Warburton, S. Ward, T. Wright. It would be possible
to add a fourth group of borderland cases in which
the existence of actual insanity was in most cases
dubious, but marked eccentricity not amounting to
insanity was unquestionable. Such were Boswell
and R. Browne and Laurence Oliphant. William
Blake clearly lived on the borderland of insanity,
and Dr. Maudsley indeed declared many years ago
that if the story of his sitting naked with his wife
in his summer house is to be believed, he was certainly insane; this, however, one may be permitted
to doubt. Blake had strong opinions regarding the
action of the sun on the skin, and in a day in which
sun baths are regarded as beneficial we may view
more intelligently the action of a man who was in
many respects a pioneer. I leave this group out of
account. Nor are the cases of suicide, at least ten
in number, necessarily to be regarded as cases of
insanity.

If we count every case of probable insanity
which may be inferred from the data supplied by
the national biographers, and even if we include
that decay of the mental faculties which in pre-
disposed subjects is liable to occur before death
in extreme old age, we find that the ascertainable

number of cases of insanity is 44, so that the incidence of insanity among our 1030 eminent persons is 4.2 per cent.

It is probably a high proportion. I do not know the number of cases among persons of the educated classes living to a high average age in which it can be said that insanity has occurred at least once during life, but it is stated that among the general population there are only from 1 to 2 per cent cases of insanity. It may be lower, but at the same time it can scarcely be so very much lower that we are entitled to say that there is a special and peculiar connection between genius and insanity. The association of genius with insanity is not, I believe, without significance, but in face of the fact that its occurrence is only demonstrable in less than 5 per cent cases, we must put out of court any theory as to genius being a form of insanity.

It may be said that although the proportion of insane men of genius is so small, a different result would be attained if we took account of those who sprang from insane stocks, or showed their neuropathic unsoundness by producing insane stocks. 'It is no exaggeration to say,' Dr. Maudsley once boldly wrote, 'that there is hardly ever a man of genius who has not insanity or nervous disorder of some form in his family.' * It is many years since that statement was made, yet neither Dr. Maudsley

* H. Maudsley, 'Heredity in Health and Disease,' *Fortnightly Review*, May, 1886.

nor anyone else has ever brought forward any sound evidence in support of it. So far as the present inquiry bears on the point, it may be said that the number of those men of genius who are noted as having a father or mother who became insane, or children who became insane, is very small indeed, the cases of insanity in the descendants being about equal to those of insanity in the ascendants. Less than two per cent of our eminent persons are stated to have had either insane parents or insane children. We may certainly believe that the records are incomplete, but there is clearly no ground for believing that an insane heredity is eminently productive of intellectual ability. The notion sometimes put forward that in discouraging the marriages of persons belonging to mentally unsound stocks we are limiting the production of genius is without support.

While I cannot compare with any precision the liability of persons of genius to insanity with the similar liability of corresponding normal classes, there is one comparison which it is interesting to make. We may compare the liability of persons of genius to insanity with the similar liability of their wives or husbands. It is noted by the national biographers that in sixteen cases the wives or husband (there is only one case of the latter *) became

---

* This was Mrs. Barbauld's husband; it may be added that the man to whom Harriet Martineau was engaged became insane, and that Hannah More's marriage was prevented by what seems the morbid eccentricity of the man.

insane. We may be fairly certain that this is a decided underestimate, for while the biographers would hold themselves bound to report the insanity of their subjects, they would not consider themselves equally bound to give similar information concerning the wives, while in other cases it may well be that the record of the fact has been lost. If now, in order to make the comparison reasonably fair, we omit the second group of slight cases of insanity and only admit the first and third groups, we find that the proportion of cases of insanity among the persons of genius is 2.4 per cent. Among the conjugal partners, on the other hand (I have not made any allowance for second marriages), it is 2.2 Thus we see that on a roughly fair estimate the difference between the incidence of insanity on British persons of genius and on their wives or husbands is a negligible difference; it is scarcely hazardous to assert that British men of genius have probably not been more liable to insanity than their wives.

At the first glance it might seem that this may be taken to indicate that the liability of genius to insanity is exactly the normal liability. That, however, would be a very rash conclusion. If the wives of men of genius were chosen at random from the general population it would hold good. But there is a well-recognised tendency — observed among all the mentally abnormal classes — for abnormal persons to be sexually attracted to each other. That this tendency prevails largely among persons of eminent intellectual ability many of us may have had occasion to observe. What we see, therefore, is not so much the conjunction of an abnormal and a normal class of persons, but the presence of two abnormal classes.

With regard to the significance of insanity, it must be pointed out that even if there is a slightly unusual liability to insanity among men of genius, there is no general tendency for genius and insanity, even when occurring in the same individual, to be concomitant. Just as it is rare to find anything truly resembling genius in an asylum, so it is rare to find any true insanity in a man of genius when engaged on his best work. The simulation of it may occur — either the 'divine mania' of the artistic creator, or a very high degree of eccentricity — but not true and definite insanity. There seem to be very few certain cases — mostly poets — in which the best work was done during the actual period of insanity. Christopher Smart's one masterpiece may be said to be actually inspired by insanity, and much of Cowper's best work was written under the influence of insanity. Periods of insanity may alternate with periods of high intellectual achievement, just as gout may alternate with various neurotic conditions, but the two states are not concomitant, and genius cannot be accurately defined as a disease.

It must also be pointed out, in estimating the

significance of the relationship between genius and insanity, that the insane group is on the whole not one of commanding intellectual pre-eminence. It cannot compare in this respect with the gouty group, which is not much larger, and the individuals of greatest eminence are usually the slightest or the most doubtful cases. Among poets and men of letters, of an order below the highest, insanity has been somewhat apt to occur; marked eccentricity almost or quite amounting to insanity has been prevalent among antiquarians, but the intellectual eminence of antiquarians is often so dubious that the question of their inclusion in my list has been a frequent source of embarrassment.

If we turn from insanity to other grave nervous diseases, we are struck by their rarity. It is true that many serious nervous diseases have only been accurately distinguished during the past century, and we could not expect to find much trace of them in the *Dictionary*. But that cannot be said of epilepsy, which has always been recognised, and in a well-developed form cannot easily be ignored. Yet epilepsy is only mentioned twice by the national biographers — once as occurring in early life (Lord Herbert of Cherbury), once in old age (Sir W. R. Hamilton). Even these two cases, however, cannot be admitted. In Lord Herbert of Cherbury's case the national biographer has simply misunderstood a passage in Lord Herbert's *Autobiography*, in which he tells us how, as he believed, he escaped the epilepsy which he says is common in his family by acquiring a minor disorder in childhood, a 'defluxion of the ears' which 'purged his system'; in Sir W. R. Hamilton's case the epileptoid fits occurring in old age most certainly cannot be regarded as true epilepsy. There appears to be nothing whatever in the records of British genius favourable to Lombroso's favourite theory, that genius tends to occur on an epileptoid basis.

While, however, grave nervous diseases of definite type seem to be rare rather than common among the eminent persons with whom we are dealing, there is ample evidence to show that nervous symptoms of vaguer and more atypical character are extremely common. The prevalence of eccentricity I have already mentioned. That irritable condition of the nervous system which, in its Protean forms, is now commonly called neurasthenia, is evidently very widespread among them, and probably a large majority have been subject to it. Various definite forms of minor nervous derangement are also common.

Among the minor forms of nervous derangement stammering is of very great significance. I have ascertained that at least thirteen of the eminent persons on my list (twelve men and one woman) stammered. These were Bagehot (?), R. Boyle, Curran, Croker, Erasmus Darwin, Dodgson, Mrs. Inchbald, C. Kingsley, Lamb, Maginn, Priestley,

Sheil, Sidgwick. Seven others are noted as having defects of speech which are sometimes stated not to amount to a stammer, but in other cases were doubtless ordinary stammering. When it is remembered that the normal occurrence of stammering among adults is much below one per cent and also that my record is certainly very incomplete, it will be seen that there can be no doubt whatever as to the abnormal prevalence of stammering among British persons of ability. It may be added that twenty-five persons are described as having a high, shrill, feminine, small or weak voice; this also is certainly very decidedly less than the real number.

Stammering may be defined as a functional disturbance of the central nervous system, congenital or acquired, characterised by involuntary, disorderly spasms in certain muscles concerned in vocal utterance. In other words, it is a spastic neurosis of muscular co-ordination. E. M. Hartwell ('Report of the Director of Physical Training,' Boston *School Document*, no. 8, 1894), following Marshall Hall, describes it as a Saint Vitus's dance of the finer, more peripheral muscles of speech. Stammering is frequently distinguished from stuttering, but it is unnecessary to observe any distinction here, as our knowledge of the precise nature of the voice defects found among our men of genius is often imperfect. We may with Wyllie regard 'stammering' as the general term. Clouston, in his *Neuroses of Development*, regards stammering as specially associated with rapid brain growth, and as most likely to occur between birth and the seventh year. In his careful investigation among Boston school children Hartwell found that stammering became more prevalent at the beginning of accelerated growth, just before or just after such growth culminates, and again after its cessation, and he concludes that the irritability of the nervous system of which stammering is an expression, is correlated with the most marked upward and downward fluctuations of the power of the organism to resist lethal influences. Stammering is much less common in adults than in children and is three to four times more frequent in men. Among male adults its frequency has been most carefully investigated in recruits, and its prevalence found to be, according to the standard adopted, 3 to 6 per thousand in France (Chervin), as well as among French recruits in the American War of Secession (Baxter), 1.2 per thousand among native American recruits during the same war (Baxter), and exactly the same in Russia (Ssikorski).

In persons of neuropathic inheritance, stammering is specially liable to occur. 'Even in the very intelligent,' Wyllie remarks (*Disorders of Speech*, p. 22), 'it may be found associated with nervousness and excitability as well as sometimes with more distinct irritability of the nervous system.'

Among the nervously abnormal classes stammering and allied speech defects occur with especial frequency. This is notably the case among mental defectives. Thus in Berlin, Cassel found that 33.5 per cent of defective children showed infirmities of speech, and Dr. Eichholz, a London School Inspector, states ('The Treatment of Feeble-Minded Children,' *British Medical Journal*, 6th September, 1902) that 'quite 75 per cent of defective children speak imperfectly, ranging from complete aphasia to a mere indistinct thickening, including stammering, halting, lisping, word-clipping, mispronunciation, and the mainly purely vocal imperfections.' Most of the minor speech defects mentioned would seem to have been specially prevalent among our British men of genius.

The tendency to very high-pitched voice which is so remarkably common in men of intellectual ability may possibly be due to a slight paralysis of the vocal cords, such as is apt to occur in more marked degrees in general paralysis (as observed by Permewan, *British Medical Journal*, 24th November, 1894), unless it is caused by a general arrest of laryngeal development.

Involuntary spasmodic twitching movements, or tic, of the smaller muscles, especially of the face, would appear to occur with very unusual frequency among our British men of genius, although I have no figures of the prevalence of such convulsive movements among the ordinary population. I have noted the prevalence of this nervous disorder in seven cases: Brougham, W. Hook, Dr. Johnson, C. Kingsley, Marshall, J. S. Mill, and Paley.

In another form a tendency to nervous inco-ordination is shown, by no means necessarily by any actual tremours, in the tendency to bad hand-writing. Illegible handwriting is mentioned in nine cases which certainly need to be largely increased.

A tendency to scrawling or illegible handwriting has been frequently noted among the men of genius of many countries and is by no means due to too much writing, for it is often traceable at an early age. It must be re-membered that the handwriting is a very delicate in-dication of the nervous balance, and as such has been carefully studied during recent years by Kraepelin and his pupils, while alienists have long been accustomed to attribute significance to the remarkable changes in handwriting which often occur under the influence of insanity. As Goodhart has truly remarked (*Lancet*, 6th July, 1889), 'illegibility is a disease'; and he compares it to the defects of speech.

Writer's cramp, to which illegible handwriting is occasionally due, is also, it must be remarked, not the mere result of excessive writing, for, as Féré points out ('Professional Neuroses,' *Twentieth Century Practice of Medicine*, vol. x, p. 707), it occurs more frequently in high officials than in their subordinates who write more, and is associated with mental overwork and neurasthenic and neuropathic conditions.

Short sight, another condition frequently occurring on a basis of hereditary nervous defect, is noted as existing in an extreme degree sixteen times, and in twelve cases some other sense was defective or absent.

A condition to which I am inclined to attribute considerable significance from the present point of view is clumsiness in the use of the hands and awkwardness in walking. A singular degree of clumsiness or awkwardness is noted many times by the national biographers, although they have certainly regarded it merely as a curious trait, and can scarcely have realised its profound significance as an index to the unbalanced make-up of the nervous system. This peculiarity is very frequently noted as occurring in persons who are tall, healthy, robust, full of energy. As boys they are sometimes not attracted to games, and cannot, if they try, succeed in acquiring skill in games; as they grow up all sorts of physical exercise present unusual difficulties to them; they cannot, for instance, learn to ride; even if fond of shooting, they may be unable to hit anything; in walking they totter and shuffle unsteadily; they are always meeting with accidents. Priestley, though great in experiment, was too awkward to handle a tool; Macaulay could not wield a razor or even tie his own neck cloth; Shelley, though lithe and active, was always tumbling upstairs or tripping on smooth lawns. It would be easy to fill many pages with similar examples. It is noted of at least fifty-five eminent men and women on our list that they displayed one or more such inaptitudes to acquire properly the muscular co-ordinations needed for various simple actions of life. In numerous cases this clumsiness was combined with voice defect.

Digital clumsiness, Sir J. Bland Sutton remarks (*British Medical Journal*, 7th November, 1925), referring to its unfortunate occurrence sometimes in surgeons, is 'as much a defect as colour-blindness.'

The reality of the connection between clumsiness of muscular co-ordination and mental anomaly is clearly shown by the fact that in idiocy, the most extreme form of mental anomaly, this clumsiness is seen at its maximum. 'In general,' remarks Dr. W. W. Ireland (*The Mental Affections of Children*, 1898, p. 319), 'idiots or imbecile children are awkward in their motions and slow at learning to walk. . . . No doubt the cause of this lateness in learning to walk is in some cases owing to weakness, in others to nervous diseases; but there are still cases where the child always appeared strong and healthy.

... Their gait, too, is awkward. Idiots in general have a bad balance. ... The same awkwardness applies to the hand.' The awkwardness in the case of idiots is doubtless largely due to absence of mental power. In genius the same result is brought about not by absence of mental power, but by the streaming — not only functionally, it is probable, but organically — of the mental energy into other channels. A cause which we may even consider opposite, leads to a like defect in the muscular machinery.

IX
STATURE

Nature of the data — Tendency of British men of ability to vary from the average in the direction of short and more especially of tall stature — Apparent deficiency of the medium-sized.

As regards stature, I have succeeded in obtaining information in 363 cases; in 276 cases the information is indefinite, in 87 cases definite.

In the first and larger group, which includes women, 119 are said to be tall, 74 of average or medium height, while 84 are short. There is frequently some difference of opinion regarding an eminent person's height, and in selecting the most probable estimate I have borne in mind the common tendency to regard a man who is really of average height as short, and to regard a tall man as of average height; our standard of height, in other words, tends to be above that for the general population. There still results, however, an abnormally small proportion of medium-sized persons, although these form the bulk of the population. This discrepancy may be accounted for, in part, by a tendency among biographers to ignore stature when it shows no exceptional deviation from the average.

The smaller group of men of genius whose height is definitely known furnishes evidence of a more reliable character. The distribution of height in this group is as follows:

ft.	in.		ft.	in.	
5	0...................	2	5	9.................	7
5	1...................	3	5	10................	15
5	2...................	1	5	11................	10
5	3...................	3	6	0.................	9
5	4...................	1	6	1.................	9
5	5.......	2	6	2.................	1
5	6...................	5	6	3.................	4
5	7...	5	6	4.................	3
5	8.....	7			

It will be noted that here, as in the other group, we still have a marked deficiency of medium-sized persons, and a predominance of the tall over the short. It may be said that here also there has been a tendency to ignore the height of the average-sized men of genius, and such a tendency may be admitted as, in the past at all events, accounting for this deficiency; the very marked preponderance of the tall over the short still remains.

If we take five feet nine inches as the average of the class producing men of ability (this was the average height of the fathers of Galton's English men of science), we find that fifty-one of our men of genius are above that height and only twenty-nine below it. It will be observed that there is a very considerable proportion of individuals over six feet in height, and as various other persons on our list are described as gigantic, although their precise stature is not known, we must conclude that there really is an excess of such abnormally tall persons.

It is noteworthy that the men of genius who spring from the lower social classes tend to be abnormally tall. The lower social classes are always shorter on the average than the upper classes.* But it is remarkable that among the very small number of our British men of genius who have sprung from the lower social strata a considerable proportion are not only tall, but excessively tall. Of the seventeen British men of genius who are known to have been six feet one inch or over in height, at least seven sprang from the peasantry or a lower than middle-class social group; these include Cook, Cobbett, Trevithick and Borrow. It would appear — although I do not propose to discuss this question here — that the organic impulse to intellectual predominance, most clearly seen in those individuals on our list whose social environment has been against their development, tends in some degree to be associated with a corresponding energy in physical growth. There may well be in men of genius a tendency to physical variation in both directions, to deficiency as well as to excess, but it is predominantly in the direction of excess.†

* The evidence on this point has been brought together by H. de Varigny, art. 'Croissance,' Richet's *Dictionnaire de Physiologie*, vol. IV.

† The results here reached concerning British men of genius accord with the results reached on a somewhat wider basis in a subsequent chapter ('Genius and Stature') in which I have discussed some of the problems involved. (See pp. 271–88.)

The average height of Cambridge students is nearly five feet nine inches (cm. 174.8). Nearly all other classes of the community in England are below this height.

Porter among Saint Louis children (*Publications, American Statistical Society*, 1894) found that superior intellectual capacity is associated with superior stature, and inferior intellectual capacity with inferior stature, Christopher (*Journal, American Medical Association*, 15th September, 1900) found the same result among Chicago school children. This result has been severely criticised and cannot be accepted without qualification. Gilbert at Iowa found no such correlation but rather the reverse. It must be remembered that there are various kinds and degrees of ability and various ways of testing it. Nor can it be assumed that results that hold good of average school children — even when we have definitely ascertained what those results are — necessarily hold good also of men of genius, who are an extremely exceptional class.

Papillault (*Bulletin Société d'Anthropologie de Paris*, 1899, p. 446) has found that giantism is sometimes associated with infantilism (more or less glabrous condition of body, defective pigmentation, more or less under-development of sexual organs and impulse, etc.), although infantile persons have no necessary tendency to become giants. He believes that there is some deep underlying but yet undetermined connection between the giantism and the infantilism. This is interesting in view of the frequent association of some degree of infantilism with some degree of giantism in men of extraordinary intellectual ability.

Ewart found that children born in the first quarter of the year are the tallest and heaviest. Combe stated that individuals born in summer tend to be taller than those born in winter. Although the numbers are far too small for any decisive statement, our British men of genius

possibly show such a tendency. Unless we take the
extremely low heights, there is not indeed an absolute
majority of winter-born (October — March) over
summer-born (April — September) among the short.
But it certainly appears that while among those whose
height is below five feet five inches there are as many as
four winter-born to six summer-born, among those who
are over six feet one inch there is only one winter-born
to six summer-born.

It was found by Arthur MacDonald that in America
first-born children of school age tend to be larger than
later children. This is not in accordance with the results found at birth, nor can it be said to hold good as
regards the very meagre data furnished by the British
men of genius on my list. A strict comparison is not
possible, but it may at all events be said that the preponderance of eldest children among British men of
genius below five feet seven inches in height is somewhat
greater — if indeed there can be said to be any real
difference — than among those who are over five feet
ten inches. This may possibly be explained by the results of Ewart's inquiry among children of the ordinary
population in England. He found that at the age of six
the eldest child is the tallest and heaviest, but he attrib-
utes this to the absence of a sufficient interval between
births, and when a due interval occurs he finds that
stature and weight tend to reach a maximum with the
third child.

X

PIGMENTATION

Hair-colour and eye-colour — Method of classification — Sources of data — The index of pigmentation — Its marked variation in the different intellectual groups — Some probable causes for this variation.

IF we turn to a further anthropological character, pigmentation, or the colour of the hair and eyes, I am able to bring forward a larger body of evidence, and it is not difficult to supplement the data furnished by the *Dictionary* with the help of portraits, more especially those in the National Portrait Gallery.* I have information on this point concerning 424 of the eminent persons on our list. In classifying by pigmentation I have relied in the first place on the eye-colour, but have allowed hair-colour a certain influence in modifying the class in those cases in which there was marked divergence between the two in lightness and darkness. I have sorted the eminent persons into three classes, according as their eyes were unpigmented (blue),

* The determination of the pigmentation of portraits has been in nearly all cases by personal inspection. The only exception is in the case of several eminent Scotch personages whose portraits were exhibited at the Edinburgh Loan Exhibition of Scottish National Portraits, in 1884. Dr. Beddoe was kind enough to lend me his own carefully annotated catalogue of this Exhibition, with permission to make use of his notes. I availed myself of this permission when necessary, with, I need scarcely say, entire confidence.

highly pigmented (brown), or occupying an intermediate position (combinations of blue with yellow, orange or brown).* This intermediate class
has necessarily been large, and I have comprised
within it three subdivisions: a fair medium, a
dark medium, and, between these two, a doubtful
medium.

I found that the 424 individuals might be thus
classed as regards eye-colour: unpigmented, 71;
light medium, 99; doubtful medium, 54; dark
medium, 85; fully pigmented, 115. The question
arose as to how the results thus obtained might
be conveniently formulated, so as to enable us to
compare the different groups of eminent persons. I
finally decided to proceed with each of these groups
as follows: The doubtful medium persons in each
of these classes were divided equally between the
fair medium and the dark medium; then two-
thirds of the fair medium persons were added to
the fair class, the remaining third to the dark
class, and, likewise, two-thirds of the dark medium

* The chief terms used, popularly and in literature, to describe
eye-colour are (besides blue, which is frequently applied to eyes
by no means purely blue), grey, hazel and black. 'Grey' is applied
to light mixed eyes, *i.e.*, those which show blue with some admixture of yellow or orange; 'hazel,' to dark mixed or greenish
brown, and sometimes to fully pigmented brown eyes; 'black'
eyes do not really exist at all. It seems to me that the terms
'grey,' 'hazel,' and 'black,' should never be used when we are
attempting to define eye-colour with any degree of precision — a
somewhat difficult matter at the best. I may add that my division
of eyes into these main classes is substantially the same as Dr.
Beddoe's.

were added to the dark class, the remaining third to the fair class; the five classes were thus reduced to two, and, on multiplying the fair by 100 and dividing by the dark, we obtain what may be called an index of pigmentation. This method of notation is really simple, and is quite sufficiently accurate for the nature of the data dealt with; it will be seen that by its use an index of 100 means that fair and dark people are equally numerous in a group, while indices over 100 mean an excess of fair persons, and indices under 100 an excess of dark persons.

I may remark concerning this index of pigmentation that, while it yields results which are strictly comparable among themselves in the hands of a single observer, proceeding in a uniform manner, it is doubtful whether two observers would carry it out in a strictly identical manner. Beddoe's index of nigrescence, founded on hair-colour and applied directly to living subjects, is a convenient formula for indicating the degree of pigmentation. But in my observations, largely made on portraits (in which the hair was often whitened by age, absent, concealed beneath a wig, or obscured by the darkening of the paint), it was necessary to accept eye-colour as the primary basis of classification.

I have been able to obtain the index of pigmentation in the case of fourteen groups. I present them with their index of pigmentation in the order

of decreasing fairness, noting also the number of
individuals in each group. Some individuals, I may
remark, are included in more than one group, while
various miscellaneous persons are not included at
all.

Group, with Number of Individuals		Index of Pigmentation
Social and political reformers	(6)	400
Scholars	(7)	200
Lawyers	(15)	114
Soldiers	(23)	110
Men of science	(45)	109
Sailors	(13)	100
Philosophers	(12)	100
Painters, sculptors and architects	(38)	94
Poets	(58)	90
Men and women of letters	(98)	79
Statesmen	(49)	78
Explorers	(7)	66
Divines	(44)	48
Actors and actresses	(18)	30

Although the numbers are for some groups few,
and we must not regard the index as giving results
which are quite invariable, we may accept the
general results with some confidence. It may be
regarded as fairly certain that the first six groups
do really tend to be unusually fair, and the last
three groups unusually dark. The average index of
pigmentation for the British population generally
probably lies between eighty and one hundred, but
it varies greatly if we take separate districts, being
very high in many parts of Scotland and very low
in many parts of the West of England. It is fairly
obvious that this fact furnishes, to some extent, a

key to the position of the various groups in reference to this index. Sailors, who tend to be fair, come largely from the coast, and the inhabitants of the coast are usually fairer than people from inland districts.* Men of science come largely from regions where the population is fair. Artists tend to be fair, both in England and France, and it is at first a little surprising to find that they do not appear higher upon the list. It may be pointed out, however, that a large proportion of our most eminent painters come from East Anglia, a region in which, though the hair is not very dark, the eye-colour is very frequently brown.† Actors come largely from regions where the population is dark. But this factor, though it accounts for much, will not account for everything, nor will it explain the decisiveness of the results. Divines come from all parts of the United Kingdom, yet they tend to be distinctly dark.‡ The darkness of eminent actors is very marked, whatever their place of origin; only one of the eighteen on my list, Munden, falls in the unpigmented group, and he is certainly not an actor

* It has, I believe, been stated by Beyer that there is a preponderance of blonds among the Naval Cadets of the United States.

† During a walk from Sudbury to Hadleigh, in Central Suffolk, I noted the eye-colour of the children and adults I passed, and found that the proportion of brownish eyes to bluish eyes was about 70 per cent to 30 per cent. On the following day I found myself in Colchester, Essex, on Market day; here the proportions were reversed; there were about 70 per cent bluish eyes to about 30 per cent brownish.

‡ This result has also been reached by Dr. Beddoe.

of the highest rank. The extreme fairness of
political agitators and social reformers (religious
reformers, who tend to be decidedly dark, not being
included) is peculiar. The darkness of travellers
and explorers may be explained by a kind of natural selection, fair persons speedily succumbing
to the effects of tropical climates; it may be remarked that this group would have been still darker
if it had not been for the presence of two or three
individuals, of so-called Celtic type, who are fairly
pigmented on the whole, though their eyes are not
dark. It would, however, be out of place here to
discuss fully the very interesting question of the
significance of pigment in relation to intellectual
ability.*

I may say that I regard the results of my observations
in the National Portrait Gallery (though some of the
data are common to both series of observations) as
distinctly more trustworthy in the light they throw on
the relationship of pigmentation to intellectual occupation, not only because the numbers are larger but also
because the standard of ability is much lower, so that
the influences of predilection in the direction of the intellectual ability is less complicated by the possibly
disturbing factor of very high and versatile intellectual
ability. Thus in the small group of very eminent sailors we have several exceptional men like Cook and
Dampier, who were notably dark; the large number of

---

* I have briefly discussed it in 'The Comparative Abilities of
the Fair and the Dark,' a subsequent chapter, based on an investigation of pigmentation in the National Portrait Gallery, independent of the *Dictionary*.

more typical but less eminent sailors in the National Portrait Gallery give us a higher index, which is doubtless nearer to the truth. (I should add, however, that the index of pigmentation was here obtained in a way that at one point slightly differed from that adopted in the later series, *i.e.*, in the National Portrait Gallery groups I simply divided all the medium persons in each group equally between the unpigmented and the fully pigmented sections.)

XI

OTHER CHARACTERISTICS

Personal beauty or the reverse — The eyes — Shyness and
   timidity — Tendency to melancholy — Persecution by the
   world.

A PHYSICAL characteristic to which the national
biographers frequently allude, though I do not
propose to attempt to give it any numerical values,
is personal beauty or the absence of it. A very
large proportion of persons are referred to as
notably handsome, comely, imposing; a very
considerable, but smaller, proportion are spoken of
as showing some disproportion or asymmetry of
feature, body or limbs, as notably peculiar or even
ludicrous in appearance. A not uncommon type is
that of the stunted giant, with massive head and
robust body, but short legs.

There is one feature, however, which is noted as
striking and beautiful in a very large number of
cases, even in persons who are otherwise wholly
without physical attractions. That is the eyes.
It is frequently found that descriptions of the
personal appearance of men of genius, however
widely they may differ in other respects, agree in
noting an unusual brilliancy of the eyes. Thus the
eyes of Burns were said by one observer to be like
'coals of living fire,' and Scott writes that they

'literally glowed'; while of Chatterton's eyes it
was said that there was 'fire rolling at the bot-
tom of them.' It is significant that both of these
instances, chosen almost at random, were poets.
While, however, the phenomenon seems to be
noted more frequently and with more emphasis in
poets, it is found among men of genius of all classes.
One may suppose it to be connected with an unusual degree of activity of the cerebral circulation.

In regard to the mental and emotional disposition
of British persons of genius, the national biographers enable us to trace the prevalence of one or
two tendencies. One of these is shyness, bashful-
ness, or timidity. This is noted in sixty-eight cases,
while fifty are described as very sensitive, nervous,
or emotional, and, although this is not equivalent
to a large percentage, it must of course be remembered that the real number of such cases is
certainly very much larger, and also that the
characteristic is in many cases extremely well
marked. Some had to abandon the profession they
had chosen on account of their nervous shyness at
appearing in public; others were too bashful to de-
clare their love to the women they were attracted
to; Sir Thomas Browne, one of the greatest masters of English prose, was so modest that he was always blushing causelessly; Hooker, one of the chief
luminaries of the English Church, could never look
any one in the face; Dryden, the recognised prince
of the literary men of his time, was, said Congreve,

the most easily put out of countenance of any man he had ever met. It is not difficult to see why the timid temperament — which is very far from involving lack of courage * — should be especially associated with intellectual aptitudes. It causes a distaste for social contact and so favours those forms of activity which may be exerted in solitude, these latter, again, reacting to produce increased awkwardness in social relations. Moreover, the mental state of timidity, which may be regarded as a mild form of *folie du doute*, a perpetual self-questioning and uncertainty, however unpleasant it may be from the social point of view, is by no means an unsatisfactory attitude in the face of intellectual problems, for it involves that unceasing self-criticism which is an essential element of all good intellectual work, and has marked more or less clearly the greatest men of scientific genius. Fundamentally, no doubt, timidity is a minor congenital defect of the nervous mechanism, fairly comparable to stammering. It may be noted that the opposite characteristic of over-self-confidence, with more or less tendency to arrogance and insolence, is also noted, but with much less frequency, and usually in men whose eminence is not due to purely intellectual qualities. In some cases, it would seem, the two opposite tendencies are com-

---

* 'None are so bold as the timid when they are fairly roused,' wrote Mrs. Browning in her *Letters*. The same point has been brought out by Dugas in his essay on timidity.

bined, the timid man seeking refuge from his own timidity in the assumption of arrogance.

In a certain number of cases information is given as to the general emotional disposition, whether to melancholy and depression, or of a gay, cheerful and genial character. In eighty-five cases the disposition is noted as melancholy, in twenty as cheerful or jovial; in seven cases both dispositions are noted as occurring, in varying association, in the same person.*

This marked tendency to melancholy among persons of intellectual aptitude is no new observation, but was indeed one of the very earliest points noted concerning men of genius. According to a saying attributed to Aristotle, all men of ability are melancholy, and Reveillé-Parise, one of the first and still one of the most sagacious of the modern writers on genius, devoted a chapter to the point. It is not altogether difficult to account for this phenomenon. Melancholy children, as Marro found, are in large proportion the offspring of elderly fathers, as we have also found our persons of intellectual eminence to be. A tendency to melancholy, again, even though it may always fall short of insane melancholia, is allied to those neurotic and abnormal conditions which we have found to be not infrequent. Moreover, it certainly has a stimulating influence on intellectual work. The more normal man of cheerful disposition instinctively seeks the consolations of society. The melancholy man, like the shy man, is ill-adapted to society, and more naturally seeks his consolations in a non-social field, such as that of the intellect,

---

* We are here brought to the rather hazardous problem of temperament which has in recents years been suggestively studied by Kretschmer, *Physique and Character* (English translation), 1925.

often plunging more deeply into intellectual work the more profound his melancholy becomes. Wagner said that his best work was done at times of melancholy, and among the eminent men on our list several writers are mentioned who turned to authorship as a relief to personal depression. It may also be said that not only is melancholy a favourable condition for intellectual work, but that the sedentary and nerve-exhausting nature of nearly all forms of intellectual work in turn reacts to emphasize or produce moods of depression.

Another cause that serves largely to accentuate the tendency of men of genius to melancholy is the attitude of the world towards them. Every original worker in intellectual fields, every man who makes some new thing, is certain to arouse hostility where he does not meet with indifference. He sets out in his chosen path, ignorant of men, but moved by high ideals, content to work in laborious solitude and to wait, and when at last he turns to his fellows, saying, 'See what I have done for you!' he often finds that he has to meet only the sneering prejudices of the few who might have comprehended, and the absolute indifference of the many who are too absorbed in the daily struggle for bread to comprehend any intellectual achievement. The wise worker knows this and arms himself with benevolent contempt, alike against the few and the many. Thus of one of the great men of science on our list, Stephen Hales, it was said that he could look 'even upon those who did him unkind offices without any emotion of particular indignation, not from want of discernment or sensibility; but he used to consider them only like those experiments which, upon trial, he found could never be applied to any useful purpose, and which he therefore calmly and dispassionately laid aside.' But it has to be remembered that the prevailing temperament of men of genius is one of great nervous sensitiveness and irritability — so that, as Reveillé-Parise puts it, they are apt to 'roar at a pin-prick,' — and even when they are well aware what the opinion of the world is worth, they still cannot help being profoundly affected by that opinion. Hence a fruitful source of melancholy.

The attitude of the world toward the man of original intellect, being not merely one of disdain or indifference, but constantly tending to become aggressive, has certainly reinforced the tendency to melancholy. It is practically impossible to estimate the amount of persecution to which this group of pre-eminent British persons has been subjected, for it has shown itself in innumerable forms, and varies between a mere passive refusal to have anything whatever to do with them or their work and the active infliction of physical torture and death. There is, however, at least one form of persecution, very definite in character, which it is easy to estimate, since the national biographers have probably in few cases passed it over. I refer to imprisonment. I find that at least 160, or over 16 per cent, of our 975 eminent men were imprisoned, once or oftener, for periods of varying length, while many others only escaped imprisonment by voluntary exile. It is true that the causes of imprisonment were various, but even imprisonment for such a cause as debt may usually be taken to indicate an anomalous lack of adjustment to the social environment. The man of genius is an abnormal being, thus arousing the instinctive hostility of society, which by every means seeks to put him out of the way.

It will be seen that the various personal traits noted in this section, while completing our picture of British persons of genius, may be linked on at numerous points to other traits we have previously noted. It only remains to gather together the threads we have traced and to ascertain how far they may be harmoniously woven into a complete whole.

XII

CONCLUSIONS

The characteristics of men of genius probably to a large extent independent of the particular field their ability is shown in — What is the temperament of genius? — In what sense genius is healthy — The probable basis of inaptitude for ordinary life — In what sense genius is a neurosis.

IT may be reasonable to ask, in estimating the significance of those characteristics of British persons of genius we have here ascertained, to what degree an investigation of persons of eminent intellectual aptitude belonging to other countries would bring out different results. It is not possible to answer this question quite decisively. The fact, however, that at many points our investigation simply gives precision to characteristics which have been noted as marking genius in various countries seems to indicate that in all probability the characters that constitute genius are fundamentally alike in all countries, though it may well be that minor modifications are associated with national differences. The point is one that can only be decisively settled when similar investigations are carried out concerning similar groups of persons of superior intellectual ability belonging to various countries.

A further question may be asked: How far has confusion been introduced by lumping together persons whose intellectual aptitudes have been shown in very different fields? May not the average biological characteristics of the man of science be the reverse of those of the actor, and those of the divine at the other extreme from those of the lawyer? I believe that Galton was inclined to think that the investigation of groups of men with different intellectual aptitudes would yield different results. As, however, we have seen, the investigation of eminent British persons, when carried out without reference to the particular fields in which their activities have been exercised, yields results which, when comparable with those of Galton, do not usually show any striking discrepancies. Nor, so far as I have at present looked into the matter, does it appear that on the whole, when we consider separately the various groups of British eminent persons we are here concerned with, such groups show any widely varying biological characters. Certain variations there certainly are; we have seen that the geographical distribution of the various kinds of intellectual activity to some extent varies, and also that in pigmentation there are in some cases marked variations. On the whole, however, it would appear that, whatever the field in which it displays itself, the elements that constitute the temperament of genius show a tendency to resemble each other.

I shall probably be asked to define precisely what the 'temperament' is that underlies genius.

That, however, is a question which the material before us only enables us to approach very cautiously. There are two distinct tendencies among writers on genius. On the one hand are those who seem to assume that genius is a strictly normal variation. This is the standpoint of Galton.* On the other hand are those, chiefly alienists, who assume that genius is fundamentally a pathological condition and closely allied to insanity. This is the position of Lombroso, who compares genius to a pearl — so regarding it as a pathological condition, the result of morbid irritation, which by chance has produced a beautiful result — and who seeks to find the germs of genius among the literary and artistic productions of the inmates of lunatic asylums.

It can scarcely be said that the course of our investigation, uncertain as it may sometimes appear, has led to either of these conclusions. On the one hand, we have found along various lines the marked prevalence of conditions which can hardly be said to be consonant with a normal degree of health or the normal conditions of vitality; on the other hand, it cannot be said that we have seen any ground to infer that there is any general connection between genius and insanity, or that genius tends to proceed from families in which insanity is prevalent; for while it is certainly true

* In the preface to the second edition of *Hereditary Genius* Galton somewhat modified this view.

that insanity occurs with unusual frequency among
men of genius, it is very rare to find that periods of
intellectual ability are combined with periods of
insanity, and it is, moreover, notable that (putting aside senile forms of insanity) the intellectual
achievements of those eminent men in whom unquestionable insanity has occurred have rarely been
of a very high order. We cannot, therefore, regard
genius either as a purely healthy variation occurring within normal limits, nor yet as a radically
pathological condition, not even as an alternation
— a sort of allotropic form — of insanity. We may
rather regard it as a highly sensitive and complexly developed adjustment of the nervous system
along special lines, with concomitant tendency to
defect along other lines. Its elaborate organisation along special lines is often built up on a basis
even less highly organised than that of the ordinary
average man. It is no paradox to say that the
real affinity of genius is with congenital imbecility
rather than with insanity. If indeed we consider
the matter well we see that it must be so. The
organisation that is well adapted for adjustment to
the ordinary activities of the life it is born into is
not prompted to find new adjustments to suit itself.
The organic inhibition of ordinary activities is,
necessarily, a highly favourable condition for the
development of extraordinary abilities, when these
are present in a latent condition. Hence it is that
so many men of the highest intellectual aptitudes

have so often shown the tendency to muscular in-co-ordination and clumsiness which marks idiots, and that even within the intellectual sphere, when straying outside their own province, they have frequently shown a lack of perception which placed them on scarcely so high a level as the man of average intelligence. It is not surprising that by means of the *idiots savants*, the wonderful calcu-lators, the mattoids and 'men of one idea,' and the men whose intellectual originality is strictly confined to one field, we may bridge the gulf that divides idiocy from genius.

Since a basis of organic inaptitude — a con-dition which in a more marked and unmitigated form we call imbecility — may thus often be traced at the foundation of genius, we must regard it as a more fundamental fact in the constitution of genius than the undue prevalence of insanity, which is merely a state of mental dissolution, in nearly every case temporarily or permanently abolishing the aptitude for intellectual achieve-ment. It must not, however, be hastily concluded that the prevalence of insanity among men of genius is an accidental fact, meaningless or un-accountable. In reality it is a very significant fact. The intense cerebral energy of intellectual reaction involves an expenditure of tissue which is not the dissolution of insanity, for waste and repair must here be balanced, but it reveals an instability which may sink into the mere dissolution of insanity, if the balance of waste and repair is lost and the high pressure tension falls out of gear. Insanity is rather a Nemesis of the peculiar intellectual energy of genius exerted at a prolonged high tension than an essential element in the foundation of genius. But a germinal nervous instability, such as to the ordinary mind simulates some form of insanity, is certainly present from the first in many cases of genius and is certainly of immense value in creating the visions or stimulating the productiveness of men of genius. We have seen how significant a gouty inheritance seems to be. A typical example of this was presented by William Morris, a man of very original genius, of great physical vigour and strength, of immense capacity for work, who was at the same time abnormally restless, very irritable, and liable to random explosions of nervous energy. Morris inherited from his mother's side a peculiarly strong and solid constitution; on his father's side he inherited a neurotic and gouty strain. It is evident that, given the robust constitution, the germinal instability furnished by such a morbid element as this — falling far short of insanity — acts as a precious fermentative element, an essential constituent in the man's genius. The mistake usually made is to exaggerate the insane character of such a fermentative element, and at the same time to ignore the element of sane and robust vigour which is equally essential to any high degree of genius. We may perhaps accept the ancient dictum of Aristotle as reported by Seneca: 'No great genius without some mixture of insanity.' But we have to remember that the 'insanity' is not more than a mixture, and it must be a finely tempered mixture.

This conclusion, suggested by our survey of British persons of pre-eminent intellectual aptitude, is thus by no means either novel or modern. It is that of most cautious and sagacious inquirers. The same position was, rather vaguely, adopted by Moreau (de Tours) in his *Psychologie morbide dans ses rapports*, etc., published in 1859, though, as his book was prolix and badly written, his proposition has often been misunderstood. He regarded genius as a 'neurosis,' but he looked upon such 'névrose' as simply 'the synonym of exaltation (I do not say trouble or perturbation) of the intellectual faculties. . . . The word "neurosis" would indicate a particular disposition of the faculties, a disposition still in part physiological, but overflowing those physiological limits'; and he presents a genealogical tree with genius, insanity, crime, etc., among its branches; the common root being 'the hereditary idiosyncratic nervous state.' Professor Grasset, again, more recently (*La supériorité intellectuelle et la névrose*, 1900), while not regarding genius as a neurosis, considers that it is united to the neuroses by a common trunk, this trunk being a temperament and not a disease. The slight admixture of morbidity penetrating an otherwise healthy con-

stitution, such as the present investigation suggests
as of frequent occurrence in genius, results in an
organisation marked by what Moreau calls a
'neurosis' and Grasset a 'temperament.'

It has been necessary to state, as clearly as
may be possible, the conclusions suggested by the
present study as regards the pathological relationships of genius, because, although those conclusions are not essentially novel, the question is one
that is apt to call out extravagant answers in one
direction or another. The most fruitful part of our
investigation seems, however, to lie not in the aid
it may give towards the exact definition of genius
— for which our knowledge is not sufficient — but
in the promising fields it seems to open out for the
analysis of genius along definite and precise lines.
The time has gone by for the vague and general
discussion of genius. We are likely to learn much
more about its causation and nature by following
out a number of detailed lines of inquiry on a carefully objective basis. Such an inquiry, as we have
seen, is difficult on account of the defective nature
of the material and the lack of adequate normal
standards of comparison. Yet even with these
limitations it has not been wholly unprofitable. It
has enabled us to trace a number of conditions
which, even if they cannot always be described as
factors of the genius constitution, clearly appear
among the influences highly favourable to its
development. Such a condition seems to be the

great reproductive activity of the parents, the child destined to attain intellectual eminence in many cases alone surviving. The fact of being either the youngest or the eldest child is a condition favourable for subsequent intellectual eminence; and I may add that I could refer to numerous recent instances of large families, in which the eldest and the youngest, but no other members, have attained intellectual distinction. We have further seen that there is a tendency for children who develop genius to be of feeble health, or otherwise disabled, during the period of physical development. It is easy to see the significance of this influence, which by its unfavourable effects on the development of the limbs — an effect not exerted on the head, which may thus remain relatively large — leaves an unusual surplus of energy to be used in other directions; at the same time the child, who is thus deprived of the ordinary occupations of childhood, is thrown back on to more solitary and more intellectual pursuits. The clumsiness and other muscular inco-ordinations which we have found to be prevalent — while there is good reason to believe that they are of congenital origin — co-operate to the same end. Again, it is easy to see how the shock of contact with a strange and novel environment, which we have proved to be so frequent, acts as a most powerful stimulant to the nascent intellectual aptitudes. It is possible to take a number of other common peculiarities in the course of the development of genius and to show how they either serve to inhibit the growth of genius along unfruitful lines or to further it along fruitful lines.

Such an investigation as the present is far from enabling us to state definitely all the determining factors of genius, or even all the conditions required for its development. It suggests that they are really very numerous and that genius is the happy result of a combination of many concomitant circumstances, though some of the prenatal group of circumstances must remain largely outside our ken. We are entitled to believe that the factors of genius include the nature of the various stocks meeting together in the individual and the manner of their combination, the avocations of the parents, the circumstances attending conception, pregnancy and birth, the early environment and all the manifold influences to which the child is subjected from infancy to youth. The precise weight and value of these manifold circumstances in the production of genius it must be left to later investigation to determine.

XIII

THE CELTIC SPIRIT IN LITERATURE

Definition of the Celtic spirit — Its feeling for the remote — Its decorative sense — Irish and Welsh literature — The Nordic spirit — The *Chanson de Roland* — The blending of Celtic and Nordic spirits in English literature.

Of recent years we have heard much about the Celts, about Celtic aspirations, about the Celtic movement. Yet the people who talk with confident familiarity about these things would be puzzled if they were asked to define a Celt. Even among those who talk most confidently concerning him, there is no agreement at all as to who the 'Celt' is, where he comes from, or even where he is to be found.

I do not propose to discuss these questions here because they are extremely complicated, and involve the consideration of a mass of technical details which even at the end still leave us in some doubt as to the exact solution we are justified in accepting.* There is, however, a related question which we may approach with some reasonable prospect of solving it: I mean the precise nature of

---

* It is undesirable, and usually misleading, to employ the word 'Celt' in any precise racial sense. It is most correctly used, as I have throughout used it, in a purely conventional sense, to indicate the general population (really of very mixed race) in certain specific regions which were once of Celtic language and culture.

that generally admitted quality which is commonly
called by such vague and unsatisfactory names
as 'Celtic glamour.' If we seek to escape from the
mists with which this question is usually enveloped,
what, precisely and specifically, is this 'Celtic
glamour'?

At the outset it may be necessary to say that,
for the purposes of the question before us, there are
two bodies of literature to investigate. There are,
indeed, five regions in which more or less allied
'Celtic' traditions may be traced: Ireland, the
Highlands of Scotland, Wales, Brittany, and Cornwall. We eliminate three of these, for the High-
land traditions coalesce largely with the Irish, the
Breton are oral, and the Cornish can scarcely be
said any longer to exist at all. There remains Ireland, with a large body of literature which is for
a large part primitive in character, and Wales,
with a smaller body of literature which is later and
sometimes wrought with high artistic skill.*

It may be well, before proceeding, to quote two
passages which exhibit in a characteristic manner
the special qualities of Celtic literature. I choose
two passages in honour of women, always a favourite and felicitous theme to Celtic poets. In the

---

* The general reader who wishes to gain an idea of ancient Irish
literature may do so in Miss Eleanor Hull's collection of the chief
Irish stories or in Lady Gregory's *Cuchulain of Muirthemne* (in
which, however, there is a considerable amount of manipulation).
For the Welsh literature there is Lady Charlotte Guest's admirable translation of the *Mabinogion* (preferably in Mr. Alfred Nutt's
edition).

typical and unexcelled description of Olwen, in
the *Mabinogion*, we are told: 'She was clothed in a
robe of flame-coloured silk, and around her neck
was a collar of red gold set with precious stones and
rubies. Fairer was her hair than the flower of the
broom, whiter her skin than the foam of the waves;
brighter her hands and fingers than the blossom of
the anemone of the waters emerging with its trefoil
flower from the little basin formed by its jetting
fountain. Neither the eye of the moulted falcon
nor that of the tiercel hawk was clearer than hers.
Her bosom was whiter than the swan's, her cheek
redder than the reddest roses. It was impossible
to see her without loving her. Four white trefoils
arose beneath her feet wherever she trod. That was
why she was called Olwen, White Footprint.'

The Ossianic bard thus describes Credhe and her
household: 'A journey I have in hand to Credhe's
mansion against the mountain's breast; it is ap-
pointed for me to go thither, to Credhe, at the Paps
of Annan. Pleasant is the house where she is, with
men and boys and women, magicians and min-
strels, cup-bearer and doorkeeper and horsekeeper.
The command over all belongs to fair Credhe,
the yellow-haired. With coverlet and with down
pleasant will my lot be in her *dun*. A bowl she has
whence juice of berries flows, and therein she makes
her eyebrows black, crystal vats of fermenting
grain, cups and goblets. The colour of her *dun* is
of lime; coverlets and rushes abound there for the

beds; silk is among them, and many a blue mantle, red gold and the polished drinking horn. Her bower is of silver and yellow gold, its ridgy thatch laid without defect, of the crimson wings of ruddy birds. The door posts are green and the lintel of silver taken as spoil from the slain. Credhe's chair on thy left, overlaid with gold, stands at the foot of her delicate bed, a glittering bed, made in the East, of yellow gold and precious stones. Yet another bed, on thy right, of gold and silver, unerringly wrought, with tent-like curtains, like the foxglove's flower, running upon slender copper rods. Pleasant is the lot of her household; their mantles are neither faded nor worn; their full locks are curly and fair. Wounded men with the blood jetting out from them would fall asleep to the fairy birds' warbling in the eaves of her bower. A hundred men there are in Credhe's house from one angle to the other, and thirty fully measured feet is the width of her noble door. Credhe that owns all these things at low water or flood, hath by a spear cast's length excelled all Ireland's women.' * No one

* It will be seen that I have not gone to the Ulster Cuchulain cycle of legends for typical examples of the Celtic temper in literature. The Welsh *Mabinogion*, Renan long since said, is the true expression of Celtic genius, that is, it should be added, in its most self-consciously artistic forms. The Cuchulain stories, while from some points of view the most interesting of all, are more penetrated by mythic conceptions, and are wilder and harsher; they are genuinely Celtic in tone, but have not attained the finest colour and aroma of that temper. Moreover, it must perhaps be added, Ulster has always stood half outside the Celtic world, and that energetic and ferocious spirit that differentiates Ulster and

could doubt that these two passages possess those
peculiar qualities which we term 'Celtic.' The
Welsh fragment renders these in a more deliberately
artistic fashion, the Scoto-Munster Ossianic fragment in a more wayward, a more decadent manner,
but they both appeal to us as having those qualities
which we are pleased to term 'Celtic glamour.'

If we attempt to analyse the special characteristics of such passages, certain very constant elements are slowly revealed. In the first place, we
have what I believe to be the very fundamental
and significant fact that in Celtic literature always
there is presented to us *the remote as remote*. This
sense of remoteness is deliberately sought in the
finest Celtic romances. 'The Dream of Maxen
Wledig' leads us over mountains as high as the sky,
and down rivers, and across seas, before we reach
the far island which holds the enchanted castle of
the tale, and its vanished splendour is brought before us with an unparalleled combination of remoteness and precision. 'The Dream of Maxen
Wledig' is indeed an unsurpassable example of the
remote as remote, of the sense of mystery, of the atmosphere of 'glamour,' not attained by the use of
any cheap devices of mistiness or vagueness, but
clearly and firmly by the hand of a great artist. It

her legends may well have been infused into the Cuchulain cycle
by the stream of Scandinavian invasion pouring into northern
Ireland, an invasion which, by way of Scotland and England, has
continued during historical times.

is instructive, too, because it enables us to see how
the effect was produced. The Celtic mind demands
a great and invisible past of impossible magnificence; all Celtic literature is the search for the
satisfaction of that demand. The memory of the
splendour of Rome which had once been theirs long
haunted the Celtic and especially the Cymric mind;
the Emperor Maxen Wledig, as Loth points out, is
founded on traits of Maxentius, the adversary of
Constantine the Great, and when we realise this
the whole character of the dream at once becomes
intelligible. Sometimes, again, the land of Celtic
legend lies on the farther side of a terrifying mist.
Geraint once reached such a mist from out of
which no man had ever returned. 'Fearlessly and
unhesitatingly Geraint dashed forward into the
mist. And on leaving the mist he came to a large
orchard; and in the orchard he saw an open space,
wherein was a tent of red satin; and the door of the
tent was open, and an apple-tree stood in front of
the door of the tent; and on a branch of the apple-
tree hung a large hunting-horn; and no one was in
the tent save one maiden sitting on a golden chair.'
Such visions only come in Celtic romance to him
who fearlessly and unhesitatingly dashes forward
into the mist, it may even be but the mist of in-
toxication, if, as Renan remarked, the Celt's tendency to drunkenness is to be regarded, not as weakness for gross enjoyment which is altogether absent
in him, but to the need for illusion, the search for

the vision of the invisible world.* In nearly all
poetry, it must be remembered, the element of remoteness is introduced. This element is essential
not only for the attainment of any atmospheric
effect, but also for all elaborate architectonic construction. In the *Arabian Nights* — the only great
work which shows that special romantic quality
which we find in the Celtic legends — not only is
the ancient and highly idealised age of Haroun-al-
Raschid used as a remote mist in which every story
may be plunged to become iridescently beautiful,
but the element of distance, of long journeys, of
great mountains to be overpassed, and great
deserts and seas to be traversed, is constantly used
with elaborate skill; and when we are taken on
board a bark of red sandalwood, with mast of fine
amber and ropes of silk, we feel that we are bound
for a land of romance exactly identical with the
land that Maxen Wledig reached at the end of his
long journey, or that Rhonabwy saw in his dream
when he fell asleep on the yellow calf-skin. But
while the romantic poet, as we universally know
him, makes much use of the element of remoteness,
it is usually his endeavour to attain — what to the
Celtic mind is utterly abhorrent — *the remote as*

---

* Fiona Macleod, admitting that the Celt makes a remarkably
good emigrant, well says: 'Our people have truly loved their land.
... But it is also true that in that love we love vaguely another
land, a rainbow-land, and that our most desired country is not the
real Ireland, the real Scotland, the real Brittany, but the vague
Land of Youth, the shadowy Land of Heart's Desire.'

present. The remote as remote is alien to him, and antipathetic to the passionate sense of life which stirs him; he is not satisfied unless he has vivified it into the present, however various the devices he may adopt. The Homeric poems are so realistic that they never suggested, what we now know to be the fact, that a vast age of heroic civilization lay behind Homer. Dante placed his comedy in the supernatural world, but he is absolutely in the present and only concerned to sit in judgment on the people he had himself known, quite unlike those Celtic travellers to the underworld in whose visions the prototype of the Divine Comedy has been found. Milton sang the origin of the world, but with an incongruity that often startles us to-day he instinctively occupied himself with the ideals, the discoveries, even the mechanical appliances, of his own time.

This feeling for the remote as remote is a fundamental trait of the Celtic poet's conception of his subject. There is another allied and not less fundamental trait in his technical method of dealing with it. His method is always *decorative.* That is to say, he is always concerned to find the beautiful and harmonious detail. The pages of Celtic romance are like a woven tapestry, with bold outline and strong colour as in the Irish stories, or in the Welsh with softly harmonised colours and delicately flowing lines; in either case they produce more nearly than anything in literature the exact effect of an old tapestry.

It has to be said, one must note, that these qualities of Celtic literature rest on certain psychic qualities of the makers of Celtic literature, of which we may here especially set down inventiveness and quick sensibility, two qualities that are allied, or indeed identical. Swift mental response is shown in the delightful wit of the Celt, in his aptness to embroider statements of fact or (as some will have it) to lie, in his faculty for combining incongruous ideas.* Quick sensibility, again, or rapid feminine response in harmony with, or in reaction against, external stimuli, is of all qualities that which we most readily attribute to the Celt. It is a quality of nervous texture, even to some extent a mental quality, and by no means a pure quality of feeling. It thus becomes very misleading to speak, as Matthew Arnold repeatedly spoke in his Celtic lectures, of the *emotional* qualities of Celtic peoples and Celtic literature. If we wish to speak precisely, and to avoid any misleading confusions, it is best to reserve the term 'emotion' for the deep and inarticulate manifestations of feeling, and to use the term 'sensibility' for the more nervous and intelligent quality of quick sensation and response.†

* I may illustrate what is here meant by the example of an acquaintance of mine, a genial Irish priest, who, after gazing at an exceedingly mediocre seascape in a boarding-house dining-room — he prided himself that he was a connoisseur in painting — turned to me with charmingly blended surprise and modest confidence, and declared that he believed it was a Rossetti. The Irish 'bull' is an example of the same wilful or involuntary tendency.

† Mrs. Sophia Bryant, in an interesting study of 'The Celtic

This quick sensibility is, for instance, well illustrated by the Celtic eye for nature imagery, so often used for decorative purposes in the Welsh and especially in the Ossianic literature.

When we have clearly defined to ourselves these precise qualities of the Celtic mind as it displays itself in literature * — that in vision it regards the remote as remote and in method is decorative — we begin to realise the truth that underlies many of the rhapsodical utterances of the writers on 'Celtic glamour.' For instance, we hear much of fairyland of twilight, in this connection. Mr. Yeats has called one of his books 'The Celtic Twilight.' The atmosphere into which all genuinely Celtic things — the Ulster cycle of legends least of all — brings us is quite accurately and precisely described as one of twilight. Twilight has the curious property of making the scenes it envelops appear at once both near and remote. The glowing high lights and dark shadows of full sunlight have disappeared, as also have the commonplace reflections from the clouds of dull daylight; we are left

Mind' (Contemporary Review, October, 1897), has sought to express this in the statement that the main characteristic of the Celtic mind is a high potential, or tendency for the potential to pass swiftly into the actual.

* I here confine myself to literature, or it would be easy to show that exactly the same qualities are shown in painting by men belonging to Celtic peoples. Thus the pictures of Burne-Jones, although he was not born in a Celtic land, or bred among Celtic traditions, show conspicuously the two qualities here emphasised: the sense for the remote as remote and the fundamentally decorative method.

with a vision that is at once both delicate and precise. For a moment a kind of musical silence seems to fill the air; we are conscious of the presence of mystery; we feel as if we had caught a glimpse of a landscape in another world. This impression — fantastic as it may seem, and yet explicable by the conditions of the atmosphere during this brief period of diffused light — very exactly corresponds to the special impression which Celtic romance makes upon us.

II

So far I have tried to define the characteristics of the Celtic spirit in literature without detailed comparison with any other kind of literary temper. Our usual attempts to define the Celtic spirit tend to evaporate in mist because we make no serious effort to put the products of the Celtic imagination beside the products of any other kind of imagination.

It is idle to assert, it may be said in passing, that the characteristics of Celtic literature are simply the characteristics of primitive literature. This is altogether incorrect. In so far as Celtic literature is itself primitive it necessarily shows many features — and more especially the presence of supernatural elements — which have a certain resemblance to primitive literature generally. But it will be found that the literature of savage peoples, however charming or impressive it may be to us at moments, is nearly always essentially a bald statement of what the narrator regards as facts which have their main interest in being facts; its wildest romances are brief, naked, and business-like. Celtic literature, when it is really characteristic, is no longer merely primitive, it has become self-conscious, deliberate, artistic. It can therefore be profitably compared only with literature which has reached a like stage of development.

In Great Britain, and in the northwestern district of Europe, there is one, and only one, literary spirit which can be compared with the Celtic in magnitude, intrinsic force, and permanent influence.* I propose to call it the Nordic spirit, for it is as closely associated with the fair long-headed peoples of Northern Europe (by Deniker termed Nordic) as the Celtic spirit is with the peoples of Central and Southern Europe now or formerly speaking languages of the Celtic family. The Nordic spirit in literature is manifested at first in the Scandinavian lands, then in Northwestern France and Germany, as well as Eastern England and Scotland. The chief of its more primitive embodiments are the Icelandic Eddas, its highest artistic achievement, unmixed

---

* It would be interesting to compare Celtic literature with the Finnish *Kalevala*. But the curious similarities and dissimilarities which such a comparison would show may be due to both arising, in part, from the same sources.

with other influences, is probably the *Chanson de Roland*.

One's first feeling in turning from Celtic litera-ture to Nordic literature is one of dulness and monotony. It deals with the same main themes, battle and love, but the two elements which are almost omnipresent in the products of the Celtic mind — supernatural invention and vivid detail — and add so much charm to the Celtic narration have almost entirely fallen out of the Nordic stories. When, however, we have become really acclimatised to the Nordic atmosphere we per-ceive that the undoubted absence of these ele-ments involves a distinction, but not necessarily a loss; we are simply in another world. There is atmosphere here also, as there always is in fine literary art, not indeed the atmosphere of twilight, but of starlit nights and of storm-swept days. Celtic literature takes us into a world where bright sensations, a restless invention, dominate from first to last; profound human passion, with all its painful and stupid limitations, is not there, is not even conceivable there, for we are in a world where all things are possible. The Celtic story of Tristan and Yseult, it may be noted, only as-sumed tragic vitality and significance when it had been moulded by realistic Nordic hands. Nordic literature is dominated from first to last by emo-tion, and where emotion is there is limitation, tension, pressure; if the fountain leaps high in the air it is because of the oppression at its subterranean heart.

To illustrate the spirit of this literature we may turn to the speech of the dying Brynhild in the Volsunga Saga, the greatest primitive achievement of the Nordic mind: '"And now I beg of thee, Gunnar, one last boon. Let make a great pyre on the plain for all of us, for me and for Sigurd, and for those who were slain with him, and let it be covered over with cloth dyed red by the folk of Gaul, and burn me thereon on one side of the King of the Huns, and on the other those men of mine, two at the head and two at the feet, and two hawks withal; so all is shared equally. And lay there betwixt us a drawn sword, as in the other days when we twain stepped into one bed together; and then may we have the name of man and wife, nor shall the door swing to at the heel of him as I go behind him. Nor shall that be a niggard company if there follow him those five bondwomen and eight bondmen, whom my father gave me, and those burn there also who were slain with Sigurd. More yet would I say, but my life-breath flits; the wounds open." . . . And then died Brynhild and was buried there by the side of Sigurd, and thus their life-days ended.'

The highly charged emotional intensity of Nordic narrative — simple, realistic, heart-felt, without reliance on fantastic prodigies — inevitably involves not merely inaptitude, but dis-

dain for deliberately minute picturesque details.
It equally involves the denial of supernatural aid.
This is so because emotion is a specifically human
quality and can only be adequately manifested
under the conditions of human personality. The
Hebrew Jehovah, with his jealousy, indignation,
and pity, the dwellers in Greek Olympus, with
their restless lusts and rivalries, were alike an-
thropomorphic; a god, as Lucretius and the Epi-
cureans rightly felt, must be serene. All Nordic
literature impresses us as the expression of a
people who are in the highest degree emotional,
practical, serious, in a word intensely human.
They do not feel, as the Celtic man so easily feels,
that after all the boundary between the real and
the unreal is very vague, that the nimble invention can easily create a world for itself, that there
is no misfortune so great that it may not be
straightened out by a twist of the hand of the
juggler who has learnt to control it, and no feat
so stupendous but that somewhere the charm
to perform it may not be found. All Nordic literature is the record of some human passion
to be humanly suffered, some human right to
be humanly achieved, some human wrong to be
humanly wreaked. But Nordic literature reaps
the fruits of its abstention from the picturesque
and the supernatural in the heroic magnificence
which it is thus able to impart to its human
figures, a magnificence which the Celtic hero who

finds extra-human aid on every hand can never attain. There the Nordic poet at once reaches the springs of great art. It would be idle to search all Celtic literature for anything so poignant as the speech of the dying Brynhild.

The Nordic poet is, however, an artist in his methods as well as in his conceptions. Those realistic and emotional qualities which in the sagas grow somewhat monotonous, in the more developed manifestations of Nordic art become self-conscious and deliberate. The realism remains, but the emotion is more artfully wrought to a climax, and the monotony, instead of being a helpless accident, becomes a method of heightening the total effect, so that on the basis of the primitive realism, human emotion and monotony, it becomes possible to erect a great architectonic poem far beyond the reach of pure Celtic art.* The supreme Nordic poem of mediæval times — for the Volsunga Saga belongs to a more primitive stage of culture — is without doubt the *Chanson de Roland*. That is indeed the final manifestation of the pure Nordic spirit on a great scale. After the eleventh century literary traditions began to be widely diffused in Europe, and it was no longer

* Mrs. Sophia Bryant, admitting the artistic imperfection of the Irish, traces it, ingeniously and perhaps truly, in part at least, to their positive activity in creativeness, annulling self-criticism, and allowing imperfect work to stand, 'the vividness of the ideal making up for the inadequacy of its realisation.' The deliberation and hesitancy of the Nordic mind, on the other hand, involve perpetual self-criticism and progress.

possible for any great work of genius to grow up in isolation. The *Chanson de Roland* existed in a germinal form before the coming of the Northmen to Western Neustria — to Roland's home in the march of Brittany, where, however, as Gaston Paris suggested, the Nordic spirit probably already existed — but the work of genius in which it has come down to us was, in the opinion of good authorities, probably written by a Norman and it may be in the neighbourhood of Mont Saint Michel. The story of Charlemagne's disastrous expedition into Spain against the infidels and the defeat and death of his faithful paladins in the pass of Roncesvalles is not only the finest manifestation of the special qualities of the Nordic spirit, it is one of the great summits of literature. Rough, firm, precise, realistic, monotonous, with no charming decorative detail, with scarcely a single simile in the whole length of it, the *Chanson de Roland* might have merely been what in one aspect it really is, a record of feats of arms. But it is far more than this. The element of combat sinks into the background, and the epic poem becomes a tragic drama appealing to the universal emotion of mankind. This poet is a supreme artist, and even the baldness and monotony of his narrative, the plain hard roughness of his verse, become elements in the great effects he attains. Charlemagne in his retreat from Saragossa to his palace at Aix-la-Chapelle, unwitting of danger or treachery yet oppressed by a vague dread, places Roland and the chief of his peers at the head of the little rear-guard, innocent of the fate that is slowly winding its coils around them. In every subtle way the poet makes us realise the tragedy that is approaching as the four hundred thousand infidels slowly close round the undaunted little band of heroes cheerfully affronting their doom, and the fascination of the narrative is not in its record of feats of arms, but its massive and poignant appeal to the most fundamental human emotions, to the pity and terror of the fate of brave men who succumb beneath the stroke of fate, to the depth and the beauty of the bands of affection which bind those who have long faced together the good and the bad chances of life. To the Celtic mind bloodshed and slaughter are as empty of emotional human content as for the child who knows not what they mean; he remains light-hearted throughout, and when the hosts of Queen Meave are flung against the might of Cuchulain and thousands fall in a moment it is all sheer gaiety and not one pulse of the blood is stirred. To the Nordic mind every stroke is felt to vibrate through the fibres of human flesh, and becomes an appeal not to the decorative imagination but to all the emotions that make us men and bind together the world with links of sympathy. It is impossible to claim that the great unknown poet who wrought the *Chanson de Roland* was

ever conscious of this fact, but it is the very stuff
of his art; it is the woof in which he worked with
such splendid energy and force. When at length
the Moslems close on the band of paladins with
their men who nearly all lie dead in the pass,
and Roland consents to blow his horn, his famous *olifant*, and the aged emperor thirty leagues
away hears the long and melancholy blast that the
dying paladin sends afar till the blood starts from
his eyes, the emotional tension of the *Song of
Roland* reaches its highest point. In his own more
primitive way and with the limited resources of a
single art this poet attains the same kind of massive power in the art of playing on the throbbing
pulse of human emotion, which in more recent
times and in a more complex manner was achieved
by Wagner. We realise how it is that that remote idyllic spot in the land of the Basques, the
green plain amid wooded heights and browsing
goats, Roncesvalles, is one of the sacred places of
our race.

III

The *Chanson de Roland* represents the last
great achievement of the pure Nordic spirit on
the European mainland. In the isolation of lands
cut off by the sea, like Iceland and Ireland, it was
possible for the unmixed Nordic spirit, the unmixed Celtic spirit, to develop more or less un-
hampered by alien traditions during one or two

succeeding centuries — though it must be remembered that the traditions were never quite
pure, for even the *Mabinogion* was faintly touched
by Norman influence, and even the Icelandic
Eddas, it may be, were touched by Irish influence
— but on the Continent the growth of civilisation, the spread of written literature, the cos-
mopolitan authority of the Church, the growing
international social intercourse, soon familiarised
all the makers of literature with each other's
work, and the special themes of Celtic poet and
Nordic poet — so far as they were not too subtle
for transmission — became common property.
In England this fusion was even more complete
than in Continental Europe, for here the two
spirits, each in its finest form, were brought together. The Danish or Anglian element in Eastern
England was thus mightily reinforced when the
Normans came, and the *Chanson de Roland* has
come down to us in an English manuscript. On
the other side of England, in Wales, was the home
of the Arthurian legend, the finest manifestation
of the Celtic spirit, soon to be revealed to England
and the world in the epoch-making work of Geoffrey of Monmouth. The supremacy of England
in poetry is due to the accident which brought
about the union in our island of the Celtic spirit
and the Nordic spirit in their finest forms.

These two elements have now long been exquisitely and inextricably intertwined in our

literature; there has been a mingling of traditions and a mingling of blood. Celtic poet and Nordic poet have seemed to rival each other in aptitude to absorb the spirit and the methods of the other until sometimes in seeming, though in seeming only, each has lost the individuality of his own tribe. A curious illustration is furnished by Malory in his *Morte d'Arthur*. That, we are inclined to say offhand, is essentially a manifestation of the Celtic spirit. Yet it is nothing of the kind. Sir Thomas Malory, it is probable, belonged to the Leicestershire family of that name which settled in Cambridgeshire in the early part of the fourteenth century, a characteristically Danish and Anglian part of England,* and Malory was a man of mainly Nordic spirit. However diligently he may have absorbed the stories and the machinery of Celtic legend, he retains the baldness, the monotony, the avoidance of the supernatural, the instinctive insistence on human interest, which mark the Nordic man. In his hands the Story of King Arthur and his Knights becomes almost as Nordic in its tone as the story of Charlemagne and his paladins is in the *Chanson de Roland*. Again and again we feel in his pages the pulsing throb, the rhythmic swell of the wave of emotion, that we can nowhere hear in pure Celtic literature,

* At the same time, it is of interest to remark, there is a strong element of dark population in Leicestershire, indicating a residuum of primitive British blood.

that we feel below the surface of all Nordic literature.

It is, however, by no means only in the later course of Celtic tradition that we may observe how curiously the two spirits blended or sought to replace each other; we may trace the same phenomenon throughout English literature. Every great English poet, however much he may have leaned to the one side or the other, has combined the Celtic spirit and the Nordic spirit, whether he has absorbed the traditions or inherited the blood. Chaucer, while he certainly belongs in the main to the Nordic side — as we might expect from one so strongly touched by Norman influence and so intimately associated with Eastern England — has yet absorbed the vivacity and imaginative delicacy of the Celtic spirit. Spenser shows the same blending in a more marked and definite form all the more conspicuously since he took up a theme that was more or less Celtic in form. His county, Lancashire, is an old Celtic region greatly overrun by Scandinavian settlers, and we may well believe that he had in his blood an inherited aptitude for both these kinds of literary spirit. We may certainly find it in his work, and the Celtic tapestry of the *Faërie Queene* — happily compared by Landor to an ancient tapestried chamber — is worked with a sober, heartfelt, realistic earnestness altogether Nordic. The intimate way, indeed, in which in Spenser's great poem the web of serious human emotion is, to use his own favourite phrase, 'subtly wrought' into the woof of a legend of 'faery land' — too sweetly and sincerely conceived to be merely conventional and borrowed — is unique in our literature.

Shakespeare, however, is the supreme example of all that has been gained for our literature by the juxtaposition of the men of Nordic and Celtic spirit. Here indeed there is no intimate fusion of the two spirits, but rather, as it were, a constant dramatic opposition and contrast, a duologue which is sometimes manifested in technical minutiæ and sometimes comprehends the whole scope of a play. Fundamentally Shakespeare would appear to belong to the Celtic side, and as the district he sprang from is known to be an ancient Celtic infolding in the otherwise mainly Anglian midlands, this is not surprising. To realise the special qualities of Shakespeare's work we should bear in mind the qualities of the most conspicuous playwright among his contemporaries, Ben Jonson, a Scandinavian Lowlander with all the Nordic qualities, scarcely indeed in quite their finest form, hardly tinctured at all by any Celtic elements. What we feel by comparison in Shakespeare's work is the happy extravagance of its imagery, its extreme swiftness of thought, the light and delicate touch.* As a poet

* Chapman, a very pronounced representative of the Nordic spirit in its qualities and their defects, furnishes an equally instructive comparison.

Shakespeare is marked by his excessive freedom
from bondage to literal fact, by the audacity and
profusion of his metaphors, impressionistic rather
than precise, qualities which were habitual in old
Celtic literature, but are nowhere found in the best
English poetry to an extent which even approaches
Shakespeare.* As a dramatist, also, Shakespeare
rarely presents the typical Englishman; Hamlet,
and Falstaff, and Mercutio — all characteristically
Shakespearean creations — are emphatically all
men of Celtic rather than of Nordic temper, for
they all have in highest degree the qualities of
mental vivacity and quick sensibility. Except to
some extent in the chronicle plays, where the
dramatist was somewhat fettered, it is the same
throughout, and it is noteworthy that as Shakespeare developed and became more truly himself
the more strongly marked is the Celtic spirit in his
work. It begins as a play of elves, besides the
serious and stolid Nordic realism of *Venus and
Adonis*, and it ends by becoming a philosophy of
life. Prospero, the exiled duke who dwells in a
bare island cell and yet has control over nature,
over the world of spirits and the world of man, is
the supreme embodiment of the Celtic artist in

* I have elsewhere shown ('The Colour Sense in Literature,'
Contemporary Review, May, 1896) that Shakespeare's use of colour
words tends to be purely imaginative; they are seldom (as in
Tennyson, for instance, they usually are) an attempt to render the
precise shades of things seen; they are felicitous appeals to the
imaginative vision, not to the bodily eye, and are untranslatable
into actual fact.

literature. Shakespeare here seems to reveal a deliberate sense of the essential unreality of the visible world; imaginative vision, as in all Celtic work, becomes supreme; in the philosophy of Prospero the actual world has ceased to exist in any serious sense, for all Celtic art is the evocation of a mirage. Yet the Nordic spirit, however it may have become attenuated at the end, is very strong in Shakespeare. The unfailing humanity and concentrated emotion, as well as the architectonic qualities, are alike Nordic. The driving energy is Nordic, and one is inclined to say that while as a pure artist Shakespeare more and more definitely developed the Celtic spirit within him, as a man he remained, as revealed in his early poems and in the Sonnets, the human emotional realistic child of the North.

It is unnecessary to follow the perpetual play of the Celtic spirit and the Nordic spirit as they interweave throughout our poetic literature. Every reader may trace it for himself. It is by no means difficult to extend the inquiry to prose literature. Thus Sir Thomas Browne is the almost pure type of the Celt in literature; he has in full measure both the atmospheric remoteness and the decorative detail which we have found to mark the Celtic spirit, together with the freedom from the bondage of law and order, the pervading sense of the unreality of the world, that so usually flow from those Celtic qualities. Everywhere he sees nothing but perpetual miracle; he is an experienced physician familiar with hysteria, and a philosophic thinker as well, yet he cannot help finding the capricious movements of the Devil in human affairs, and uses his influence to burn witches when the day of witch-burning was almost over. He has spent his life in professional work among the positive and progressive East Anglians of prosperous Norwich, yet he remains always what the wild and wayward dreams of his Celtic ancestors in Cheshire have made him, the brother of Traherne and Vaughan. His books are mainly philosophic, a would-be scientific discussion of the phenomena of the universe, yet by no possibility could we suppose him to be of the same race with the genuinely Nordic East Anglian philosopher who preceded him by half a century. Bacon delighted to contemplate the natural world; it was the very instinct of his being to reduce it to law and order, to arrange and to classify; the atmosphere of perpetual miracle which Browne loved to breathe — 'Methinks there be not impossibilities enough in Religion' — would have been altogether abhorrent to him. Superficially it might seem that the jewelled speech of the two men was somewhat alike; yet in reality their styles are wholly unlike, and the soaring iridescent fountain of Browne's eloquence has nothing in common with the sombre splendour that glows through the massive prose of Bacon.

To a careless observer it may seem that the

differences between the Celtic and the Nordic spirits are so subtle as to be almost arbitrary, and that in defining their respective spheres much must be left to the play of fancy. In the psychology of literature, however, we have to learn that it is often the subtle things that are the most fundamental and the most pervasive. Moreover, there is one criterion which, when we can apply it, will always furnish an objective test of the soundness of the conclusions reached in this field by processes of psychological analysis. If the poet of mainly Celtic spirit is found to drive his ancestral roots into a Celtic district of our land, the mainly Nordic poet into a Nordic district, or if the poet who conspicuously combines the two spirits is found to belong ancestrally to districts of both characters, then we may reasonably conclude that our psychological analysis is justified. And this is what we constantly find when the facts are within reach. It is certainly no accident that the two poets of the early nineteenth century who have most definitely rendered the Celtic spirit, Keats and Coleridge, come from the southwestern peninsula of England, a region which we know to be still largely occupied by a people once of Celtic speech. Neither poet would have regarded himself as a Celt, and neither had any adequate opportunity of realising what Celtic speech and literature are. Yet, with whatever other demand the genius of Keats held, some of his longer poems take on the dreamy though decorative character which we have found to characterise all genuine Celtic literature in its finest manifestations and are full of delight in detail which has never been realised; while of his shorter poems 'La Belle Dame sans Merci' is the typical expression of the Celtic imaginative mood, and the 'magic casements' have rightly become the classical example of the kind of vision which characterises the Celt in literature. Coleridge, similarly, in the 'Ancient Mariner,' 'Kubla Khan,' and a few other pieces, has in his own peculiar and personal way attained the expression of like qualities although his genius was less purely confined within poetic limits. How truly the spirit of a poet's work is an inborn grace and not an entirely acquired accomplishment we realise when we turn to Tennyson, who was fascinated by the Celtic Arthurian legend, as Milton had once been, but less wise than Milton determined to adapt himself to the task of a new presentation of it, only to achieve a work of feminine elegance in which the fine qualities of his own art almost altogether disappeared. Tennyson was rooted in the most purely Nordic district of England, his art was Nordic, and all his skill could not enable him to weave a poem in the tapestried manner which to William Morris, for instance, who united the Celtic and Nordic elements, was an effortless task.

It is in Ireland that we should expect to find a typical modern Celtic poet, and it is interesting to observe how intimately Thomas Moore, who throughout the nineteenth century was the most popular and typical of Irish poets, exactly reproduces the qualities which we find in the old literature of Ireland. This is the more notable since — unlike the more recent poets — Moore certainly knew and cared very little indeed about the ancient literature of Ireland, however happily he sometimes adapted old folk melodies. He had, he once said, 'that kind of imagination which is chilled by the real scene and can but describe what it has not seen.' The attitude of the Celtic poet could not be better defined. The Nordic poet is a realist; he can describe nothing that he has not realised and felt pulsing in his own blood; he cares nothing for the remote as remote; 'I saw it, I was there,' is his perpetual implicit affirmation. The Celtic poet's imagination is 'chilled by the real scene and can but describe what it has not seen.' It is noteworthy that in Mr. Stephen Gwynn's volume on Moore the qualities attributed to Moore's work in verse are precisely those which we have found to mark the Celtic spirit from the first: remoteness, the lack of reality, the taste for decorativeness and ornamentation, a certain diffuseness and lack of concentration and structure, together with an absence of the personal weight which the sense of reality brings. It is true that the author of the 'Loves of the Angels' was a small man in the world of imagination, while the author of, let us say, 'Hyperion,' was a great poet and imaginative artist, but differences in quality must not blind us to identity of kind.

In another writer of the early nineteenth century we find the Celtic spirit in a finer form than Moore can give it to us, and the example is instructive because it shows how independent spirit is of environmental circumstances. There is no purer example of the Celtic spirit in literature than is furnished by Hawthorne, and even if we never knew that his family sprang from the Welsh Border we could read it in any page of his romances. The early Welsh bards had found their effects in looking back to a remote past when the shadow of the splendour of old Rome had been thrown across their land; their New England child was for ever haunted by a vanished past that was peopled by the sombre heroes driven oversea as exiles from their old English homes. Yet in *The House of the Seven Gables* and the rest, after the lapse of a thousand years we find the exact qualities that we found in the *Mabinogion:* the remote as remote, the minutely realised and decorative detail, the atmosphere of twilight, of a life that is lived in a strange and delicate dream.

I have said nothing of the 'Celtic Movement.' The reason may perhaps be clear. From the point of view of great literature there is no 'Celtic movement' in the petty sense in which it is generally understood, nor are great poets the outcome of such movements. If at the present time we possess one poet at all events who adequately represents the Celtic spirit, it is equally true that the same poetic qualities may be traced throughout the whole of our literature. This is clear even to one who has, personally, no part or lot in the Celtic world. It may indeed be said that until we realise clearly what the Celtic spirit means and what the Nordic spirit means we are without the clue to guide us through our literature. Sagacious observers in the past have from time to time vaguely seen the significance, now of this element, now of that, perhaps occasionally even of both. But the literary historian of the past has failed to grasp that significance in any broad or definite manner. The clue can only be found when we place ourselves at a standpoint at once psychological and ethnological. As we follow it, our rich and varied literature, for the first time, falls into harmonious order.

XIV

THE EVOLUTION OF PAINTING IN ENGLAND

The two European centres of painting — Main characteristics of these centres — The position of Great Britain in relation to them — The Traditional School of the West Coast — The Naturalistic School of the East Coast.

WE cannot understand the course which the art of painting has followed in England, and the influences which have affected that course, unless we understand the main lines along which the art has proceeded in Europe generally. Broadly speaking, there are two primary centres of painting in Europe, differing widely as regards both the races that have constituted them and the conditions that have affected their development. The first of these centres is that of the Mediterranean, that which arose in Greece and Etruria. The other centre is that of the Rhine, more especially the Lower Rhine and the regions extending from its estuary, now known as Holland and Belgium. It is from these two centres that the European art of painting has spread. There are no other primary centres of painting in Europe, and, unless we go back to palæolithic times, it cannot be said that there are any other primary centres of the arts of design generally. There are, however, two secondary centres, of very considerable importance — that of

Venice, which, geographically speaking, merges into that of Etruria, and that of Spain, which is mainly significant through the supreme achievement of a single artist, Velasquez, at his finest point of inspiration in half a dozen pictures. These two secondary centres owe their great interest and charm to the fact that they represent a successful combination of the methods of the North and of the South. Otherwise the two primary centres remain distinct, even although it may be that, if we could go far enough back into the neolithic age, we should find a link of connection between them, for in pre-historic times, as Montelius and others have shown, there were very important commercial routes between the Mediterranean and north-western Europe.

The course of each of the art currents arising in these two centres has been long, in the case of the older of them demonstrably extending over thousands of years, though this southern art-impulse has now been exhausted for several centuries, leaving the northern centre still vigorous and widely diffused. Both continue to exert the influence of their traditions wherever the methods of European painting are practised.

The general characters of the southern and the northern centres are, however, widely different. The southern way of painting expressed the instincts of a people who had not always a close and vivid perception of reality, but who were

artists to the finger-tips. The northern way of
painting expressed the instincts of a people who
were not apt to create beauty of form or line, but
who were infinitely patient in detecting and representing the details of beauty, in colour and light,
of the world that was familiar to them. These
differences were fostered, if they were not even
to some extent caused, by the varying conditions
under which the people of these two races lived.
In the dry and bright air of the South it was possible to paint external wall spaces. Thus arose
a decorative method in which details were sub-
ordinated or suppressed for the creation of flowing
harmonies; this method found its full expression
in fresco painting. In the cold and damp and dark
air of the North such a method was impossible; here
arose oil painting, and by this method were produced small cabinet works in which were sought
the highly elaborated brilliance and colour of great
jewels wherewith to decorate the interior of houses.
The varying climate of the North and the South
influenced the characteristics of these two art-
centres in another way. In the South, where the
light is nearly always equally brilliant, the problem
of light less easily presents itself to the painter. It
is merely a datum which, until his art reaches a
high degree of development, he accepts and ig-
nores. Light, indeed, in the South, is a blessing so
bountifully bestowed on man that he is constantly
seeking to minimise it; so it is that while we find

the architects of northern France always striving
to make their church windows larger and larger,
in the South of France and in Spain they were
always striving either to reduce their windows or
so to dispose them that they let in as little light
as possible. In the North, light is not only comparatively rare and precious, its manifestations
are more varied, and therefore more conspicuous
than in the South. The painter is thus irresistibly
attracted to the manifold and difficult problems
of light, and as his work is small and meant to
be seen indoors, instead of seeking the flat and
broadly flowing harmonies of the southern artist,
he strives to elaborate into one jewel, deeply glowing with light and colour, some single aspect of the
visible world floating in its own atmosphere. Thus
the southern painter is predominantly a decorative
artist who attenuates, traditionalises, or, as we
conventionally term it, 'idealises' the actual world;
the northern artist is predominantly what we are
accustomed to call a 'realist' who seeks to concen-
trate some corner of the actual world in a dazzling
and highly elaborated focus of light and colour.
The southern artist has always tended to restrain
nature within forms demanded by his own traditional conceptions; the northern artist has always
worshipped nature, and has always found it easy
to modify his traditions, and to model his own
conceptions, to the forms of the natural world. It
is dangerous to attempt to set up any all-embrac-

ing formula, but it remains true that we cannot understand the fundamental characteristics of the southern and the northern centres of painting unless we remember that the most typical and significant artists of the one have always set up the canon of tradition, whatever personal modification their own temperaments may have brought to tradition, while the others have at the decisive moment always set up the canon of nature.

I

Great Britain, separated from the Continent, has in painting, as in other matters, been exposed to different influences. It has been affected by the influx alike of races and of traditions from the South and from the North. As regards painting, however, racial impulses remained latent, and traditions non-existent, for very many centuries after the composition of the population had been definitely determined. Mural paintings were no doubt common in English churches, but they are usually of a primitive, crude, and conventional character, and a few fine portraits, a field in which later the English excelled, were produced at an early period. There appears to have been no interest in foreign painting, and no desire to imitate or rival it. At last, towards the middle of the sixteenth century, Holbein was induced by Erasmus to visit England. In all respects an admirable and significant representative of the northern school of painting, he was the greatest painter who had up to that time visited this country. He painted much in England, drew many portrait sketches, left some of his finest work behind him. But it remains doubtful whether he found here more than a very limited appreciation of his work, and of influence he had absolutely none. So far as the development of painting in England is concerned, Holbein might never have visited our shores at all. He seems to have been forgotten, and some of the most important pictures he left behind, like the portrait group of More's family, have disappeared, while to other pictures his name was affixed at random, as a synonym for 'unknown early master.' A few years later, when Shakespeare tries to think of some great artist, it is not the Rhine master nor indeed any Northerner whose name occurs to his mind, but Julio Romano, Raphael's weak follower of ambiguous reputation, is the name that comes to him in a halo of remote Italian romance.

The decisively initiative moment in the evolution of English painting came indeed from the North, but it was the North at a time when the final southern Renaissance wave was now about to spend itself, last of all, on England.

In 1625 there came to the throne a monarch who, whatever his defects as a constitutional ruler, certainly showed a finer taste in painting and a greater enthusiasm in collecting works of art than any English monarch before or since. In this,

indeed, he was but representing a spirit widely
spread in the courts he had visited in youth, but he
represented that spirit with great judgment and
energy. His collections were dispersed to form the
nuclei of some of the most famous foreign galleries;
had they been preserved, England would now
possess the most magnificent collection of pictures
in Europe. Charles I was not content merely to
collect pictures; he desired to have great artists
around him, and though he was not successful
in securing the not very eminent masters whose
presence he sought, chance favoured him by bringing to London the most princely and magnificent
figure that has perhaps ever reached the highest
eminence in painting, the man who still shares with
Velasquez the pinnacle of art in that age. Rubens
came to London as an ambassador, but at Charles's
invitation he stayed to paint. He was thus the
second great painter who worked in England. But
although Rubens doubtless found among the few
cultured English nobles a far more appreciative
public than Holbein could find, he was not destined
to initiate English painting; his own art was too
original and audacious to be understood in a
country where the only paintings at all well
known were the stiff and angular portraits of the
early Flemish and French schools. It was the
influence of a pupil of Rubens who shortly followed
him to England, as a promising place to achieve
fortune, that the taste for painting and the aptitude

to paint in accordance with recognised European methods first appeared in England. Vandyke arrived in London in 1632 at the age of thirty-two, and remained in England many years. He speedily became the fashion; he not only painted the King and the Queen and their family repeatedly, but a great number of persons of quality. He was the first of the long series of fashionable portrait-painters, and unlike his successors he practically had the whole field to himself.

There was good reason why Vandyke rather than either of the two greater painters who preceded him should have exercised this decisive influence on the development and direction of English taste in painting. His unquestionably great and facile talents, his quick impressionability, his accomplished eclecticism, even his monotonous mannerisms, won admiration and applause when more profound and original artists would only have met with indifference and contempt. A public just beginning to awake to æsthetic perception found here exactly what it needed and could understand. To an aristocracy painfully conscious of its unpolished roughness and the barbarism from which it had only just emerged, the particular mannerism of Vandyke and the air of elegant and refined distinction which he shed over his sitters, without too absurdly disguising these robust models, must indeed have been enchanting.* So it is that Van-

* Very significant indeed of Vandyke and of Vandyke's art is

dyke has had the good fortune to leave his mark for
ever on the English men and women of that age;
and the people who were shortly after found vigorous enough to cut each other's throats in the name
of king or country will always appear to us with
the idle attenuated hands and the lackadaisical
affectations which Vandyke has endowed them
with.

Vandyke not only exercised a decisive influence on moulding English taste in painting; it was
under his influence that the first genuinely English portrait-painters, Dobson and Walker, arose.
Dobson, both in date and importance, came first;
although he owed much to Vandyke he was an
artist of virile temperament and slow deliberate
perceptions, very honest and solid in his methods,
with a horror of trickery. So at least he appears in
the excellent pictures by which he is represented in
our National and National Portrait Galleries. He
worthily occupies the place of the first genuinely
English painter. Dobson attached himself to the
King's party; Walker belonged to the Parliamentary
party; it was a seemingly paradoxical division, for

the contrast between his own portrait as painted by himself and as
painted by a careful but undistinguished fellow artist — I forget
his name — whose picture now hangs in the great gallery at
Vienna, which contains so many of the most beautiful and interesting pictures in the world. On himself Vandyke bestowed the same
careless air of distinction that he found it so easy to bestow on his
sitters, together with an even greater degree of refinement. For
his fellow artist the glamour is non-existent, and Vandyke appears
before us with an unforgettably veracious face, small-mouthed,
sensual, assertive, the face of a clever and ambitious *parvenu*.

whereas Dobson was something of a Puritan in his
methods, Walker had the instincts of the Cavalier;
he was a follower of Vandyke and nothing more, an
artist of feminine sensitive temperament, whose
portraits remain pleasing and as portraits interesting, though they can never command the respect
and admiration which Dobson still wins from us.

We thus see that the English native school of
painting arose under a stimulus that came from
the north European centre, though in a form
profoundly modified by influences from the secondary centre of Venice. This mixed character
has marked most of the art influences that have
reached England; they have been predominantly
northern, but to some extent southern. When
the Civil Wars cut short for the time the native
development in painting, the England of Restora-
tion days, like the England of Elizabethan days,
fell back on artists more or less of the northern
school. For nearly a century after the death of
Dobson the art of painting was almost extinct;
there were no English artists of merit or of reputation, and the foreign artists who took the place
of Vandyke — Lely and Kneller — possessed more
reputation than merit.

When English painting arose again it was
along new lines. Hogarth, indeed, stands apart;
he showed how an artist, while distinctly of the
northern school, could yet be genuinely English;
but though our first absolutely English artist, he

was somewhat out of the main line of evolution.
The painters who carried on this main line of development were still under the inspiration of the
northern school as affected by southern influences.
Richard Wilson had seen the pictures of the
French landscape artists and had lived in Rome;
those two facts chiefly moulded his work. While,
however, he remained convinced throughout that
the typical landscape is a classical landscape with
Roman architecture as an essential item, and
while he generally assumed that it should be seen
as the French landscape painters saw it, he yet
went somewhat beyond these canons. He began
to perceive the beauty of English landscape and
he was fascinated by the problems of atmosphere.
His very powerful personality is clearly revealed
in his work, which has the sobriety, calm, and
thoroughness of an artist who had clearly realised
what it was he wanted to do and knew how to do
it. Wilson is the Dobson of English landscape,
and these two figures are the chief initiators in
English painting.

Wilson's work was almost unnoticed in his
time, it was eclipsed by the much more brilliant
work of a much more brilliant man. Reynolds,
indeed, knew and cared very little about landscape; he claimed for himself supremacy in portrait-painting, and compounded for that position
by declaring that in landscape Gainsborough
was supreme. It is impossible to overrate the in-

fluence of Reynolds on the evolution of English painting. Every English artist before him, even Hogarth with all his originality and aggressive independence, had been but as it were a patient and laborious craftsman. Reynolds took both himself and his art proudly; he desired to show that an English artist can assume something of the princely stateliness of a Titian or a Rubens. The same feeling went into his work; he dealt in traditions, but freely, almost recklessly, and with an accomplished command of his methods which enabled him to infuse his work easily with the sentiment of his own personality. He thus became a sort of English Vandyke, that is to say, a less severely trained Vandyke.

It is no doubt because of the immense services to painting which were directly and indirectly rendered by Reynolds's brilliant and accomplished personality, that his work has always been very indulgently treated in England. The seductive qualities which it must have possessed in the highest degree when fresh from his hand intoxicated his contemporaries, and in more recent times there has never been any inclination to judge harshly a figure in our art history at once so imposing and so amiable. It must, however, be said that the part played by Reynolds in the development of English painting — with which we are alone here concerned — was indirect rather than direct. His seductive brilliancy was not, and could not be, accompanied by any penetrating and earnest vision of the world, or any desire to see things truly. The judgments on painting contained in his discourses and other writings, and — notwithstanding his professed worship of Michelangelo, Raphael and the 'grand style' — his real admiration for the late Bolognese school reveal a taste which was that of his age, and confirm the impression produced by his paintings. He was fascinated by the epidermis of things, and his desire was to render the fascination of that epidermis, the sheen and bloom of the world. His preoccupation with these aspects rendered it easy for him to adopt the incongruous affectations of a pseudo-classicality which led him into very vapid absurdities, as well as much restless experimentalism in the use of pigments which has brought its own revenge. Delightful and admirable as much of his work still remains, there could scarcely be any progress along those lines.

The line of progress was more truly represented by a less showy if not less accomplished artist. Although Gainsborough doubtless owed much to a sympathetic personality, he lacked the commanding and somewhat superficial personal qualities which contributed so greatly both to the work and the position of Reynolds. A man of sensitively acute æsthetic perceptions and, like so many of the other great painters, a passionate lover of music, he was saved from committing the pseudo-classicalities and specious superficialities which commended themselves so often and so easily to Reynolds.* He was neither so indiscriminate an admirer of tradition as Reynolds, nor so bold an innovator in technical methods; his penetrating and sensitive love of nature seems indeed usually to have been under a certain restraint due partly to the limitations of a temperament which was not marked by its daring impulses or its ability to withstand the tendencies of the day, but showed a very sound and sober judgment in following the most genuinely English or at all events northern traditions (including that of Vandyke) and in making real progress possible along these lines. Gainsborough was much more English than Reynolds, and even apart from his actual achievements he is a very important figure in the development of English art. In his hands portrait-painting reached a sensitive delicacy combined with intellectual distinction which no Englishman had achieved before, if, indeed, it ever has since; while in land-

* A comparison of Reynolds's 'Mrs. Siddons as the Tragic Muse' (in the Dulwich Gallery and the Duke of Westminster's Collection) with Gainsborough's portrait of Mrs. Siddons (in the National Gallery) may alone serve to indicate this profound difference of personal temperament, and — as may be clearer in the sequel — something even deeper than personal temperament. Reynolds instinctively sought to convey the genius of the actress by the external aid of clouds, a throne, allegorical figures, and a theatrical attitude. It was equally natural to Gainsborough to seek the same end, with no external aids but colour and light, by simply concentrating his vision on the woman herself.

scape he leads directly to the delightful art of
Morland, the first English landscape painter
who had a kind of international reputation, and,
indeed, one' cannot help thinking, directly influenced the development of French landscape art.

It may be doubted, however, whether the truly
original note was reached in the development of
English landscape art until we come to the water-
colour painters of the end of the eighteenth century. Here we find an art of very simple and
humble origin still unencumbered by traditions.
This freedom from traditions, the nature of the
media employed, the small and unpretentious
scale on which the art was carried out, made it
easy for water-colour work to obtain a freshness
and naturalness, a swift and delicate reproduction of natural effects, which were to become a
little later the characteristics of English painting
at its highest point of culmination.

Turner, who is one of these culminating points
of English painting, is a very interesting figure
from the present point of view, because he represents the fusion of the aboriginal English water-
colour manner with the more traditional oil-
colour manner. On the one hand, he was a more or
less successful disciple of the school of Poussin
and Claude, painting the old-fashioned classical
scenes, and seeing them in the old-fashioned way,
introducing at the same time impossible human
figures which were all his own; on the other hand,

taking up the art of water-colour at its highest point of development, he made it the happiest of mediums for expressing his own highly individual vision of the world. He continually tended to leave behind the traditional method and to weld oil-painting more and more into a medium for expressing what he had first learnt to express in water-colour. It may seem an illegitimate impulse, but in Turner's hands it was fully justified by its success, and it certainly achieved the immense service of finally emancipating English painting, rendering it at once the most personal and the most realistic representation of the natural world. Turner is thus the most significant figure in the development of English art.

It may well have been the emancipating influences of Turner which rendered Constable possible, though we have to remember that Constable really represents the climax of a great and fruitful though local movement in landscape art, and is most intimately linked on to Crome, and thereby to the great Dutchmen. In Constable we have the most absolutely and purely English manifestation of the art of landscape painting at its highest point. The exotic and traditional elements that are still clearly traceable in Turner have in Constable disappeared; he painted distinctively English things under truly English aspects, in a characteristically English spirit. And, as ever happens, by force of being national

he became international. He was not only the
first great English landscape painter who was
completely national, but the first to have really
international significance. Whatever pioneering
part may be assigned to Huet, it was largely under
Constable's influence that the French school of
romantic landscape arose.*

After Constable the current of English evolution in painting was transferred to France, and
proceeded there on more or less English lines,
some of which have flowed back and are still with
us. One of the chief purely British initiators in
English painting since Constable has been Ford
Madox Brown. A singularly forceful temperament, with a very personal vision of the world,
Madox Brown possessed a genius that was essentially simple and homogeneous, though very
versatile in its manifestations. Whether he turned
his hand to landscape, or to dreams of past life, or
to scenes of present-day life, his touch remained
hard, firm, brilliant, personal, a little fantastic,
but essentially realistic. It was once the fashion
to belittle Madox Brown's influence, and to
question his initiatory impulse on the so-called
Pre-Raphaelite movement. The fashion had its
excuse in the somewhat unsympathetic character

* Constable's international significance is shared by his contemporary, Bonington, a painter of versatile and accomplished
genius who began to do many things which have often been
repeated since. Bonington's early association with Delacroix
makes it a little difficult to define his originality.

of Brown's genius. Although Rossetti brought
an eager receptivity, the sensitive temperament
of the poet, the sensuous attitude of the lover of
physical beauty (which in turn influenced Brown),
much of the force and fibre of his work exists
already in Brown before 1848. The term 'Pre-
Raphaelite' may have been happily chosen in so
far as its inventors sought to fling a slight at the
popular ideals of their day, but otherwise it was a
misnomer; the movement was indeed not so much
Pre-Raphaelite as Flemish. Madox Brown's
training was Flemish, his traditions were fundamentally northern, though transformed in his
perfervid Scottish temperament; Holbein was the
artist who most decisively influenced him and sent
him to nature, and though he studied in Rome
the visit left no permanent impress on his art.
Rossetti, again, remained true to the same
northern tradition; he visited no foreign centre
of art except Belgium, which ever after left its
mark on his work, and though on this basis it is
true that his Italian temperament led him to
developments which seem sometimes to recall the
work of the North Italian masters (those most
closely in touch with the Flemish masters), the
Italian by blood was still a Northerner by artistic
training and tradition. Millais and Holman Hunt
also remained essentially Northerners; the one
true Pre-Raphaelite was Burne-Jones, and the
profound fascination which the Tuscan or Etrus-

can spirit exerted on him swiftly drew him away
from those northern influences under which his
genius had begun to develop.*

II

It has seemed necessary to trace this rapid
sketch of the development of painting in England
and the chief traditions and forces that have influenced it, even although it may have recalled
many facts that are familiar. When, however, we
proceed to study the geographical distribution of
the great painters who have played the chief part
in this evolution, we reach ground that is comparatively untrodden, and we attain results that
are so precise and definite that they furnish pecul-

* The reader will not need to be told that this was written over
twenty years ago. To-day the Pre-Raphaelite movement is
seldom mentioned save with contempt, and the painters of that
group are scarcely considered painters at all. (See, for example,
Mr. Clive Bell in the London *Nation* for 19th December, 1925.)
But this is a rather shallow view, which will pass, and I see no need
to change what I have written. Forty years ago English art was
in a sadly moralistic and story-telling way, with a completely dull
and slipshod technique. A reaction to a more genuinely æsthetic
outlook was necessary, and the Pre-Raphaelites in initiating that
reaction were performing a valuable function. For those who were
then young Burne-Jones came as the inspiring revelation of a new
beauty, by no means as the mere imitator of an old beauty. Some
thirty years ago, I remember, a French critic, as he passed an
engraving of Burne-Jones's 'Merlin' on my walls, remarked: 'In
future ages when men think of English art they will say — "Burne-
Jones!"' The French art historian of to-day, like Elie Faure,
would not agree. He would be more inclined to say: 'Gainsborough!' and, for my own part, I hope he would be right. The
Pre-Raphaelite movement had no significance for European art,
but for English art it had an importance we must not belittle
though it has now passed away.

iarly brilliant evidence of the intimate connection between race and even the subtlest manifestations of the human spirit.

In the study of British genius we have found that the British painters and designers (I here leave out of account sculptors and architects) of sufficiently high rank to come within the limits of eminence I had set, and concerning whose place of origin adequate information was forthcoming, are forty-five in number. If now, bearing in mind the characteristics of the great English artists, and remembering that they may be roughly divided into the two classes of those who have been mainly influenced by nature, and those who have been mainly influenced by tradition, we proceed to inquire into their origins, we find that the geographical distribution runs as nearly as possible parallel with the distribution by characteristics. In other words, while the painters who have chiefly followed nature came from one part of the British Islands, the painters who have chiefly followed tradition came from another part. Speaking roughly, it may be said that of the two great foci of genius which may be found in England, the East Anglian focus is the headquarters of the painters of nature and the south-western focus, more especially Devonshire, the headquarters of the painters of tradition. The East Anglian district is the centre of an influence which extends along the whole east coast of England

and Scotland and to some distance inland, while
Devonshire is, so far as painting is concerned, the
centre of a district which may be said to include the
whole of the rest of the country including Ireland.

There may be some query as to the propriety of
dividing painters into two classes accordingly as
they are mainly affected by nature or by tradition.
It may be said that no painter is cut off from
tradition, and that the worship of nature may
itself become a tradition. Although this is true,
the distinction between the painter who is mainly
influenced by what other painters have done, or
by his own imagination, and the painter who is
mainly influenced by what his eye actually sees,
is fairly clear, both to those who are and those
who are not painters, and it may well be retained.
A few examples may illustrate both the distinction itself and the accuracy with which it coin-
cides with geographical distribution. Reynolds
belonged so far as is known almost entirely to
Devonshire, the centre of the south-western focus of British genius; he is likewise the king of
the English painters of tradition; his ideals of art
were Italian; in theory he was an ardent admirer
of Michelangelo, in practice he was a strayed
disciple of the later Venetians. A painter, he
was accustomed to say, should form his rules
not from books or precepts, but (from nature? oh,
no!) 'from pictures.' 'Rules,' he would add, 'were
first made from pictures.' Very different, indeed,

were the maxims and the practice of Constable. Like Gainsborough, Constable belonged to Suffolk; he was absolutely untouched by Italian tradition, and certainly never formed his rules by the study of pictures. 'Truth only will count,' he said, and he loathed every attempt at *bravura*, the striving to go beyond nature. As a more complex illustration, we may take Turner. It may seem a little difficult to say whether Turner belongs pre-eminently to the school of tradition or the school of nature. His early work was distinctly in large measure traditional; through the greater part of his life he carefully preserved a predilection for pseudo-classical conventions. Yet at the same time he revealed a passionate devotion to nature which in his latest work has altogether survived the classical traditions. The key to this complexity in Turner's genius is, however, at once apparent when we turn to consider his ancestry. His father, like Reynolds, belonged to Devon, coming in early life to London, where he married; the mother's place of origin does not appear to be definitely known, but as her relations were scattered in the eastern counties, we are probably correct in supposing that her family belonged to the east coast. There are no greater names in English painting than Reynolds, Constable, and Turner, and we thus see that all three furnish evidence — at nearly every point definite evidence — of the intimate connection between a painter's method of painting and his racial heredity.

It would be somewhat tedious to go through the whole group of the forty-five artists in the same manner to show how they illustrate this distribution, even if my own knowledge of second-rate British artists were sufficiently extensive to enable me to do this with complete assurance. In order that the reader may judge for himself, I print the list here:

Barry........Cork.
Bewick.......Northumberland and Cumberland.
Blake........Somerset (?).
Bonington....Nottingham.
H. K. Browne.Norfolk.
Cattermole...Norfolk.
Constable....Suffolk.
Cotman......Norfolk.
Copley.......Limerick and Clare, but originating in Yorkshire and Lancashire.
Cox.........Birmingham.
Crome.......Norfolk.
Cruikshank...Leith.
Danby.......Wexford.
Dawson......Nottingham.
Dobson......Hertfordshire.
Doyle........Dublin.
Dyce ....Aberdeen.
Eastlake .....Devon.
Etty.........Yorkshire.
Flaxman .....Norfolk.
Gainsborough.Suffolk.
Gillray.......Lanark.
Haydon......Devon.
Hogarth .....Suffolk.
Keene.......Westmoreland.

Landseer....Lincoln.
Lawrence ...Worcester.
Leech.......Irish.
Maclise.....Elgin and Cork.
Morland....Norfolk (?) (mother apparently French).
Mulready...Clare.
Northcote...Devon.
Opie........Cornwall.
Phillip......Aberdeen.
Raeburn....Edinburgh and Annandale.
Reynolds....Devon.
Romney ....Westmoreland and Cumberland.
Sandby.....Nottingham and Lincoln.
Scott (D.)...Lanark.
Stothard....Yorkshire and Shropshire.
Turner......Devon and Nottingham (?).
Varley......Nottingham.
Wilkie......Midlothian and Fife.
Wilson......Montgomery.
Wright......Derby.

It will, I believe, be found that if a line is drawn from London (for the south-eastern corner of England is singularly bare of painters) to Liverpool, the naturalistic painters will be found mainly to the east of that line and the traditionalistic and idealistic painters to the west. There are of course a few dubious and complex cases. Flaxman, for instance, scarcely appears to show the special characteristics of the east country. The case of Wilson, again, seems to resemble that of Turner; he was at once a conserver of traditions and an ardent lover of nature; on his mother's side he was undoubtedly Welsh; his father was a clergyman, and bears a Teutonic or Scandinavian name, which, though widespread, belongs mainly to the east coast. It may be noted that, while the two divisions are nearly equal in size, the whole of Scotland falls into the eastern division; this is due to the fact that the west of Scotland has produced so few painters; if painters were forthcoming here I should expect them to fall mainly into the western group.

If we turn to more recent painters — not included in the present list because still living when the body of the *Dictionary of National Biography* was issued — we shall scarcely find any marked exceptions to the tendency already found to prevail. The chief movement in British painting during the latter half of the nineteenth century was that associated with the 'Pre-Raphaelites.'

Leaving Rossetti, as mainly of Italian race, out of account,* we find that the leaders and precursors of the movement, like Ford Madox Brown and Millais, belonged in character mainly to the followers of nature, and in race mainly to the east country group. But Burne-Jones, notwithstanding all the influences around him, is strictly distinguished from the others by his love of tradition and his affection for early Italian art. In the light of our present knowledge concerning race it is impossible not to connect this fact with his Welsh ancestry.

It is probably unnecessary to elaborate a point which when once indicated is seen to be very clear and simple. The British Islands, roughly speaking, may be said to be divided between two races; one, more ancient, predominantly dark in complexion and commonly called 'Celtic,' but in reality, while containing what may fairly be called Celtic elements, doubtless more correctly denominated Mediterranean. The other element, fairer than the first, lying in its most concentrated form along the east coast of England and Scotland, is Teutonic in its affinities, closely related to the Flemish, Dutch and Scandinavians, as well as to the people of northern France. It is clear that the instincts of one of these two great sections of our popula-

* It is not known (W. M. Rossetti told me) where the Peirces, to whom the Rossettis belong on the English side, came from, and the name itself is not very distinctive.

tion urge them to adopt a traditional or idealistic
vision of the world in painting, while the people of
the other section are impelled to the direct study
of nature, their tradition, when they have one,
being the naturalistic tradition of the North
European centre of painting to which the other
men are insensitive. The first are concerned with
what, as it seems to them, ought to be; the others
with what is. The first are moved by great ideals
or follow lofty traditions; the second are, however,
more closely in sympathy with the impulses of
the important art-centre, that of North Europe,
with which Great Britain is in such close contact;
they have produced twice as many notable artists
as the men of the western district.* And it is from
them, rather than from the others, that the decisively progressive movements in the evolution
of British painting have come.† As I have previously pointed out, the east country and the fair
element in our population have shown a special
predilection for the scientific study of nature,

* That it should be so is not surprising when we recall that even
in mediæval times this part of the country was the chief English
art-centre. I am inclined to think that more remains of mural
painting are found here than elsewhere; it is certain that East
Anglia is the chief district for brasses; while the same region, as is
recognised, almost alone in our country, has produced an original
and attractive architectural style.

† The French school of romantic landscape, which received its
impetus from the east coast of England, spread almost exclusively
among painters of fair race belonging to northern and north-
western France, the regions of France most closely allied to
eastern England in race.

though they have no such special pre-eminence in the field of poetry. Now we see the same fundamental racial distinction even in so subtle a matter as methods of painting and modes of æsthetic feeling. Nearly all English painters have been subjected to similar environmental and traditional influences, and have been educated in the same large art-centres. Yet the racial factor, while not all-powerful, still persists. A man's æsthetic feelings are the most delicate, seemingly the most capricious, of his mental possessions. Yet they are, we see, among his most radical and unchangeable possessions; and through a long series of ancestors born to till the soil or to consume its fruits, he may yet retain a spiritual kinship, only waiting for circumstances to make it clear, with the greatest artists of his race, even in foreign lands.*

* When 'The Evolution of English Painting' was first published, Mr. D. S. MacColl sought to explode the view therein put forward in the pages of the *Saturday Review* (22d March, 1902). It may not be necessary to take seriously this playful effort. But if one does so, Mr. MacColl's criticisms are found to resolve themselves into two: (1) there is no 'antenatal necessity' for the character of a painter's art; and (2) we must not accept any 'single cause' of what men do in art. Both these propositions may be accepted without the need for changing a single word in my statement. If the men on the west coast of Great Britain tend on the whole to follow traditional methods in art and those on the east coast naturalistic methods — Mr. MacColl made no serious attempt to deny the fact — that implies no fatal necessity; they were following their own natural bent; that indeed was my point. As to the factor which I had invoked, and which Mr. MacColl would himself admit the existence of, not being a 'single cause,' I had myself already clearly stated that it was 'not all-powerful.' I was dissecting out a single cause, and analysis is not synthesis.

XV

GENIUS AND STATURE

Fallacies of the inquiry — The stature of normal persons — Tall, middle-sized, and short persons of genius — Undue infrequency of the middle-sized — The variational tendency of genius — Some of the problems involved.

THE anthropometry of 'genius' — using the word here and throughout merely to indicate the most highly valued variations of intellectual faculty — is in a much more elementary condition than our knowledge of the physical characters of criminals. There are sufficient reasons why this should be so. The man of genius less obviously belongs to the 'dangerous classes' than the criminal, the idiot, and other varieties of abnormal man; so that we seldom obtain him under favourable conditions for precise measurement. Moreover, persons of artistic genius, at all events, usually possess to an even greater extent than criminals a kind of vanity distinctly opposed to all such proceedings; and few have been found to imitate Zola, who complacently lent himself to the minute scientific investigations of Dr. Toulouse. If, however, there is one anthropological character of genius which ought to be fairly well ascertained, it is stature; for that is the coarsest of all anthropometric characters, and in its roughest degrees can be judged by the unaided eye. This is so obvious that from time to time the subject has been discussed; but, so far from any agreement having been reached, the conclusions of those who have dealt with the matter are absolutely opposed. And the reflection is inevitable that, if so simple a question as this will not admit of solution, it is impossible to determine any character of genius; and any attempt to consider the study of genius a scientific study is merely an affectation of pseudo-scientific journalists.

When, however, we come to look into the attempts made to settle this question, the cause of their failure is sufficiently obvious. The apparent simplicity of the problem has put the inquirer off his guard. In such a matter it has seemed enough to collect anecdotes concerning little or big 'great men,' to look into a few histories and biographies, or to fall back on one's own reminiscences. No one has attempted to treat the matter in a really serious and methodical manner. So far as I am aware, not a single writer who has undertaken to inquire whether men of genius are 'tall' or 'short' has taken the trouble to explain what he means by 'tall' or 'short.' It is easy to understand the contempt which anyone with the faintest tincture of scientific training must feel for such inquiries. The study of the stature of famous men threatens to resolve itself largely into a psychological analysis of the fallacies of human perception. Men are wont to belittle the physical height of the man of genius in order to emphasise his intellectual stature; or they magnify the Jovian altitude of both. Moreover, we all have different standards of height; and it is possible for the same person to be short, middle-sized, and tall, for different observers who all knew him well at the same period of his life. Middle height, as judged by the eye, is a peculiarly uncertain quantity. Thus Rossetti seemed to his brother to be of 'rather low middle stature'; to Mr. Hall Caine, of 'full middle-height'; and to Mr. Sharp, 'rather over middle height.' His actual height was barely five feet eight inches; so that, considered as an Englishman, he was of precisely middle height, though to most persons he would appear somewhat below it, since we instinctively and reasonably compare a man with his own class, and the professional classes are somewhat above the general average in height. This is, indeed, a very frequent source of error, and a large number of persons of genius who have been called short must, it is probable, strictly be regarded as of middle height, or even as tall.

It is scarcely credible, but seems to be true, that of the numerous writers who have come forward to settle this question, not one has taken the medium-sized 'great' man into consideration, and not one has considered what proportion of tall, medium-sized, and short men are found in the community generally. Yet, until we know these

facts, it is idle to pile up lists of either short or
tall men of genius.

I propose to try to avoid some of the grosser of
the fallacies just mentioned. We may fairly attempt to approach the problem on a British basis,
because, although British stature is slightly higher
than that most prevalent in Europe, it is fairly
near the average; and, moreover, I shall chiefly be
concerned with British men of genius.*

Thanks to the Anthropometric Committee of
the British Association, the stature of the inhabitants of the British Islands is fairly well
ascertained. The average for the United Kingdom
(I speak throughout of males only) is 67.66 inches,
while the mean (*i.e.*, the most frequent) height is
5 feet 7–8 inches, the professional and commercial
classes having a mean height about 2–3 inches
over this, and the labouring classes about an inch
or two below; racially both the Scotch and the
Irish are somewhat taller than the English, and
the Welsh shorter. When we examine the Anthropometric Committee's tables, we find that
not less than 68 per cent of the inhabitants of

* Stature is one of those measurements which may be investigated with excess of precision. There are still investigators who
laboriously carry out extended inquiries into height measured by
millimetres, while quite unaware that the daily variation in height,
especially in youth, is so gross as to be itself measurable in centi-
metres. In a boyish attempt of my own to be scientifically exact I
discovered this daily variation; but it had been carefully investigated a very long time before by a clergyman named Wasse
(*Philosophical Transactions*, 1724), who correctly attributed it to
the elasticity of the intervertebral cartilages of the spine.

Great Britain are between 5 feet 4 inches and 5 feet 9 inches in height; while 16 per cent are below 5 feet 4 inches and 16 per cent above 5 feet 9 inches. It is, therefore, both convenient and sufficiently accurate to say that all persons between 5 feet 4 inches and 5 feet 9 inches are of medium height. There is thus very little variability in the stature of the inhabitants generally. As Galton has pointed out, one-half of the population differs less than 1.7 inches from the average of all of them, while not less than 68 per cent come within what I have called medium height. Therefore if stature counts for nothing in men of extraordinary intellectual ability, or 'genius,' and assuming for the present that such men spring from the population generally, we must expect to find that 68 per cent of such persons are of medium stature (not above 5 feet 9 inches, nor below 5 feet 4 inches); while small but equal numbers should be found below and above that height, forming a symmetrical curve.

There are, of course, several possibilities. Instead of this normal convex curve, we might have an oblique downward curve (due to a preponderance of tall persons), or an oblique upward curve (due to a preponderance of short persons), or a concave curve (due to a preponderance of both tall and short persons). The first possibility, *i.e.*, that the majority of men of genius like the majority of ordinary men are of medium height — although apparently the most obvious assumption — has not, so far as I know, ever been advanced. No one has yet brought forward a list of average-sized men of genius, and argued that they form the majority. The second possibility has aroused most enthusiastic faith:* the advocates of the theory that men of genius are short of stature have shown a fiery activity often characteristic of their clients, and have sometimes claimed celebrities to whom they are not entitled. The third type has found numerous, though less energetic, champions. The fourth type, according to which the short and tall would alike prevail at the expense of the middle-sized, seems to have found no advocate. Yet, as we shall see, it is this type which most nearly represents the state of things we actually find.

The names and measurements contained in the following lists have been drawn from many sources, and, although I am prepared to learn that some have been mistakenly entered, I believe that in the main they may be relied upon as accurate. Many names given in previous lists have been excluded, either because the evidence seemed feeble, or the intellectual ability displayed trifling. I have thus exercised a certain degree of selection; that is inevitable when the value of evidence has to be sifted. But such selection has no disturbing in-

---

* This is true (as the late Surgeon-Major W. J. Buchanan told me) not only of Europe but of India, and it is an old idea of the Hindu shastras that genius, or ability, goes with short stature.

fluence on the results when it is not exercised in favour of a prejudice; and I must admit that, though the result I have reached seems to me the most simple and the most probable result, it had not occurred to me beforehand as probable. So far as I had any expectation, it was that the small men of genius would predominate; for I remembered Balzac's saying that 'nearly all great men are little,' and the emphasis with which Lombroso and others have followed on this side — which has, indeed, certain biological considerations in its favour. I have included no names which are not really eminent in some field or another. Except in a few unquestionable cases, the names of the living were excluded.

It will be seen that the names are grouped alphabetically into two classes differing in value. The first class contains only those whose height is definitely known, so that we are here free from the influence of mere impressions. It is undoubtedly true that such a list is abnormally deficient in persons of medium height, for it more rarely occurs to the biographers of such to mention the precise height; this is a source of error to be borne in mind, and we may put against it a compensatory error in the second class, for here many of the persons alleged to be of middle height were probably tall, *i.e.*, over five feet nine.

The second class contains those who seemed tall, of medium height, or short to their contemporaries, whose judgments we are not able to control by precise measurements. Notwithstanding the fallacies I have already mentioned, such judgments have a certain value.*

TALL

George Borrow (6 ft. 2)
J. Bruce (6 ft. 4)
Burke (5 ft. 10)
Burns (nearly 5 ft. 10)
Sir R. Burton (nearly 6 ft.)
Carlyle (5 ft. 11)
Cobbett (over 6 ft.)
Coleridge (5 ft. 9½)
O. Cromwell (5 ft. 10)
Darwin (about 6 ft.)
Dumas *fils* (5 ft. 10)
Fielding (over 6 ft.)
Hawthorne (5 ft. 10½)
J. Hogg (5 ft. 10½)
A. Lincoln (6 ft. 1)
Marryat (5 ft. 10)
Peter the Great (6 ft. 8½)
Sir William Petty (over 6 ft.)
Sir W. Raleigh (about 6 ft.)
C. Reade (over 6 ft.)
Sir W. Scott (about 6 ft.)
Shelley (5 ft. 11)
Southey (5 ft. 11)
Thackeray (6 ft. 4)
Trevithick (6 ft. 2)

A. Trollope (5 ft. 10)
G. Washington (6 ft. 3)
Whitman (6 ft.)
John Wilson (5 ft. 11½)

Hans Andersen ('the Long Poet')
Arago
T. Arnold
Audubon
D'Azeglio
Beaumarchais
Bismarck
Joseph Black
Bolingbroke
Bonington
Boyle
Lord Brougham
Bunyan
Bishop Burnet
Julius Cæsar
Champollion
Charlemagne
Clive
Columbus

---

* In the case of men belonging to the past we have to reckon with the possibility that the average height of the population may have somewhat changed. In the present century F. D. Maurice was described by his son as 'distinctly below the middle height, not above five feet seven.' In 1745 Otway was described as 'of the middle height, about five feet seven inches'; while Swift at five feet eight was considered tall. But from the present point of view the mainly interesting point is not the absolute height, but the relative height of a certain group of men in comparison with their contemporaries.

Condorcet
Corot
Crabbe
Dalton
Delacroix
Denham
Sir Kenelm Digby ('gigantic')
Dumas *père*
J. Edwards
Emerson
Flaubert
Foscolo
Froude
Gilbert
Goethe
E. de Goncourt
Gounod
Helmholtz
A. von Humboldt
Leigh Hunt
Huxley
Edward Irving
Sir Henry Irving
Dr. Johnson
Ben Jonson
Lamartine
Lavoisier
Lessing
Li Hung Chang ('a giant among Chinamen')
Longfellow
Mazarin
Millet

Mirabeau
Molière
Moltke
Monti
Henry More
A. de Musset
Nietzsche
Petrarch
Poussin
Puvis de Chavannes
Richelieu
J. P. Richter
Romilly
Ruskin
Schiller
Schopenhauer
Adam Sedgwick
Sheridan
Sir Philip Sidney
Smollett
Sterne
Taine
Tasso
Tennyson
St. Thomas Aquinas
J. Thomson
Torrigiano
Tourgueneff
Volta
Waller
D. Webster
William the Silent
Wordsworth

MEDIUM

Lord Beaconsfield (5 ft. 9)
Byron (5 ft. 8½)
Sir A. Cockburn (5 ft. 6)
Dickens (5 ft. 9)
Gladstone (about 5 ft. 9) *

Jeffrey (5 ft. 6)
Bulwer Lytton (about 5 ft. 9)
F. D. Maurice (5 ft. 7)
J. S. Mill (5 ft. 8)
Otway (5 ft. 7)

* It appears, however, that this was Gladstone's height in old age, but that earlier in life he was 5 ft. 11 in., and should therefore be in the tall group.

S. Richardson (about 5 ft. 5)
D. G. Rossetti (barely 5 ft. 8)
Swift (5 ft. 8)
Voltaire (5 ft. 7)
Wellington (5 ft. 7)
Wesley (5 ft. 6)
Zola (5 ft. 7)

Alexander the Great (or short)
Lord Bacon
Baudelaire
St. Bernard
Sir Thomas Browne
Browning
Lord Burleigh
S. Butler
Camoëns
Lord Chesterfield
Chopin
William Collins
Confucius
Cowper
Dante
Defoe

St. Francis of Assisi (rather below)
Hazlitt
Heine
Hood
Keble
Lagrange
Linnæus
J. R. Lowell
Luther
Marvell
Guy de Maupassant
Clerk Maxwell
Michelangelo
J. Mill
Newton (or short)
Poe (or short)
Renan
J. Sansovino
Sydney Smith
Spinoza
Steele
Suckling
Verlaine
Watteau

SHORT

Balzac (nearly 5 ft. 4)
Beethoven (5 ft. 4)
W. Blake (barely 5 ft.)
Hartley Coleridge (about 5 ft.)
St. Francis Xavier (4 ft. 6)
J. Hunter (5 ft. 2)
Kant (about 5 ft.)
Keats (5 ft.)
Meissonier (about 5 ft.)
T. Moore (5 ft.)
Napoleon (5 ft. 1¾)
Nelson (5 ft. 4)
De Quincey (5 ft. 3 or 4)
Thiers (5 ft. 3)
Bishop Wilberforce (5 ft. 3)

Aetius

Albertus Magnus
Aristotle
Augustus Cæsar
Barrow
Baskerville
Beccaria
Beddoes
Bentham
Admiral Blake
Louis Blanc
Bocchoris
Brunelleschi
Burbage
Calvin
Lord Camden
T. Campbell
Chamfort

Chillingworth
Chrysippus
Comte
Condé
Crome
Cruikshank
Curran
David of Angers
Descartes
Sir Francis Drake
Dryden
H. Milne Edwards
Erasmus
Faraday
M. Ficinus
Fromentin
Fuseli
Garrick
Gibbon
Giotto
Godwin
Goldsmith
Gray
Hales
W. Harvey
Warren Hastings
Haüy
Herzen
E. T. A. Hoffmann
Hogarth
O. W. Holmes
Horace
D. Jerrold
Gottfried Keller
Kepler
Admiral Keppel
Lalande
C. Lamb
Lamennais

Larrey
Laud
Lipsius
Locke
Lulli
Marshal Luxembourg
Macaulay
Charles Martel
Melancthon
Mendelssohn
Menzel
Mézeray
Mezzofanti
Milton (or medium)
Montaigne
Sir T. More
Montesquieu
Mozart
Narses ('the body of a child')
Philopœmen
Pomponazzi
Lord John Russell
A. del Monte Sansovino
Shaftesbury (first Lord)
C. Smart (called himself a dwarf)
Socinus
Lord Somers
Spencer
Dean Stanley
Timour
Turner
Voiture
Wagner
H. Walpole
Lord Westbury
Wilberforce
Woolner
Wren

By uniting the two classes, and doubling the number of those in the first class, so as to give due weight to their superior accuracy, we reach a result which may, I think, be regarded as a fair approximation to the actual state of things. It will be found that we thus obtain 142 tall men of genius, 74 of middle height, while 125 are short.*

We may safely conclude from these figures that the faith cherished by many, that nearly all great men are little — a very venerable faith, as indicated by the ancient sayings collected in Burton's *Anatomy of Melancholy* concerning great wits with little bodies — is absolutely incorrect. Some deduction must doubtless be made in view of the fact that our medium is made on the basis of the general population, while the majority of men of genius belong to the educated classes. This deduction would tend to equalise the two extremes; but that it would not destroy the slight pre-eminence of the tall men of ability is perhaps indicated by the fact, shown by the Anthropometric Committee, that the stature of 98 Fellows of the Royal Society (who from the present point of view may be counted as men of genius) was nearly half an inch above that of the professional class to which they usually belong. At the same time it is clear that the belief in the small size of great men was not absolutely groundless. There is an abnormally large propor-

---

* This result finds confirmation in the examination of a volume entitled *Word Portraits of Famous Writers* (by their contemporaries), which shows out of 116 famous writers 24 short persons, 20 of middle height, and 40 who are tall — *i.e.*, the same general result in a more irregular form. Even if we assume that the remaining 32 were all of middle height, we still have an undue excess of the tall and short.

tion of small 'great men.' It is mediocrity alone
that genius seems to abhor. While among the
ordinary population the vast majority of 68 per
cent was of middle height, among men of genius,
so far as the present investigation goes, they are
only 22 per cent, the tall being 41 per cent, instead
of 16, and the short 37 instead of 16. The approximate equivalence of the two extremes is probably
in favour of the results so far as those extremes
are concerned; and although, on grounds already
mentioned, the figures I have given probably do
not represent the exact state of affairs so far as
middle height is concerned, there is considerable
ground for believing that, while its precise amount
may be doubtful, there is really a considerable
deficiency of the middle-sized among men of
genius.* The curve of height for genius is thus the
opposite of that for the ordinary population; and
both extremes are present to an abnormal extent.

The final result is, therefore, not that persons
of extraordinary mental ability tend either to be
taller or shorter than the average population, but
rather that they tend to exhibit an unusual tendency to *variation*. Even in physical structure,
men of genius present a characteristic which on
other grounds we may take to be fundamental in
them: they are manifestations of the variational

* This is confirmed by a later inquiry, which I have not seen
(*Grand Magazine*, June, 1906), showing that of 250 men and
women of intellect, 89 were tall, 83 short, and only 78 of middle
size.

tendency, of a physical and psychic variational diathesis. In a slight and elusive shape, a shape so elusive that it is rarely hereditary, the man of genius represents the same kind of phenomenon which, in organic nature generally, appears to have slowly built up the animated world we know. Just as the visible world is the outcome of the accumulated gross variations of plants and animals, so the world of tradition and culture is the outcome of the accumulated delicate variations of men of genius. The product is different, but it has been obtained by the same method.

It would be interesting if we could trace in a more detailed and precise manner the factor of physical stature in the constitution of the genius variation, and ascertain its precise significance. This is still difficult. One or two points may be noted.

It must be remembered that genius, however it may be defined, is certainly only an excessive development of characteristics which may be traced in much more rudimentary forms. It is thus not impossible to throw light on the subject of genius by investigating the peculiarities of physical stature generally, and the common intellectual accompaniments of under-development and over-development. The conclusion we have reached, that both tall and short individuals tend to predominate unduly among persons of genius, is confirmed and to some extent explained by observa-

tion of the general population. The observations
so far made, indeed, are few, but so far as they
go perfectly definite. Thus Bohannon — who, under the inspiration of Professor Stanley Hall,
collected data concerning over one thousand
abnormal children in the United States, dividing
them into various groups according to the predominant abnormal character — found that both
tall children and short children are intellectually
superior to children of medium height. The tall
(except in cases of very excessive tallness, which
may be regarded as pathological) showed their
superiority both in general health and mental
ability; at the same time they were notable for
their sensitiveness, good nature, even temper, and
popularity with others. The small were less often
healthy, and consequently were apt to be delicate, ugly, or vicious; but when fairly healthy they
tended to show very great activity both of body
and mind.

These observations, which will no doubt be confirmed, are in harmony with the results of daily
experience with children, and they serve not only
to support the conclusion we have reached with
regard to men of genius, but they also indicate that
genius itself is merely the highest form of a common
tendency which puts forth its tender buds in every
schoolroom.

It would still remain to show the causes of this
tendency; for it is scarcely possible to hold that the

health and ability of the tall is due (as has apparently been suggested) to forced association with their elders in youth, and quite absurd to hold that the activity and mental quickness of the small is due to the arrested development caused by forced association with their juniors. In both cases it seems probable that the primary cause is a greater vital activity, however we may ultimately have to define 'vital activity.' Among the tall such intensity of vital action has shown itself in unimpeded freedom; in the short it is impeded and forced into new channels by pathological or other causes. The latter case is perhaps the more interesting and complicated. An anthropometric examination of short men of genius would throw much light on this question. There are certainly at least two types of short men of genius: the slight, frail, but fairly symmetrical type (approaching what is called the true dwarf), and the type of the stunted giant (a type also to be found among dwarfs proper). The former are fairly symmetrical, but fragile; generally with little physical vigour or health, all their energy being concentrated in the brain. Kant was of this type. The stunted giants are usually more vigorous, but lacking in symmetry. Far from being delicately diminutive persons, they suggest tall persons who have been cut short below; in such the brain and viscera seem to flourish at the expense of the limbs, and while abnormal they often have the good fortune to be

robust both in mind and body. Lord Chesterfield
was a man of this type, short for his size, thick-set,
'with a head big enough for a Polyphemus'; Hartley Coleridge carried the same type to the verge of
caricature, possessing a large head, a sturdy and
ample form, with ridiculously small arms and legs,
so that he was said to be 'indescribably elfish and
grotesque.' Dryden — 'Poet Squab' — was again
of this type, as was William Godwin; in Keats the
abnormally short legs co-existed with a small head.
The typical stunted giant has a large head; and
such stunting of the body has, indeed, a special
tendency to produce large heads, and therefore
doubtless those large brains which are usually
associated with extraordinary intellectual power.
It is a curious fact — as a distinguished anatomist,
the late Sir George Humphrey, remarked many
years ago — that when from any cause the growth
of the rest of the body is stunted, the head not
only remains disproportionately large, but often
becomes actually larger than in ordinary persons.
'Thus short persons and persons with imperfectly
developed lower extremities are not uncommonly
remarkable for the size of their heads, as though
the expenditure of growing force being too great
in one direction, other parts are ill-cared for.'* It
may be added that the commonest type of dwarf

---

* Humphrey, *The Human Skeleton*, p. 96. We may perhaps
regard these people as highly developed on a basis of infantilism.
They need to be studied along the lines laid down by Kretschmer.

possesses a proportionally large head and short legs.

It would doubtless be an attractive task to attempt to trace the causes which lead genius to be associated at once with both abnormal extremes of stature. It must probably be found at an early period of embryonic development, when, as we know from the researches of Dareste and others, the causes of dwarfism may also be found, sometimes in arrest of growth resulting from precocious development. Here, however, it is enough to have ascertained the facts in a roughly approximate fashion. It need only be pointed out, in conclusion, that the result we have reached, although apparently new, is such a result as should have been expected. Geoffroy Saint-Hilaire long since, and Ranke more recently, have pointed out that both giants and dwarfs — the abnormally tall and the abnormally short — are usually abnormal in other respects also. From the biological point of view we know nothing of 'genius,' what is so termed being simply an abnormal aptitude of brain function; so that among those variations and abnormalities which, as is already generally agreed, we find with unusual frequency among the very tall and the very short, extraordinary mental aptitude ought sometimes to occur.

XVI

THE COMPARATIVE ABILITIES OF THE FAIR AND THE DARK

The hair-colour and eye-colour of the British population — The National Portrait Gallery — Eye-colour the chief criterion — The index of pigmentation — The royal family — The aristo- cracy — The pigmentary character of different groups — Characteristics of the fair and the dark.

WE know something concerning the hair-colour and eye-colour of the general population. Many observations have been made on this point during recent years, not only among continental nations but in all parts of the British Islands. It may in- deed be said that it was an Englishman, Dr. John Beddoe, who first realised the interest of such ob- servations, and carried them out on a wide scale. To him chiefly we owe the map which shows the relative fairness and darkness of the population of our islands.* When we look at this map we see that there is a certain order in the distribution of the fair population and the dark population, that the fair people are, on the whole, arranged along the eastern sides of the two islands and the dark people along the western sides, so that in each island as we go from east to west the population tends to become darker.

* Much more thorough surveys of special regions have since been made, such as Tocher's 'Pigmentation Survey of School- Children in Scotland,' *Biometrika*, vol. VI, 1908.

At this point, however, it may be said that our
knowledge ends. We know which districts of the
country are mainly fair and which mainly dark;
we even know where particular types of fairness
and darkness are chiefly to be found, but we do not
know how different classes of the population differ
from each other in this respect. It is true that
certain results have been reached here too, and for
these also we are indebted to Dr. Beddoe, though
they were not obtained by the method of direct
observation. Dr. Beddoe found, by examining a
very large number of the descriptions of 'Persons
Wanted' in the *Police Gazette*, that there is a great
difference in average degrees of fairness between
people of different occupations, more especially
that while men connected with horses and cattle,
such as grooms and butchers, are notably fair,
shoemakers and tailors tend to be notably dark.
No doubt such observations will in time be made
directly on the general population, and we shall
know the relative proportions of the fair and the
dark among people following every occupation.

I have not attempted any inquiry of this kind.
But I have endeavoured to carry out a somewhat
allied inquiry by examining the portraits of eminent
persons, and comparing the fairness or darkness of
different groups of such persons. The National
Portrait Gallery contains portraits of several
thousand persons who in some way or other have
acquired eminence during the past six hundred

years, and I therefore selected this Gallery for study as furnishing a specially favourable field for the investigation of the question.

This inquiry was by no means so easy as it might appear at the first glance. I have spent many hours in the Gallery, during a period extending over nearly two years, in making the necessary observations. I cannot regret the hours spent in the company of so many wise and noble and gracious personages. But I have acquired a certain scepticism as to the fidelity both of those who paint and those who write portraits. In many cases the painted statements concerning the same person are absolutely unlike; in many cases the painted statements are absolutely unlike the written statements of those who knew the originals. In other cases the discrepancies, though less marked, are still sufficiently considerable to be painful to a careful investigator. I soon realised that the artist was on the whole much more reliable than the literary observer, but, on the other hand, if the artist happens to be dominated by the desire to obtain his own effects at all costs to truth, he may lead us hopelessly astray. An amusing instance of the confusion thus produced many be seen in the neighbouring National Gallery, where Millais in his portrait of Gladstone has represented one eye blue, the other brown. Nor are these the only difficulties with which the anthropologist must contend in the National Portrait Gallery. The age of a picture may dim or discolour what was once clear and definite, and the same result is attained when a picture is hung high up on the walls in the murky London air. Again, the age of the sitter often enables us to do no more than guess at the probable colour of his hair, or the fashion of his time may have covered it with a wig. Yet when all allowance is made for these causes of error, and a certain amount of care and discretion has been exercised, dubious cases severely disregarded, differing portraits of the same person duly compared, it is still possible to obtain fairly reliable results in the majority of instances.

I decided to take eye-colour as the chief criterion of pigmentation, in preference to hair-colour, mainly on the ground that the eyes were visible in a larger number of cases than the hair. At the same time, hair was also taken into consideration as a secondary criterion, and the judgment as to fairness or darkness obtained from the eyes was modified, if necessary, by that obtained from the hair; thus a person of the so-called 'Celtic' type, with light eyes and dark hair, would be classed as medium. It was scarcely practicable to take into account the actual complexion, and as the depth of colouring of the skin on the whole follows that of the hair and the eyes, it was unnecessary. I found that the degree of precision attainable with my material enabled me to classify my subjects into three classes: light, medium, dark.

The ordinary words used to describe the colour of the eyes, it may not be unnecessary to remark, are very vague and inaccurate. In reality the iris varies from blue (in which case there is a total lack of pigment), through blue-yellow, blue-orange, blue-orange-brown in various combinations, to brown (in which case there is full pigmentation). I find that descriptive writers speak of 'blue' eyes with considerable licence, even when the eye is only very partially blue, while they use the unsatisfactory word 'grey' to describe what is really a blue-yellow eye; 'black' is also liberally applied, usually to brown eyes. There are in reality no black eyes; in examining portraits, however, one sometimes meets with apparently black eyes, which may either be brown or blue, a serious source of confusion, for we thus run the risk of making a totally wrong classification. Thus the eyes of Charles I sometimes seem to be black; in reality they were dark blue.* I have of course omitted the cases in which this important distinction cannot be made with fair probability. Of the three classes — light, medium, dark — into which I have classified all those individuals in the National Portrait Gallery whose portraits enable us to classify them, the first class contains those with completely or almost completely blue eyes and fair

---

* The same may be said of his daughter Henriette d'Angleterre, whose eyes were greatly admired in France, but while by most of those who knew her they were called blue, by some they were called black.

or brown hair; the last class includes those with completely or almost completely brown eyes and brown or black hair; the medium class includes those whose eyes are of intermediate colour and who usually have brown hair. As already mentioned, any striking contrast between hair-colour and eye-colour involved some shifting of class.

In this way it was possible to ascertain that so many among the distinguished persons represented in the Gallery were fair, so many dark, and so many of intermediate colouring. This result, however, was obviously of no very extraordinary interest. To realise its significance we should have to obtain for comparison a corresponding series of undistinguished persons, and even then we should have to recognise that the personages represented in the Gallery are an extremely miscellaneous collection. In order to obtain results that are really of interest we must break up our data into groups. I have therefore divided the individuals whose colouring I have been able to ascertain into sixteen different groups, according to social rank, occupation, etc., these groups in some cases overlapping, so that one individual sometimes appears in more than one group. It was then possible to ascertain the number of fair, medium, and dark persons in each of the sixteen groups. But it was still necessary to find a convenient method of comparison by reducing the three figures in each group to one figure. To attain this I divided the medium persons in each group equally between the fair and dark persons, thus reducing the three figures to two, and then I multiplied the fair persons in each group by 100 and divided by the number of dark persons. Thus — in accordance with a method well recognised in anthropology and by which, for instance, the cephalic index is ascertained by measuring the breadth and length of the head — I obtained what may be called the index of pigmentation.*

With these preliminary explanations I can present the results of my investigation. In the following enumeration the groups are arranged in the order of decreasing fairness:

Group with Number of Individuals	Index of Pigmentation
Political Reformers and Agitators (20)	233
Sailors (45)	150
Men of Science (53)	121
Soldiers (42)	113
Artists (74)	111
Poets (56)	107
Royal Family (66)	107
Lawyers (56)	107
Created Peers and their Sons (89)	102
Statesmen (53)	89
Men and Women of Letters (87)	85
Hereditary Aristocracy (149)	82
Divines (57)	58
Men of Low Birth (12)	50
Explorers (8)	33
Actors and Actresses (16)	33

An index of more than 100 means that the fair

* It was not possible for me to adopt Beddoe's index of nigrescence, used for tabulating the results of direct observation of hair-colour on living persons, since I had not found it feasible to make hair-colour the primary basis of classification.

element predominates over the dark in that group, an index of less than 100 means that the dark element predominates. I may add that the lists include persons of both sexes.

The results presented in this simple table — results which in part give precision to recognised tendencies and in part are entirely novel — might well be expounded at considerable length. It will, however, be enough to comment on a few of the conclusions which most clearly emerge.

In the first place, as regards the royal family and the aristocracy, it may seem that the prevalent belief which credits the upper classes with a pronounced tendency to blondness — and which finds expression in the ancient belief, of Spanish origin, in the 'blueness' of noble blood, *sangre azul*, because the veins of fair people are blue — is here shown to be fallacious. That, however, is not the case. It must be remembered that the ordinary population of the middle and lower classes is only slenderly represented in the National Portrait Gallery. It is, however, noteworthy that the small group of persons springing from the working classes is among the darkest of the groups, decidedly darker than any of the aristocratic groups. As regards the royal family, it has also to be remembered that the results have been affected by perpetual infusions of foreign blood from nearly every European country, and as most European populations are darker complexioned than the

English, it is not surprising that the tendency of the royal family to fairness has thus been somewhat reduced. The study of the physical characteristics of the royal family through many centuries is of considerable interest. The early tendency was towards fairness, but by late Tudor times there was a tendency towards darkness, for Henry VIII seems to have inherited his mother's dark eyes, and though Mary I possessed the blue-grey eyes of her Spanish mother and Edward VI's light eyes were presumably inherited from Jane Seymour, Queen Elizabeth inherited brown eyes, probably from both parents. James I brought in a muddy blue Scotch eye, which was probably derived from his father, but Charles I's dark blue eyes were apparently identical with those of his Danish mother. Charles married Henrietta Maria, whose eyes were a clear brown, and two of the children followed the father, two the mother, while two others, in early life at all events, apparently possessed eyes of intermediate colour. The last representatives of the Stuart family were brown-eyed, for though James II (unlike his brother Charles II) inherited his father's eyes, he married a dark Italian wife, whose influence was impressed on all the descendants. William III (like most of the Dutch Orange family) was very dark, and so was Mary II. George I, with his mixed German, Stuart, and Orange blood, brought in a type of mixed eye which had hitherto been apparently rare in the royal family; in his case it was a dark greenish-brown eye; he married a French wife who appears to have been dark, but while his daughter inherited his eyes, his son, George II, though still showing a mixed eye, is unaccountably fair. This is one of the few slight anomalies we meet with in studying the royal family, and perhaps indicates a return to the fair German grandfather. This light mixed type of eye, usually blue-yellow, has remained persistent, accentuated or increased by German intermarriages, and still prevails at the present day.

The study of the royal family in the National Portrait Gallery is of considerable interest, for, except during the early periods, few links are missing, and it is easy to see how strictly eye-colour is inherited, the rule being — as was noted by Galton and is familiar, indeed, to every observant person — that the eye-colour of the child follows that of one or other of the parents and is very seldom a blend of both parents.

The review of these facts clearly shows also that the average blondness of the English royal family has been modified mainly by intermixture with darker foreign royal stocks, though it may well be that these stocks were fairer than the average population of the countries they belonged to. Our evidence, therefore, indicates that the blondness of the English royal family has been maintained at a considerable height in spite of opposing foreign influences.

If we turn to the hereditary aristocracy, we again find a lower index of pigmentation than we should have been inclined to expect. Foreign intermixture here also may have had some influence. I think it probable, however, that another cause has come into operation; peers have been in a position to select as wives, and have tended to select, the most beautiful women, and there can be little doubt that the most beautiful women, at all events in Great Britain, have tended more to be dark than to be fair. This is proved by the low index of pigmentation of the famous beauties in the Gallery, the selection being made solely on the basis of reputation, independently of any personal judgment of the portraits; while women of letters (fifteen in number) are inclined to be fair and have an index of 100, the index of thirteen famous beauties is as dark as 44. The same tendency is, indeed, illustrated by any series of famous beauties by Reynolds or Romney, and has probably been an important factor, though not the only one, in darkening the old aristocracy.

Our index of pigmentation shows, however, that the new aristocracy is fairer than the old. This seems to be one of the most novel and interesting facts revealed in the whole of this investigation. It answers the question: Why are the aristocracy fair? We see that the aristocracy tend to be fairer than the ordinary population because it is from the fair elements in the ordinary population that the aristocracy is chiefly recruited. In other words, the fair tend to attain greater success than the dark in those careers which most frequently lead to the peerage. Thus it is that both created peers and their sons (whether taken together or in two separate groups) are decidedly fairer than the old aristocracy. For the same reason lawyers, soldiers and sailors, who all tend towards the peerage, more especially lawyers, also markedly tend to be fair; statesmen, it is true, are not much fairer than the old aristocracy, but that is because they are largely taken from that very class.

A very significant fact, it seems to me, is the extremely high index of pigmentation of the group of political reformers and agitators. These are not persons who reach the House of Lords; their opinions are too radical, they are too violently opposed to the powers that be. But they possess in an extreme degree the sanguine irrepressible energy, the great temporal ambitions, the personal persuasive force, the oratorical aptitudes that in a minor degree tend to mark the class that rises to the aristocracy; it is therefore a notable and curious fact that their index of pigmentation should be as extreme as their mental attitudes and convictions.

If we turn away from the groups which are or tend to become aristocratic, we find that men of science (among whom are here included philosophers and inventors) present a strikingly high index. This seems to be due to the fact that scientific aptitude occurs with especial frequency in the north of England and in Scotland, the most peculiarly fair region of Great Britain, the region, it may be noted also, which has contained the most progressive and successful populations. The fairness of the group of artists, again, must be associated with the fact that artists tend largely to come from among the fair populations along the east coast of England and Scotland. I have noted a similar fairness in an even more marked degree among modern artists in France, who also tend to come from the fairest parts of their country. The fairness of the group of poets can scarcely be put down to a similar cause, for poets are produced by every part of the country.

The large and important group of men of letters, on the other hand, cannot be called predominantly fair; the divines are still darker, and this is so even as regards those among them (like Knox) who were reformers and agitators. The class of men of low birth (including numerous persons of intellectual distinction) is very dark. The actors and the explorers are the darkest of all.

If for the present we neglect the consideration of separate groups and seek to look more broadly at the matter, it seems to me that we may find one or two tendencies fairly well marked. It is clear that a high index of pigmentation, or an excess of fairness, prevails among the men of restless and ambitious temperament, the sanguine energetic men, the men who easily dominate their fellows and who get on in life, the men who recruit the aristocracy and who doubtless largely form the plutocracy. It is significant that the group of low-class men — artisans and peasants — and the men of religion, whose mission in life it is to practise and preach resignation to a Higher Will, are both notably of dark complexion.

While the men of action thus tend to be fair, the men of thought, it seems to me, show some tendency to be dark. This latter tendency is by no means so clear from the data before us as the other tendency. Still it is indicated, and it would be still clearer if we were to subdivide our groups according to the intellectual eminence of the individuals comprised within them; it would then generally be found, I believe, that in each group the more intellectual showed a somewhat lower index of pigmentation. It is noteworthy that the men of letters, whose intellectual achievements are on the whole decidedly greater, if less brilliant, than those of the poets, show a lower index of pigmentation. It may be said, also, regarding the men of low social class, that though their darkness is partly explainable, as we have seen, on other grounds, they are mostly men of marked intellectual force. If this is so, the dark people may be said to have their consolations; they are by no means lacking in intellectual force, and probably possess such power in a higher average degree than the fair men. The latter, by virtue of their greater executive energy, are often able to achieve success in the world with the possession of a comparatively minor, though often very considerable, inheritance of intelligence. But the dark men are better able to learn the wisdom that teaches the vanity of worldly success.*

I have hitherto said nothing concerning two groups which may seem somewhat anomalous. I refer to the two darkest groups of all, the explorers and the actors. It may be thought that the darkness of the explorers contradicts the conclusion we have just reached that the people of restless energy tend to be fair. But here a totally new consideration enters into the question. Pigmentation, it is well recognised, is a protection. The veil of dark pigment which the organism weaves for itself against the sun in summer bears evidence to this fact, and there is some reason to believe also that dark persons resist disease better than the fair. The pioneering exploits of sailors, being aided by the climatically modifying influence of the sea and being mostly in cold climates, involve no selection of dark persons. Our group of explorers, however, mostly travellers in the extremely trying climates of tropical lands, especially Africa, have needed all the assistance that constitutional

---

* As a reader is apt to suspect that any writer on such points as this is moved by personal bias, it may, perhaps, be well to state that the present writer belongs to the medium group, and is therefore able to view this series of phenomena with, as Huxley expressed it, the serene impartiality of the mongrel.

peculiarities furnish; and the life has proved too arduous for the fair, who have mostly succumbed or been discouraged. Thus it is that our most eminent and experienced explorers in hot climates are mostly men of dark eyes and hair.

I cannot furnish so unquestionable an explanation of the darkness of actors, though the phenomena are here at least equally well marked. There have been a few moderately fair actors and actresses of eminence, but scarcely any of them have been of the highest eminence. The Kemble family, to which Mrs. Siddons belonged, was dark, and Garrick was extremely dark. So far as I am aware, no really fair person has ever risen to the highest dramatic eminence in England, and so far as I have been able to observe, it is equally rare for fairness to be associated with histrionic ability in Europe generally. It may certainly be said that in Great Britain the darkest populations are those most fertile in ability of this kind, and also that actors tend, to a considerable extent, to spring from the lower, and darker, social classes. Whether these facts suffice to account for this phenomenon, or whether we must go deeper and assume that the special metabolic processes associated with the organic manufacture of pigment are also associated with dramatic faculty is not clear. I am not at present disposed to accept it, though it is scarcely beyond the bounds of possibility that, other things being equal, a certain kind of nervous texture, involving a predisposition to certain intellectual aptitudes, may be directly connected with the greater or less tendency to manufacture pigment. It is necessary to introduce the proviso, 'other things being equal,' for we certainly could not assert generally that the unpigmented person or albino shows a native tendency to enter the aristocracy (notwithstanding the case of Lord Sherbrooke), while the existence of highly pigmented lower races suffices to show that pigment alone will not confer intellectual aptitude.

The more reasonable supposition at present seems to be that the relation between pigmentation and mental aptitude is chiefly indirect, and due to race. In other words, the fair man tends to be bold, energetic, restless and domineering, not because he is fair, but because he belongs to an aboriginal fair stock of people who possess those qualities; while the dark man tends to be resigned and religious and imitative, yet highly intelligent, not because he is dark, but because he belongs to a dark stock possessing those characteristics.

An interesting sidelight is thrown on this question by considering the phenomena as they exist in a country having a racial composition in some respects comparable to Great Britain, and, without doubt, closely related to its peoples. In Norway there are, as in Great Britain, fair and dark stocks, the former usually long-headed, the latter broad-headed, and there also the darker stock is, on the whole, placed more to the south and west of the country. It so happens that a very interesting and acute psychological study of the fair and dark populations of Norway has been made by Dr. A. M. Hansen. This investigation has revealed differences even more marked between the fair and the dark than may easily be discovered in our own islands, and this is not surprising since our racial elements have been more thoroughly mixed. The fair population, he tells us, is made up of born aristocrats, active, outspoken, progressive, with a passion for freedom and independence, caring nothing for equality; the dark population is reserved and suspicious, very conservative, and lacking in initiative, caring little for freedom, but with a passion for equality. The fair people are warlike, quarrelsome when drunk, and furnish, in proportion to numbers, three times as many men for the volunteer force as the dark people; the latter, though brave sailors, abhor war, and are very religious, subscribing to foreign missions nearly three times as much per head as is furnished by the fair people, who are inclined to be irreligious. The fair people value money and all that money can buy, while the dark people are indifferent to money. The reality of the mental distinction is shown by the fact that a map of the proportion of Conservative voters in elections to the Storthing exactly corresponds to an anthropological map of the country, the Conservative majority being found in the dark and broad-headed districts. While, however, the fair population is the most irreligious and progressive, the dark population is by no means behind in the production of intellect, and the region it inhabits has produced many eminent men.

I have referred to Hansen's remarkable study of Norwegian psychology because it shows that, in a country somewhat allied to England in racial composition, much the same tendency for definite intellectual aptitude to be associated with definite physical types may be traced. There are some discrepancies, it is true; England's dark population is not attracted to seafaring and is by no means specially apt to take the Conservative side in politics. It is probable, indeed, that while the fair population of Norway is without doubt closely allied to our own fair population, the dark population may only be remotely related to ours, which is not broadheaded. Thus, this parallel by no means proves conclusively that the association between special mental aptitudes and pigmentary tendencies can be resolved entirely into a question of race. It may also be remarked that the characteristics of the fair population are especially masculine qualities, while the characteristics of the dark population are more peculiarly feminine qualities; it so happens also that women, as is now beginning to be generally recognised by anthropologists, tend to be somewhat darker than men. Even this fact, however, may possibly receive a racial explanation.

It would, in any case, be rash to state any broad and far-reaching conclusions concerning an inquiry which is still so novel. It is enough for the present that, when we carefully study so large a collection of the representations of eminent British persons as that constituting the National Portrait Gallery, it is possible to show that in the different classes of mental aptitude the proportion of fair and dark persons varies widely, and in some cases to indicate why this is so.

THE END

APPENDICES

APPENDIX A

LIST OF EMINENT BRITISH PERSONS OF ABILITY

(The names of women are italicised.)

Abbot, G. (1562–1633)
Abercromby, Sir R. (1734–1801)
Abington, F. (1737–1815)
Adam, R. (1728–1792)
Adams, J. C. (1819–1892)
Adamson, P. (1537–1592)
Addison, J. (1672–1719)
Adrian IV. (——1159)
Ainsworth, H. (1571–1622)
Airy, Sir G. (1801–1892)
Alcuin (735–804)
Alesius, A. (1500–1565)
Alexander of Hales (——1245)
Alexander, W., Earl of Stirling (1567–1640)
Allen, W. (1532–1594)
Amherst, J., Baron (1717–1797)
Andrewes, L. (1555–1626)
Anson, G., Baron (1697–1762)
Arblay, F. d' (1752–1840)
Arkwright, Sir R. (1732–1792)
Arne, T. (1710–1778)
Arnold, M. (1822–1888)
Arnold, T. (1795–1842)
Arthur, Sir G. (1784–1854)
Ascham, R. (1515–1568)
Atterbury, F. (1662–1732)
Austen, J. (1775–1817)
Austin, J. (1790–1859)

Babbage, C. (1792–1871)
Bacon, A. (1558–1601)
Bacon, F., Lord Verulam (1561–1626)
Bacon, Sir N. (1509–1579)
Bacon, R. (1214?–1294)
Bagehot, W. (1826–1877)
Baillie, J. (1762–1851)
Baily, F. (1774–1844)
Baker, Sir S. (1821–1893)
Balfe, M. W. (1808–1870)
Balfour, F. (1851–1882)
Bancroft, R. (1544–1610)
Banim, J. (1798–1842)
Banks, Sir J. (1743–1820)

Banks, T. (1735–1805)
Bannister, J. (1760–1836)
Barbauld, A. (1743–1825)
Barbour, J. (1316?–1395)
Barclay, A. (1475?–1552)
Barclay, J. (1582–1621)
Barclay, R. (1648–1690)
Barham, R. (1788–1845)
Barnes, W. (1801–1886)
Barnfield, R. (1574–1627)
Barrow, I. (1630–1677)
Barrow, Sir J. (1764–1848)
Barry, A. (1734–1801)
Barry, Sir C. (1795–1860)
Barry, E. (1658–1713)
Barry, J. (1741–1806)
Baskerville, J. (1706–1775)
Bateman, W. (1298?–1355)
Bates, H. W. (1825–1892)
Baxter, R. (1615–1691)
Beardsley, A. (1872–1898)
Beaton, D. (1494–1546)
Beaumont, F. (1584–1616)
Becher, E., Lady (1791–1872)
Beckford, W. (1759–1844)
Beddoes, T. (1803–1849)
Bede (673–735)
Bedell, W. (1571–1642)
Behn, A. (1640–1689)
Bell, A. (1753–1832)
Bell, Sir C. (1774–1842)
Bennett, Sir W. S. (1816–1875)
Benson, E. (1829–1896)
Bentham, G. (1800–1884)
Bentham, J. (1748–1832)
Bentley, R. (1662–1742)
Berkeley, G. (1685–1753)
Bessemer, Sir H. (1813–1898)
Bethell, R., Lord Westbury (1800–1873)
Betterton, T. (1635–1710)
Bewick, T. (1753–1828)
Bingham, J. (1668–1723)
Birch, S. (1813–1885)

Bishop, Sir H. (1786–1855)
Black, J. (1728–1799)
Blackmore, R. (1825–1900)
Blackstone, Sir W. (1723–1780)
Blake, R. (1599–1657)
Blake, W. (1757–1827)
Blow, J. (1648–1708)
Boece, H. (1465?–1536)
Boniface, St. (680–755)
Bonington, R. P. (1801–1828)
Bonner, E. (1500?–1569)
Booth, B. (1681–1733)
Borrow, G. (1803–1881)
Boscawen, E. (1711–1761)
Boswell, J. (1740–1795)
Bowen, C., Baron (1835–1894)
Bowring, Sir J. (1792–1872)
Boyce, W. (1710–1779)
Boyle, A., Earl of Cork (1566–1643)
Boyle, R. (1627–1691)
Bracegirdle, A. (1663–1748)
Bradford, W. (1590–1657)
Bradlaugh, C. (1833–1891)
Bradley, J. (1693–1762)
Bradshaw, H. (1831–1886)
Bradshaw, W. (1571–1618)
Bradwardine (1290?–1349)
Breton, N. (1545?–1626)
Brewster, Sir D. (1781–1868)
Bright, J. (1811–1889)
Broke, Sir P. (1776–1841)
Brontë, C. (1816–1855)
Brontë, E. (1818–1848)
Brooke, Sir J. (1803–1868)
Brougham, Lord (1778–1868)
Brown, F. M. (1821–1893)
Browne, H. K. (1815–1882)
Browne, R. (1550?–1633?)
Browne, Sir T. (1605–1682)
Browne, W. (1591–1643?)
Browning, E. B. (1806–1861)
Browning, R. (1812–1889)
Bruce, H., Baron Aberdare (1815–1895)
Bruce, J. (1730–1794)
Bruce, M. (1746–1767)
Buchanan, G. (1506–1582)
Buckle, H. T. (1821–1862)
Bull, J. (1563?–1628)
Bunyan J. (1628–1688)
Burbage, R. (1567?–1619)
Burges, C. (1589–1665)
Burke, E. (1729–1787)
Burne-Jones, Sir E. (1833–1898)
Burnet, G. (1643–1715)
Burns, R. (1759–1796)
Burton, Sir R. (1821–1890)

Burton, R. (1577–1640)
Butler, J. (1692–1752)
Butler, S. (1612–1680)
Butterfield, W. (1814–1900)
Byng, G., Viscount Torrington (1663–1733)
Byrd, W. 1538–1623)
Byron, G., Lord (1788–1824)

Cade, J. (——1450)
Cadogan, W., Earl (1675–1726)
Cædmon (*fl.* 670)
Cairns, H., Earl (1819–1885)
Caius, J. (1510–1573)
Calamy, E. (1671–1732)
Camden, W. (1551–1623)
Campbell, Sir C. (1792–1863)
Campbell, Sir G. (1824–1892)
Campbell, J., Baron (1779–1861)
Campbell, T. (1777–1844)
Campion, E. (1540–1581)
Campion, T. (——1619)
Candlish, R. (1806–1873)
Canning, C., Earl (1812–1862)
Canning, G. (1770–1827)
Canning, S., Viscount S. de Redcliffe (1786–1880)
Cantelupe, St. T. de (1218?–1282)
Canton, J. (1718–1772)
Carey, W. (1761–1834)
Carleton, W. (1794–1869)
Carlile, R. (1790–1843)
Carlyle, T. (1795–1881)
Carpenter, M. (1807–1877)
Carpenter, W. B. (1813–1885)
Carrington, R. (1826–1875)
Carstares, W. (1649–1715)
Cartwright, T. (1535–1603)
Case, T. (1598–1682)
Cattermole, G. (1800–1868)
Cavendish, H. (1731–1810)
Cavendish, M., Duchess of Newcastle (1624?–1674)
Cavendish, T. (1555?–1592)
Caxton, W. (1422?–1491)
Cayley, A. (1821–1895)
Cecil, W., Lord Burghley (1520–1598)
Centlivre, S. (1667?–1723)
Challoner, R. (1691–1781)
Chalmers, T. (1780–1847)
Chantry, Sir F. (1781–1842)
Chapman, G. (1559?–1634)
Chatterton, T. (1752–1770)
Chaucer, G. (1340?–1400)
Cheke, Sir J. (1514–1557)
Cheselden, W. (1688–1752)
Chesney, F. (1789–1872)

Chichele, H. (1362–1443)
Chichester, A. Lord (1563–1625)
Childers, H. (1827–1896)
Chillingworth, W. (1602–1644)
Church, R. (1815–1890)
Churchill, C. (1731–1764)
Churchill, J., Duke of Marlborough (1650–1722)
Cibber, C. (1671–1757)
Cibber, S. (1714–1766)
Clapperton, H. (1788–1827)
Clare, J. (1793–1864)
Clarke, S. (1675–1729)
Clifford, W. G. (1845–1879)
Clive, K. (1711–1785)
Clive, R., Lord (1725–1774)
Clough, A. (1819–1861)
Cobbett, W. (1762–1835)
Cobden, R. (1804–1865)
Cockburn, Sir A. (1802–1880)
Cockerell, C. (1788–1863)
Coke, Sir E. (1552–1634)
Colby, T. (1784–1852)
Colebrooke, H. T. (1765–1837)
Colenso, J. (1814–1883)
Coleridge, H. (1796–1849)
Coleridge, S. T. (1772–1834)
Colet, J. (1467–1519)
Collier, J. (1630–1726)
Collins, W. (1721–1759)
Collins, W. W. (1824–1889)
Colman, G., the elder (1732–1794)
Columba, St. (521–597)
Columban, St. (543–615)
Congreve, W. (1670–1729)
Conington, J. (1825–1869)
Constable, J. (1776–1837)
Cook, J. (1728–1779)
Cooke, G. F. (1756–1811)
Cooke, H. (1788–1868)
Cooper, A., First Lord Shaftesbury (1621–1683)
Cooper, A., Third Lord Shaftesbury (1671–1713)
Cooper, Sir A. (1768–1841)
Cooper, S., (1609–1672)
Copley, J. S. (1737–1815)
Copley, J. S., Lord Lyndhurst (1772–1863)
Cosin, J. (1594–1672)
Cotes, R. (1682–1716)
Cotman, J. (1782–1842)
Cotton, Sir A. T. (1803–1899)
Cotton, C. (1630–1687)
Cotton, Sir R. (1571–1631)
Coutances, W. de (——1207)
Coverdale, M. (1488–1568)

Cowley, A. (1618–1667)
Cowley, H. (1743–1809)
Cowper, W. (1731–1800)
Cox, D. (1783–1859)
Cozens, J. R. (1752–1799)
Crabbe, G. (1754–1832)
Cranmer, T. (1489–1556)
Crashaw, R. (1612–1649)
Creighton, M. (1843–1901)
Crichton, J. (1560–1585?)
Croker, J. W. (1780–1857)
Crome, J. (1768–1821)
Cromwell, O. (1599–1658)
Cromwell, T. (1485?–1540)
Cross, M. A. (1819–1880)
Cruikshank, G. (1792–1878)
Cudworth, R. (1617–1688)
Cullen, W. (1710–1790)
Curran, J. P. (1750–1817)
Cuthbert, St. (——687)

Dalrymple, J., Viscount Stair (1619–1695)
Dalton, J. (1766–1844)
Dampier, W. (1652–1715)
Danby, F. (1793–1861)
Daniel, S. (1562–1619)
Darwin, C. (1809–1882)
Darwin, E. (1731–1802)
D'Avenant, Sir W. (1606–1668)
Davies, Sir J. (1569–1626)
Davy, Sir H. (1778–1829)
Dawson, H. (1811–1878)
Day, T. (1748–1789)
Deane, R. (1610–1653)
Dee, J. (1527–1608)
Defoe, D. (1659–1731)
Dekker, T. (1570?–1641?)
De Morgan, A. (1806–1871)
Dempster, T. (1579?–1625)
Denham, Sir J. (1615–1669)
Denman, Lord (1779–1854)
De Quincey, T. (1785–1859)
D'Ewes, Sir S. (1602–1650)
Dibdin, C. (1745–1814)
Dickens, C. (1812–1870)
Digby, Sir K. (1603–1665)
Dobell, S. (1824–1874)
Dobson, W. (1610–1646)
Doddridge, P. (1702–1751)
Dodgson, C. (1832–1898)
Dodwell, H. (1641–1711)
Dolben, J. (1625–1686)
Donne, J. (1573–1631)
Douglas, G. (1474?–1522)
Dowland, J. (1563?–1626)
Doyle, R. (1824–1883)

Drake, Sir F. (1540?–1596)
Drayton, M. (1563–1631)
Drummond, T. (1797–1840)
Drummond, W. (1585–1649)
Dryden, J. (1631–1700)
Dudley, J., Duke of Northumberland (1502–1553)
Duff, A. (1806–1878)
Dugdale, Sir W. (1605–1686)
Du Maurier, G. (1834–1896)
Dunbar, W. (1465?–1530?)
Duncan, A., Viscount (1731–1804)
Dundas, H., Viscount Melville (1742–1811)
Dunning, J., Baron Ashburton (1731–1783)
Duns, J. S. (1265?–1308?)
Dunstan, St. (924–988)
D'Urfey, T. (1653–1723)
Dyce, W. (1806–1864)

Eastlake, Sir C. (1793–1865)
Eastlake, Lady (1809–1893)
Edgeworth, M. (1767–1849)
Edmund, St. (1170?–1240)
Edwardes, Sir H. (1819–1868)
Edwards, A. B. (1831–1892)
Eliot, Sir J. (1592–1632)
Elliston, R. W. (1774–1831)
Elyot, Sir T. (1490–1546)
Emlyn, T. (1663–1741)
Erskine, E. (1680–1754)
Etherege, Sir G. (1634–1691?)
Etty, W. (1787–1849)

Faber, F. (1814–1863)
Falconer, H. (1808–1865)
Fanshawe, Sir R. (1608–1666)
Faraday, M. (1791–1867)
Farquhar, G. (1678–1707)
Faucit, H. (1817–1898)
Fawcett, H. (1833–1884)
Ferguson, J. (1710–1776)
Fergusson, R. (1750–1774)
Ferrar, N. (1592–1637)
Ferrier, S. (1782–1854)
Fielding, H. (1707–1754)
Fitzgerald, E. (1809–1883)
Fitzgibbon, J., Earl of Clare (1749–1802)
Flamsteed, J. (1646–1719)
Flaxman, J. (1755–1826)
Fletcher, A. (1655–1716)
Fletcher, J. (1579–1625)
Flinders, M. (1774–1814)
Flood, H. (1732–1791)
Flower, Sir W. (1831–1899)

Foote, S. (1720–1777)
Forbes, E. (1815–1854)
Forbes, J. D. (1809–1868)
Ford, J. (1586–1639?)
Forster, W. E. (1818–1886)
Fortescue, Sir J. (1394–1476?)
Fox, C. J. (1749–1806)
Fox, G. (1624–1691)
Foxe, J. (1516–1587)
Foxe, R. (1448?–1528)
Francis, Sir P. (1740–1818)
Frankland, Sir E. (1825–1899)
Franklin, Sir J. (1786–1847)
Franks, Sir A. (1826–1897)
Freeman, E. (1823–1892)
Frere, Sir B. (1815–1884)
Frobisher, Sir M. (1535–1594)
Froude, J. A. (1818–1894)
Fry, E. (1780–1845)
Fuller, T. (1608–1661)

Gainsborough, T. (1727–1788)
Galt, J. (1779–1839)
Gardiner, S. (1483?–1555)
Garnett, H. (1555–1606)
Garrick, D. (1717–1779)
Gascoigne, G. (1523?–1579)
Gaskell, E. C. (1810–1865)
Gauntlett, H. (1805–1876)
Gay, J. (1685–1732)
Geoffrey of Monmouth (1100?–1154)
Gibbon, E. (1737–1794)
Gibbons, O. (1583–1625)
Gibson, J. (1790–1866)
Gifford, W. (1756–1826)
Gilbert, Sir H. (1539?–1583)
Gilbert, Sir J. (1817–1897)
Gilbert, W. (1540–1603)
Gillray, J. (1757–1815)
Giraldus Cambrensis (1146?–1220?)
Girtin, T. (1775–1802)
Gladstone, W. E. (1809–1898)
Glisson, F. (1597–1677)
Godwin, M. W. (1759–1797)
Godwin, W. (1756–1836)
Goldsmith, O. (1728–1774)
Gordon, C. G. (1833–1885)
Gower, J. (1325?–1408)
Graham, Sir G. (1831–1899)
Graham, J., Viscount Dundee (1649?–1689)
Grattan, J. (1746–1820)
Gray, T. (1716–1771)
Green, J. R. (1837–1883)
Greene, R. (1560?–1592)
Grenville, G. (1712–1770)
Grenville, W., Baron (1759–1834)

Gresham, Sir T. (1519?–1579)
Grew, N. (1641–1712)
Grey, Sir G. (1812–1898)
Grocyn, W. (1446?–1519)
Grosseteste, R. (1175?–1253)
Grote, G. (1794–1871)

Hale, Sir M. (1609–1676)
Hales, J. (1584–1656)
Hales, S. (1677–1761)
Hall, J. (1574–1656)
Hallam, H. (1777–1859)
Halley, E. (1656–1742)
Halliwell-Phillips, J. (1820–1889)
Hamilton, A. (1646?–1720)
Hamilton, S. W. (1788–1856)
Hamilton, Sir W. R. (1805–1865)
Hamilton, T., Earl of Haddington (1563–1637)
Hamley, Sir E. (1824–1893)
Hampden, J. (1594–1643)
Hardinge, H., Viscount (1785–1856)
Harrington, J. (1611–1677)
Hartley, D. (1705–1757)
Harvey, W. (1578–1657)
Hastings, W. (1732–1818)
Havelock, Sir H. (1795–1857)
Hawke, E., Lord (1705–1781)
Hawkins, Sir J. (1532–1595)
Hawkwood, Sir J. de (——1304)
Haydon, B. W. (1786–1846)
Hazlitt, W. (1778–1830)
Hemans, F. (1793–1835)
Henderson, A. (1583?–1646)
Herbert, A., Earl of Torrington (1647–1716)
Herbert, of Cherbury, E., Lord (1583–1648)
Herbert, G. (1593–1633)
Herrick, R. (1591–1674)
Herschel, Sir J. (1792–1871)
Heylin, P. (1600–1662)
Heywood, J. (1497?–1580)
Heywood, T. (1650)
Hickes, G. (1642–1715)
Hill, Sir R. (1795–1879)
Hinton, J. (1822–1875)
Hoadley, B. (1676–1761)
Hobbes, T. (1588–1679)
Hodgson, B. (1800–1894)
Hogarth, W. (1697–1764)
Hogg, J. (1770–1835)
Holcroft, T. (1745–1809)
Holl, F. (1845–1888)
Hood, S., Viscount (1724–1816)
Hood, T. (1799–1845)
Hook, T. (1788–1841)

Hook, W. (1798–1875)
Hooke, R. (1635–1703)
Hooker, R. (1554–1600)
Horner, F. (1778–1817)
Horrocks, J. (1617?–1641)
Hort, F. (1828–1892)
Howard, J. (1726–1790)
Howell, J. (1594–1666)
Hubert Walter (——1205)
Hughes, T. (1822–1896)
Hume, D. (1711–1776)
Hunt, L. (1784–1859)
Hunter, J. (1728–1893)
Hunter, Sir W. (1840–1900)
Huskisson, W. (1770–1830)
Hutcheson, F. (1694–1746)
Hutton, J. (1726–1797)
Hutton, R. H. (1826–1897)
Huxley, T. H. (1825–1895)
Hyde, E., Earl of Clarendon (1609–1674)

Inchbald, E. (1753–1821)
Ireton, H. (1611–1651)
Irving, E. (1792–1834)

Jameson, A. (1794–1860)
Jeffrey, F., Lord (1773–1850)
Jenner, E. (1749–1823)
Jerrold, D. (1803–1857)
Jervis, J., Earl of St. Vincent (1735–1823)
Jevons, W. S. (1835–1882)
Jewel, J. (1522–1571)
John of Salisbury (——1180)
Johnson, S. (1709–1784)
Johnston, A., Lord Warriston (1610?–1663)
Jones, I. (1573–1652)
Jones, Sir J. T. (1783–1843)
Jones, Sir W. (1746–1794)
Jones, W. B. (1822–1897)
Jonson, B. (1573–1637)
Jordan, D. (1761–1816)
Joule, J. P. (1818–1889)
Jowett, B. (1817–1893)
Juxon, W. (1582–1663)

Kean, E. (1787–1833)
Keats, J. (1795–1821)
Keble, J. (1792–1866)
Keeley, M. A. (1805–1895)
Keene, C. (1823–1891)
Kelly, F. (1790–1882)
Kemble, F. A. (1809–1893)
Kemble, J. M. (1807–1857)
Kemble, J. P. (1757–1823)

Kemp, J. (1380–1447)
Ken, T. (1637–1711)
Kennett, W. (1660–1728)
Kenyon, L., Lord (1732–1802)
Killigrew, T. (1612–1683)
King, T. (1730–1805)
King, W. (1650–1729)
Kingsley, C. (1819–1875)
Kingsley, M. (1862–1900)
Kirkcaldy, Sir W. (1573)
Knight, G. (1713–1772)
Knollys, Sir R. (1407)
Knowles, J. S. (1784–1862)
Knox, J. (1505–1572)

Lake, G., Viscount (1744–1808)
Lamb, C. (1775–1834)
Lambert, J. (1619–1683)
Lancaster, J. (1778–1838)
Lander, R. (1804–1834)
Landon, L. E. (1802–1838)
Landor, W. S. (1775–1864)
Landseer, Sir E. (1802–1873)
Lane, E. (1801–1876)
Langland, W. (1330?–1400?)
Langton, S. (1228)
Langton, W. (1321)
Lardner, N. (1684–1768)
Latimer, H. (1485?–1555)
Laud, W. (1573–1645)
Law, E., Baron Ellenborough (1750–1818)
Law, E., Earl of Ellenborough (1790–1871)
Law, J. (1671–1729)
Law, W. (1686–1761)
Lawes, H. (1596–1662)
Lawes, Sir J. B. (1814–1900)
Lawrence, Sir H. (1806–1857)
Lawrence, J., Lord (1811–1879)
Lawrence, S. (1698–1775)
Lawrence, Sir T. (1769–1830)
Layard, Sir A. H. (1817–1894)
Leake, Sir J. (1656–1720)
Lee, N. (1653?–1692)
Leech, J. (1817–1864)
Lefroy, Sir J. (1817–1890)
Leighton, F., Baron (1830–1896)
Leighton, R. (1611–1684)
Leland, J. (1506?–1552)
Leslie, A., Earl of Leven (1582–1661)
Leslie, C. (1650–1722)
Leslie, J. (1527–1596)
L'Estrange, Sir R. (1616–1704)
Lever, C. J. (1806–1872)
Lewes, G. H. (1817–1878)
Lewis, Sir G. C. (1806–1863)

Lewis, J. F. (1805–1876)
Lewis, W. T. (1748?–1811)
Liddon, H. P. (1829–1890)
Lightfoot, J. B. (1828–1889)
Lilburne, J. (1614?–1657)
Lillo, G. (1693–1739)
Linacre, T. (1460?–1524)
Lindsay, Sir D. (1490–1555)
Linguard, J. (1771–1851)
Linnell, J. (1792–1882)
Linton, E. L. (1822–1898)
Linton, W. J. (1812–1898)
Lister, J. (1786–1869)
Liston, J. (1776–1846)
Littleton, Sir T. (1422–1481)
Livingstone, D. (1813–1873)
Lloyd, J. (1627–1717)
Locke, J. (1632–1704)
Lockhart, J. (1794–1854)
Lodge, T. (1558–1625)
Loftus, A. (1533–1605)
Lovelace, R. (1618–1658)
Lover, S. (1797–1868)
Lowe, R., Viscount Sherbrooke (1811–1892)
Lowth, R. (1710–1787)
Lucus, C. (1713–1771)
Ludlow, E. (1617–1692)
Lydgate, J. (1370?–1451)
Lyell, Sir C. (1797–1875)
Lyly, J. (1554?–1606)
Lytton, E. B., Earl of (1831–1891)
Lytton, E. B., Lord (1803–1873)

Macaulay, T., Lord (1800–1859)
Macdonald, Sir J. A. (1815–1891)
Macfarren, Sir G. (1813–1887)
Mackay, H. (1640?–1692)
Mackintosh, Sir J. (1765–1832)
Mackenzie, H. (1745–1831)
Macklin, C. (1697?–1797)
Maclaurin, C. (1698–1746)
Maclise, D. (1806–1870)
Macnaghten, Sir W. (1793–1841)
Macready, W. C. (1793–1873)
Maginn, W. (1793–1842)
Maine, Sir H. S. (1822–1888)
Malcolm, Sir J. (1769–1833)
Malone, E. (1741–1812)
Malthus, T. (1766–1834)
Manning, H. E. (1807–1892)
Map, W. (*fl.* 1200)
Marlowe, C. (1564–1593)
Marryat, F. (1792–1848)
Marsh, H. (1757–1839)
Marshall, S. (1594?–1655)
Marston, J. (1575–1634)

Marten, H. (1602–1680)
Martineau, H. (1802–1876)
Martineau, J. (1805–1900)
Marvell, A. (1621–1678)
Massinger, P. (1583–1640)
Mathews, C. (1776–1835)
Mathews, C. J. (1803–1878)
Maurice, F. D. (1805–1872)
Maxwell, J. C. (1831–1879)
Mayow, J. (1643–1679)
Mead, R. (1673–1754)
Melville, A. (1545–1622)
Merivale, C. (1808–1893)
Middleton, C. (1683–1750)
Middleton, T. (1570?–1627)
Mill, J. (1773–1836)
Mill, J. S. (1806–1873)
Millais, Sir J. (1829–1896)
Miller, H. (1802–1856)
Milman, H. (1791–1868)
Milner, I. (1750–1820)
Milner, J. (1752–1826)
Milton, J. (1608–1674)
Mitchell, Sir T. (1792–1855)
Mitford, M. (1787–1855)
Moffat, R. (1795–1883)
Monck, G., Duke of Albemarle (1608–1670)
Monson, Sir W. (1569–1643)
Montagu, C., Earl of Halifax (1661–1715)
Montagu, E. (1720–1800)
Montagu, R. (1577–1641)
Moore, Sir J. (1761–1809)
Moore, T. (1779–1852)
More, H. (1745–1833)
More, Sir T. (1478–1535)
Morgan, Sir G. O. (1826–1897)
Morgan, Sir H. (1635?–1688)
Morgan, Lady S. (1783?–1859)
Morland, G. (1763–1804)
Morland, Sir S. (1625–1695)
Morley, G. (1597–1684)
Morris, W. (1834–1896)
Morton, T. (1564–1659)
Mulready, W. (1786–1863)
Mun, T. (1571–1641)
Munday, A. (1553–1633)
Mundella, A. J. (1825–1897)
Munden, J. (1758–1832)
Munro, Sir T. (1761–1827)
Murchison, Sir R. (1792–1871)
Murdock, W. (1754–1839)
Murray, J. (1778–1843)
Myers, F. W. (1843–1901)

Nairne, C., Baroness (1766–1845)

Napier, Sir C. (1786–1860)
Napier, Sir C. J. (1782–1853)
Napier, J. (1550–1617)
Napier, Sir J. (1804–1882)
Napier, R. C., Lord (1810–1890)
Napier, Sir W. J. P. (1785–1860)
Nash, T. (1567–1601)
Nasmyth, J. (1808–1890)
Nasmyth, P. (1787–1831)
Naylor, J. (1617?–1660)
Neale, E. V. (1810–1892)
Neale, J. M. (1818–1866)
Needham, M. (1620–1678)
Neill, J. G. S. (1810–1857)
Neilson, J. (1792–1865)
Neilson, L. A. (1848–1880)
Nelson, H., Lord (1758–1805)
Newcomen, T. (1663–1729)
Newman, F. W. (1805–1897)
Newman, J. H. (1801–1890)
Newton, Sir I. (1642–1727)
Nicholson, J. (1821–1857)
Northcote, J. (1746–1831)
Norton, T. (1532–1584)
Nott, Sir W. (1782–1845)
Nowell, A. (1507?–1602)
Noye, W. (1577–1634)

Ochterlony, Sir D. (1758–1825)
Ockham, W. (——1349?)
Ockley, S. (1678–1720)
O'Connell, D. (1775–1847)
Oglethorpe, J. E. (1696–1785)
Oldcastle, Sir J. (——1417)
Oldfield, A. (1683–1730)
Oldys, W. (1696–1761)
O'Leary, A. (1729–1802)
Oliphant, L. (1829–1888)
Oliphant, M. (1828–1897)
O'Neill, D. (1612–1664)
Opie, A. (1769–1853)
Opie, J. (1761–1807)
Ordericus Vitalis (1075–1143?)
Otway, T. (1652–1685)
Oughtred, W. (1575–1660)
Outram, Sir J. (1803–1863)
Owen, J. (1616–1683)
Owen, Sir R. (1804–1892)
Owen, R. (1771–1858)

Paget, Sir J. (1814–1899)
Paget, W., Baron (1505–1563)
Paine, T. (1737–1809)
Paley, W. (1743–1805)
Palmer, E. H. (1840–1882)
Palmer, J. (1742?–1798)

Palmer, R., Earl Selbourne (1812–1895)
Palmer, S. (1805–1881)
Paris, M. (——1259?)
Park, M. (1771–1806)
Parker, M. (1504–1575)
Parker, T., Earl Macclesfield (1667–1732)
Parkes, E. A. (1819–1876)
Parkes, Sir H. S. (1828–1885)
Parkes, Sir H. (1815–1896)
Parnell, C. S. (1846–1891)
Parr, S. (1747–1825)
Parsons, R. (1546–1610)
Parsons, W. (1736–1795)
Pater, W. H. (1839–1894)
Paterson, W. (1658–1719)
Patmore, C. (1823–1896)
Patrick, St. (373–463)
Pattison, M. (1813–1884)
Payne, P. (1380?–1455)
Pearson, J. (1613–1686)
Pearson, J. L. (1817–1897)
Pecock, R. (1395?–1460?)
Peel, Sir R. (1788–1850)
Peele, G. (1558?–1597?)
Peirce, J. (1674?–1726)
Pellew, E., Viscount Exmouth (1757–1833)
Penn, Sir W. (1621–1670)
Penn, W. (1644–1718)
Penry (1559–1593)
Pepys, S. (1633–1703)
Perkins, W. (1558–1602)
Perry, J. (1756–1821)
Peters, H. (1598–1660)
Petty, Sir W. (1623–1687)
Phelps, S. (1804–1878)
Phillip, J. (1817–1867)
Picton, Sir T. (1758–1815)
Pitman, Sir I. (1813–1897)
Pitt, W., Earl of Chatham (1708–1778)
Pitt, W. (1759–1806)
Pococke, E. (1604–1691)
Pollock, Sir G. (1786–1872)
Pope, A. (1688–1744)
Popham, Sir H. R. (1762–1820)
Porson, R. (1759–1808)
Pott, P. (1714–1788)
Powell, V. (1617–1670)
Pownall, T. (1722–1802)
Pratt, C., Earl Camden (1714–1794)
Preston, J. (1587–1628)
Prestwich, Sir J. (1812–1896)
Price, R. (1723–1791)
Priestley, J. (1733–1804)

Prior, M. (1664–1721)
Prynne, W. (1600–1669)
Pugin, A. W. (1812–1852)
Pulteney, W., Earl of Bath (1684–1764)
Purcell, H. (1658?–1695)
Pusey, E. B. (1800–1882)
Pym, J. (1584–1643)

Quarles, F. (1592–1644)
Quin, J. (1693–1766)

Radcliffe, A. (1764–1823)
Raeburn, Sir H. (1756–1823)
Raffles, Sir T. (1781–1826)
Raleigh, Sir W. (1552?–1618)
Randolph, T. (1605–1635)
Ray, J. (1627–1705)
Reade, S. (1814–1884)
Reid, T. (1710–1796)
Reid, Sir W. (1781–1858)
Reynolds, Sir J. (1723–1792)
Richardson, S. (1689–1761)
Ridley, N. (1500?–1555)
Ritson, J. (1752–1803)
Robertson, W. (1721–1793)
Robinson, H., Baron Rosmead (1824–1897)
Rodney, G., Baron (1719–1792)
Roe, Sir T. (1581?–1644)
Rogers, S. (1763–1855)
Romney, G. (1734–1802)
Roscoe, W. (1753–1831)
Rose, G. (1744–1818)
Ross, Sir H. D. (1779–1868)
Ross, R. (1766–1814)
Rossetti, C. (1830–1894)
Rossetti, D. G. (1828–1882)
Rowe, N. (1674–1718)
Rowlandson, T. (1756–1827)
Ruskin, J. (1819–1900)
Russell, C., Baron (1832–1900)

Sabine, Sir E. (1788–1883)
Sacheverell, W. (1638–1691)
Sadler, M. T. (1780–1835)
St. John, O. (1598?–1673)
St. Leger, Sir A. (1496?–1559)
Sale, Sir R. (1782–1845)
Salesbury, W. (1520?–1600?)
Sancroft, W. (1617–1693)
Sandby, P. (1725–1809)
Savage, R. (——1743)
Savile, Sir H. (1549–1622)
Scarlett, J., Baron Abinger (1769–1844)
Scott, D. (1806–1849)

Scott, Sir G. G. (1811–1878)
Scott, J., Earl of Eldon (1751–1838)
Scott, Sir W. (1771–1832)
Scott, W., Lord Stowell (1745–1836)]
Scotus Erigena (*fl.* 850)
Sedgwick, A. (1785–1873)
Seeley, Sir J. (1834–1895)
Selden, J. (1584–1654)
Shakespeare, W. (1564–1616)
Sharp, J. (1645–1714)
Sheil, R. L. (1791–1851)
Sheldon, G. (1598–1677)
Shelley, P. B. (1792–1822)
Sheridan, R. B. (1751–1816)
Shirley, J. (1596–1666)
Siddons, S. (1755–1831)
Sidgwick, H. (1838–1899)
Sidney, Sir P. (1554–1586)
Simpson, Sir J. Y. (1811–1870)
Sinclair, Sir J. (1754–1835)
Skelton, J. (146–?–1529)
Smart, C. (1722–1771)
Smith, A. (1753–1790)
Smith, Sir H. G. (1787–1860)
Smith, H. J. S. (1826–1883)
Smith, R. A. (1817–1884)
Smith, Sydney (1771–1845)
Smith, Sir T. (1513–1577)
Smith, W. (1769–1839)
Smith, W. R. (1846–1894)
Smith, Sir W. S. (1764–1840)
Smollett, T. (1721–1771)
Somers, J., Lord (1651–1716)
Somerville, M. (1780–1872)
South, R. (1634–1716)
Southey, R. (1774–1843)
Southwell, R. (1561?–1595)
Speke, J. (1827–1864)
Spelman, Sir H. (1564?–1641)
Spencer, E. (1552?–1599)
Sprat, T. (1635–1713)
Stanhope, W., Earl of Harrington (1690?–1756)
Stanley, A. P. (1815–1881)
Steele, Sir R. (1672–1729)
Steevens, G. (1736–1800)
Stephen, Sir J. F. (1829–1894)
Stephenson, G. (1781–1848)
Sterne, L. (1713–1768)
Stevens, A. (1818–1875)
Stevenson, R. L. (1850–1894)
Stewart, D. (1753–1828)
Stothard, T. (1755–1834)
Stow, J. (1525–1605)
Street, G. E. (1824–1881)
Stubbs, G. (1724–1806)
Sturgeon, W. (1783–1850)

Suckling, Sir J. (1609–1642)
Sullivan, Sir A. (1842–1900)
Swift, J. (1667–1745)
Sydenham, T. (1624–1689)
Symonds, J. A. (1840–1893)

Tait, A. C. (1811–1882)
Tallis, T. (1510?–1585)
Tarleton, Sir B. (1754–1833)
Taylor, Sir H. (1800–1886)
Taylor, J. (1613–1667)
Taylor, W. (1765–1836)
Telford, T. (1757–1834)
Temple, Sir W. (1628–1699)
Tennyson, A., Baron (1809–1892)
Thackeray, W. M. (1811–1863)
Thirlwall, C. (1797–1875)
Thomas, W. (——1554)
Thompson, W. (1785?–1833)
Thomson, J. (1700–1748)
Thurloe, J. (1616–1668)
Thurlow, E., Baron (1731–1806)
Tillotson, J. (1630–1694)
Toland, J. (1670–1722)
Tone, T. W. (1763–1798)
Tooke, J. H. (1736–1812)
Trelawney, E. J. (1792–1881)
Trevithick, R. (1771–1833)
Trollope, A. (1815–1882)
Trollope, Sir H. (1756–1839)
Tunstall, C. (1474–1559)
Turner, J. M. W. (1775–1851)
Tye, C. (1497?–1572)
Tyndale, W. (1490?–1536)
Tyndall, J. (1820–1893)

Udall, N. (1505–1556)
Urquhart, Sir T. (1611–1660)
Ussher, J. (1581–1656)

Vanbrugh, Sir J. (1663–1726)
Vane, Sir H., the younger (1613–1662)
Varley, J. (1778–1842)
Vaughan, H. (1622–1695)
Vere, Sir F. (1560–1609)
Vere, Sir H. (1565–1635)
Vernon, E. (1684–1757)

Wakley, T. (1795–1862)
Walker, F. (1840–1875)
Wallace, Sir W. (1272?–1305)
Waller, E. (1606–1687)
Waller, Sir W. (1597?–1668)
Wallis, J. (1616–1703)
Walpole, H., Earl of Orford (1717–1797)

Walpole, R., Earl of Orford (1676–1745)
Walsh, P. (1618?–1688)
Walsingham, Sir F. (1530?–1590)
Walter, J. (1739–1812)
Walton, I. (1593–1683)
Warburton, W. (1698–1779)
Ward, M. (1585–1645)
Ward, S. (1617–1689)
Ward, W. G. (1812–1882)
Warham, W. (1450?–1532)
Warton, T. (1728–1790)
Watson, R. (1737–1816)
Watson, T. (1557?–1592)
Watt, J. (1736–1819)
Waynflete, W. of (1395?–1486)
Webster, B. (1797–1882)
Wedgwood, J. (1730–1795)
Wentworth, W. C. (1793–1872)
Wesley, C. (1707–1788)
Wesley, J. (1703–1791)
Westmacott, Sir R. (1775–1856)
Whately, R. (1787–1863)
Wheatstone, Sir C. (1802–1875)
Whewell, W. (1794–1866)
Whiston, W. (1667–1752)
Whitbread, S. (1758–1815)
White, G. (1720–1793)
White, J. B. (1775–1841)
Whitefield, J. (1714–1770)
Whitehead, G. (1636?–1723)
Whitelocke, B. (1605–1675)
Whitgift, J. (1530?–1604)
Whittington, R. (——1423)
Whitworth, Sir J. (1803–1887)
Wilberforce, S. (1805–1873)
Wilberforce, W. (1759–1833)
Wilde, O. (1856–1900)
Wilfrid, St. (634–709)
Wilkes, J. (1727–1797)
Wilkie, Sir D. (1785–1841)
Wilkins, J. (1614–1672)
Wilks, R. (1665?–1732)
Willet, A. (1562–1621)
William of Malmesbury (——1143?)
William of Newburgh (1136–1198?)
Williams, Sir C. H. (1708–1759)

Williams, D. (1643?–1716)
Williams, Sir R. (1540?–1595)
Williams, R. (1604?–1683)
Williams, Sir W. (1634–1700)
Williamson, Sir J. (1633–1701)
Williamson, W. C. (1816–1895)
Willoughby, Sir N. J. (1777–1849)
Wilson, J. (1785–1854)
Wilson, R. (1714–1782)
Wilson, Sir R. (1777–1849)
Wilson, T. (1663–1755)
Windham, W. (1750–1810)
Winthrop, J. (1588–1649)
Winwood, Sir R. (1563?–1617)
Wiseman, N. (1802–1865)
Wishart, G. (1513?–1546)
Wither, G. (1588–1667)
Woffington, M. (1714?–1760)
Wolcot, J. (1738–1819)
Wolfe, J. (1727–1759)
Wollaston, W. H. (1766–1828)
Wolsey, T. (1471?–1530)
Woodward, H. (1714–1777)
Woolner, T. (1825–1892)
Wordsworth, Charles (1806–1892)
Wordsworth, Christopher (1807–1885)
Wordsworth, W. (1770–1850)
Wotton, Sir H. (1568–1639)
Wotton, N. (1497?–1567)
Wren, Sir C. (1632–1723)
Wright, J. (1734–1797)
Wright, T. (1810–1877)
Wulfstan, St. (1012?–1095)
Wyatt, Sir T. (1503?–1542)
Wycherley, W. (1640?–1716)
Wycliffe, J. (1324?–1384)
Wykeham, W. of (1324–1404)
Wyse, Sir T. (1791–1862)

Yates, M. A. (1728–1787)
Yorke, P., Earl of Hardwicke (1690–1764)
Young, A. (1741–1820)
Young, E. (1683–1765)
Young, T. (1773–1829)

At various points it has been necessary to classify our eminent persons into groups, according to the character of their intellectual activities. It may be convenient here to present these groupings. It should be noted that a few individuals (distinguished by an asterisk) appear in more than one list, and that some miscellaneous persons have been omitted altogether. In a large number of cases the question of classification is difficult and remains doubtful, although a considerable amount of care has been exercised in such cases. Difference of opinion must also necessarily exist on the question of duplication and the extent to which it should be carried. The eminent women have been grouped separately.

Actors. — Bannister, Betterton, Booth, Burbage, Cibber, Cooke, Elliston, Foote, Garrick, Kean, Kemble, King, Lewis, Liston, Macklin, Macready, C. Mathews, C. J. Mathews, Munden, Palmer, Parsons, Phelps, Quin, Webster, Wilks, Woodward.

Artists. — Adam, Banks, C. Barry, J. Barry, Beardsley, Bewick, Blake,* Bonington, Brown, Browne, Burne-Jones, Butterfield, Cattermole, Chantrey, Cockerell, Constable, Cooper, Copley, Cotman, Cox, Cozens, Crome, Cruikshank, Danby, Dawson, Dobson, Doyle, Du Maurier, Dyce, Eastlake, Etty, Flaxman, Gainsborough, Gibson, Gilbert, Gillray, Girtin, Haydon, Hogarth, Holl, Inigo Jones, Keene, Landseer, Lawrence, Leech, Leighton, Lewis, Linnell, Linton, Maclise, Millais, Morland, Morris,* Mulready, Nasmyth, Northcote, Opie, Palmer, Pearson, Phillip, Pugin, Raeburn, Reynolds, Romney, Rossetti,* Rowlandson, Sandby, D. Scott, G. Scott, Stevens, Stothard, Street, Stubbs, Turner, Vanbrugh,* Varley, Walker, Westmacott, Wilkie, Wilson, Woolner, Wren, Wright.

Divines. — Abbot, Adrian IV, Ainsworth, Alesius, Allen, Andrewes,* Atterbury, Bancroft, Barclay, Barrow,* Baxter, Bedell, Benson, St. Boniface, Bonner, Bradshaw, Browne, Burges, Burnet,* Butler,* Campion, Candlish, St. Thomas de Cantelupe, Carey, Cartwright, Challoner, Chalmers, Chichele, Chillingworth, Church, Clarke, Colenso, St. Columba, St. Columban, Cooke, Cosin, Coverdale, Cranmer, Cudworth, St. Cuthbert, Dolben, Doddridge, Donne,* Duff, St. Dunstan, St. Edmund, Emlyn, Erskine, Faber, Ferrar, Fox, Foxe,* Fuller, Garnett, Henderson,* Heylin, Hoadley, Hook, Hooker, Irving, Jewel, Jones, Juxon, Keble,* Ken, King, Knox,* Langton,* Lardner, Latimer, Laud, Law, Leighton, Leslie, Liddon, Lightfoot, Lloyd, Loftus, Manning, Marsh, Marshall, Martineau, Maurice, Melville, Middleton, Milner, Moffat, Montagu, Morley, Naylor, Neale, Newman, Nowell, Owen, Paley,* Parker, Parsons, St. Patrick, Payne, Pearson,* Pecock, Peirce, Penry, Perkins, Peters, Powell, Preston, Pusey, Ridley, Sancroft, Sharp, Sheldon, South, Stanley,* Tait, Taylor, Tillotson, Tyndale,* Walsh, Warham, C. Wesley, J. Wesley, Blanco White, Whitefield, Whitehead, Whitgift, Wilberforce, St. Wilfrid, Willett, D. Williams, R. Williams, Wilson, Wiseman, Wishart, Wordsworth, St. Wulfstan, Wycliffe.*

Doctors. — Caius,* Cheselden, Cooper, Cullen, Linacre,* Mead, Paget, Pott, Simpson, Sydenham. (Others are included among *Men of Science.*)

Lawyers. — Abinger, Ashburton, Austin, Blackstone, Bowen, Cairns, Camden, Campbell, Clare, Cockburn, Coke, Curran, Denman, Eldon, Ellenborough, Fortescue, Haddington, Hale, Hardwicke, Kenyon, Littleton, Lyndhurst, Macclesfield, Maine, More,* J. Napier, Noye, Russell, St. John, Selbourne, Selden, Somers, Stair, Stephen, Stowell, Thurlow, Westbury, Williams.

Men of Letters. — Addison, Alcuin, Ascham, Bagehot, Banim, Barclay, Beckford, Bede, Blackmore, Borrow, Boswell, Browne, Buchanan,* Buckle, Bunyan, Burton, Calamy, Camden, Carleton, Carlile, Carlyle, Cibber,* Cobbett,* Collier, Wilkie Collins, Colman, Congreve, Cotton, Cowley, Crocker, D'Avenant, Day, Defoe, Dekker, Dempster, De Quincey, D'Ewes, Dickens, Digby, Dodgson,* Dugdale, Elyot, Etherege, Fanshawe, Farquhar, Fielding, Foxe, Francis, Freeman, Froude, Galt, Geoffrey of Monmouth, Gibbon, Gifford, Giraldus, Goldsmith, Green, Grote, Hall, Hallam, Halliwell-Phillips, Hamilton, Harrington, Hazlitt, Herbert, Holcroft, Hood, Hook, Howell, Hughes, Hume,* Hunt, Hunter, Hutton, Jeffrey, Jerrold, Johnson, Jonson, Kemble, Kennett, Killigrew, Kingsley, Knowles, Lamb, Landor, Lee, Leland, L'Estrange, Lever, Lewes, Lillo, Lingard, Lockhart, Lodge, Lover, Lyly, Lytton, Macaulay, Mackenzie, Maginn, Malone, Map, Marryat, Marston, Miller,* Merivale, Milman, More,* Myers, W. J. P. Napier, Nash, Needham, Newman, Oliphant, Oldys, Ordericus Vitalis, Paine, Paris, Pater, Pepys, Perry, Prynne, Raleigh,* Reade, Richardson, Ritson, Robertson, Roscoe, Ruskin, Scott, Seeley, Sheil, Sheridan,* Smollett, Southey, Sprat, Sidney Smith, Stanley,* Steele, Sterne, Steevens, Stevenson, Stow, Swift, Symonds, H. Taylor, W. Taylor, Temple,* Thackeray, Thirlwall, Trelawney, Trollope, Tyndale, Udall, Urquhart, Vanbrugh,* Wakley,* H. Walpole, Walton, Warburton, Warton, Whately, Wilde, William of Malmesbury, William of Newburgh, Williams, Wilson, Wolcot, Wright, Wycherley.

Men of Science. — Adams, Airy, Arkwright, Armstrong, Babbage, R. Bacon,* Baily, Balfour, Banks, Barrow,* Baskerville, Bates, Bell, Bentham, Bessemer, Birch, Black, Boyle, Bradley, Brewster, Canton, Carpenter, Carrington, Cavendish, Cayley, Caxton, Clifford, Colby, Cotes, Cotton, Dalton, C. Darwin, E. Darwin, Davy, Dee, De Morgan, Dodgson,* Drummond, Falconer, Faraday, Ferguson, Flamsteed, Flinders,* Flower, E. Forbes, J. D. Forbes, Frankland, Franks, Gilbert, Glisson, Grew, Hales, Halley, Hamilton, Harvey, Herschel, Hodgson, Hooke, Horrocks, Hunter, Hutton, Huxley, Jenner, Jevons, Joule, Knight, Lawes, Lefroy, Lister, Lyell, Maclaurin, Malthus, Mayow, Maxwell, Miller,* Milner, Morland, Mun, Murchison, Murdoch, Napier, Nasmyth, Neilson, Newcomen, Newton, Oughtred, Owen, Parkes, Petty, Priestley, Ray, Sabine,* Sadler, Sedgwick, Sidgwick, Sinclair, A. Smith, H. J. Smith, R. A. Smith, W. Smith, Stephenson, Sturgeon, Telford, Thompson, Trevithick, Tyndall, Wallis, Ward, Watson, Watt, Wedgwood, Wheatstone, Whewell, White, Whitworth, Wilkins, Williamson, Wollaston, A. Young, T. Young.

Musical Composers. — Arne, Balfe, Bennett, Blow, Boyce, Byrd, Dowland, Gauntlett, Gibbons, Lawes, Macfarren, Purcell, Sullivan, Tallis, Tye.

Philosophers. — Alexander of Hales, F. Bacon, Roger Bacon,* Bentham, Berkeley, Bradwardine, Butler,* Duns, Erigena, Godwin, Hamilton, Hartley, Hinton, Hobbes, Hume,* Hutcheson, Locke, Mackintosh, J. Mill, J. S. Mill, Ockham, Paley,* Price, Reid, Shaftesbury, Stewart, Toland, Ward, Wycliffe.*

Poets. — Arnold, Barbour, Barclay, Barham, Barnes, Barnfield, Beaumont, Beddoes, Blake,* Breton, Browne, Browning, Bruce, Burns, Butler, Byron, Cædmon, Campbell, Campion, Chapman, Chatterton, Chaucer, Churchill, Clare, Clough, H. Coleridge, S. T. Coleridge, Collins, Cotton, Cowper, Crabbe, Crashaw, Daniel, Davies, Denham, Dibdin, Dobell, Donne,* Douglas, Drayton, Drummond, Dryden, Dunbar, D'Urfey, Fletcher, Ford, Fergusson, Fitzgerald, Gascoigne, Gay, Gower, Gray, Greene, Herbert, Herrick, J. Heywood, T. Heywood, Hogg, Hood, Keats, Keble,* Langland, Lindsay, Lovelace, Lydgate, Marlowe, Marvell, Massinger, Middleton, Milton, Moore, Morris,* Munday, Norton, Otway, Patmore, Peele, Pope, Prior, Quarles, Randolph, Rogers, Rossetti,* Rowe, Savage, Shakespeare, Shelley, Shirley, Sidney,* Skelton, Smart, Southwell, Spenser, Suckling, Tennyson, Thomson, Vaughan, Waller, Watson, Wither, Wordsworth, Wotton, Wyatt, Young.

Politicians, etc. — Arthur, A. Bacon, N. Bacon, Bateman, Beaton, Bradford, Bradlaugh, Bright, Brooke, Brougham, Bruce, Burke, Burghley, Burnet,* Cade, Campbell, Canning, Earl Canning, Carstares, Chatham, Chichester, Childers, Clarendon, Clive, Cobbett,* Cobden, Cork, Coutances, O. Cromwell, T. Cromwell, Eliot, Ellenborough, Fawcett, Fletcher, Forster, Fox, Foxe,* Frere, Gardiner, Gladstone, Grattan, G. Grenville, W. Grenville, Grey,* Hampden, Harrington, Hastings, Henderson,* Horner, Hubert Walter, Huskisson, Ireton, Kemp, Kirkcaldy, Knox,* S. Langton, W. Langton, Law, Lawrence, Leslie, Lewis, Lilburne, Lucas, Ludlow, Lytton, Macdonald, Macnaghten, Malcolm, Marten, Melville, C. Montagu, Morgan, Mundella, Northumberland, O'Connell, Oldcastle, O'Leary, O'Neill, Paget, Sir Harry Parkes, Sir Henry Parkes, Parnell, Peel, Penn, Pitt, Pownall, Pulteney, Pym, Raffles, Reid,* Robinson, Roe, Rose, Sacheverell, St. Leger, Shaftesbury, Sherbrooke, Sheil,* Sheridan,* T. Smith,* Stratford de Redcliffe, Stirling, Temple,* Thurloe, Tone, Tooke, Tunstall, Vane, Wallace,* Walpole, Walsingham, Warriston, Waynflete, Wentworth, Whitbread, Whitelocke, Wilberforce, Wilkes, Williamson, Windham, Winthrop, Winwood, Wolsey, Wotton, Wykeham, Wyse.

Sailors. — Anson, Blake, Boscawen, Broke, Byng, Cavendish, Cook, Dampier, Deane, Drake, Duncan, Exmouth, Flinders,* Franklin, Frobisher, Gilbert, Hawke, Hawkins, Hood, Leake, Monson, C. Napier, Nelson, Penn, Popham, Raleigh,* Rodney, Smith, St. Vincent, Trollope, Vernon, Willoughby.

Scholars. — Andrewes,* Adamson, Barrow,* Bentley, Bingham, Boece, Bradshaw, Buchanan,* Caius,* Cheke, Colebrooke, Colet, Conington, Creighton, Crichton, Dodwell, Grocyn, Grosseteste, Hales, Hickes, Hort, John of Salisbury, Jones, Jowett, Lane, Lightfoot, Linacre,* Lowth, Montagu, Morton, Ockley, Palmer, Pattison, Pearson,* Pococke, Porson, Salesbury, Savile, T. Smith, W. R. Smith, Spelman, Thomas, Ussher, Whiston, Wordsworth.

Soldiers. — Abercromby, Amherst, Cadogan, Campbell, Dundee, Edwards, Gordon, Graham, Hamley, Hardinge, Havelock, Hawkwood, Jones, Knollys, Lake, Lambert, H. Lawrence, S. Lawrence, Leven, Mackay, Marlborough, Monck, Moore, Morgan, Munro, Napier of Magdala, C. J. Napier, Neill, Nicholson, Nott, Ochterlony, Oglethorpe, Outram, Picton, Pollock, Raleigh,* Reid, H. D. Ross, R. Ross, Sabine,* Sale, Sidney,* Smith, Tarleton, F. Vere, H. Vere, Wallace,* Waller, Williams, Wilson, Wolfe.

Travellers. — Baker, Barrow, Bowring, Bruce, Burton, Chesney, Clapperton, Grey,* Lander, Livingstone, Mitchell, Park, Speke.

The women fall into the following groups:

Actresses. — Abington, Anne Barry, Elizabeth Barry, Becher, Bracegirdle, Cibber, Clive, Faucit, Jordan, Keeley, Kelly, Kemble, Neilson, Oldfield, Siddons, Woffington, Yates.

Philanthropists. — Carpenter, Fry.

Poets. — Baillie, Browning, Hemans, Landon, Nairne, Rossetti.

Religious. — Ward.

Traveller. — Kingsley.

Women of Letters. — D'Arblay, Austen, Barbauld, Behn, C. Brontë, E. Brontë, Cavendish, Centlivre, Cowley, Cross, Eastlake, Edgeworth, Edwards, Ferrier, Gaskell, Godwin, Inchbald, Jameson, Linton, Martineau, Mitford, Montagu, More, Morgan, Oliphant, Opie, Radcliffe.

Woman of Science. — Somerville.

APPENDIX B

ORIGINS OF BRITISH PERSONS OF ABILITY

THE significance of the place-names in the following list varies with their position. When the place-name occurs between that of the grandfather and grandmother it refers to the father (or the mother), our knowledge not going back so far as the grandparents. When the place-name comes in the centre of the page our knowledge is still more imperfect, only comprehending the fact that the eminent person's family belonged to the district in question. A query mark (?) means that the statement is fairly probable, and has been accepted in the body of the book, but is not absolutely certain. The place-names in square brackets indicate origins that are either doubtful or further back than the grandparents; no account of such origins has been taken in the summaries given in the body of the book.

	Paternal grandfather.	Paternal grandmother.	Maternal grandfather.	Maternal grandmother.
Abbot				
Abercromby	Clackmannan			
Abington		Surrey		
Adam		England		
Adams		Scotland		
Adamson	Cornwall	Perth		Cornwall
Addison		England [? Herts]		
Adrian IV	Westmoreland			
Ainsworth	Lancashire			Yorks
Airy	Lincs [Westmoreland and Yorks]	Yorks		Suffolk
Alcuin		Midlothian		
Alesius		Gloucester		
Alexander				
Alexander of Hales				
Alexander (W.)	Clackmannan			
Allen	Lancashire			
Amherst	Kent			Yorkshire
Andrewes	Suffolk [Essex]			
Anson	Staffs			
Arblay, D'	Shropshire		France	Derbyshire
Arkwright	Cumberland	Lancashire		
Armstrong				Northumberland (?)
Arne		England		

	Paternal grand-father.	Paternal grand-mother.	Maternal grand-father.	Maternal grand-mother.
Arnold (M.)	Hants and Suffolk [Ireland]			Cornwall
Arnold (T.)	Suffolk and Hants			Ireland [Huguenot]
Arthur			Devon [? Cornwall]	
Ascham	Yorks		England	Yorks
Atterbury	Kent			Warwick
Austen	Suffolk		Devon	
Austin				
Babbage			Somerset	
Bacon (A.)	Suffolk	Suffolk		Essex
Bacon (F.)	Suffolk	Suffolk		Essex
Bacon (N.)				Suffolk
Bacon (R.)				
Bagehot	Somerset			Somerset
Baillie				Ayr and Lanark
Baily			England	Middlesex
Baker	Gloucester			England
Balfe			Ireland	
Balfour	Haddington			
Bancroft	Lancashire			
Banim	Kilkenny		England	
Banks (J.)	Lincs			
Banks (T.)				

	Paternal grandfather.	Paternal grandmother.	Maternal grandfather.	Maternal grandmother.
Bannister	Yorks	Gloucester (?)		
Barbauld				
Barbour				
Barclay (A.)		Scotland	Aberdeen	
Barclay (J.)		Elgin	Scotland	
Barclay (R.)		Kent		
Barham		Dorset		France
Barnes		Shropshire		
Barnfield		Suffolk		
Barrow (I.)		Lancashire		Dorset
Barrow (J.)				Kent
Barry (A.)			Somerset	Lancashire
Barry (C.)			England	
Barry (E.)			England (?)	
Barry (J.)			Cork	
Baskerville			Worcester	
Bateman			Norfolk	
Bates		Leicester		
Baxter		Shropshire		Shropshire
Beardsley		Scotland		England
Beaton		Fife		
Beaumont		Leicester		
Becher		Ireland		
Beckford	Glo'ster			
Beddoes		Shropshire		England and Ireland
Bede			Durham	

	Paternal grandfather.	Paternal grandmother.	Maternal grandfather.	Maternal grandmother.
Bedell				
Behn	Essex			Essex
Bell (A.)	Fife			Holland
Bell (C.)	Lanark			
Bennett	Kent			
Benson			Kent	Cambs
Bentham (G.)	Hants			Hants
Bentham (J.)				
Bentley	Yorks			
Berkeley	England			Ireland (?)
Bessemer			England [Huguenot]	
Bethell	Wilts		England	
Betterton	Northumberland			Cumberland
Bewick			Yorks	
Bingham			England	
Birch	Shropshire			
Bishop	Antrim [Scotland]			Aberdeen
Black	Devon			
Blackmore				Glamorgan [and Devon & Glo'ster]
Blackstone	Wilts			Wilts
Blake (R.)	Somerset			
Blake (W.)	Somerset (?)			

	Paternal grand-father.	Paternal grand-mother.	Maternal grand-father.	Maternal grand-mother.
Blow				
Boece				
Boniface				
Bonington				
Bonner	Notts		Notts (?)	Notts
Booth	Lancashire		Forfar	
Borrow	Cornwall		Devon	
Boscawen	Cornwall		England	
Boswell	Ayr			Norfolk [Huguenot]
Bowen	Mayo			
Boyle (A. Earl of Cork)	Hereford	Kent		Ireland and Austria
Boyle (Robert)	Hereford	Hereford		Kent
Bracegirdle	Northants			
Bradford	Yorks			
Bradlaugh	Suffolk			Wilts
Bradley	Durham			Antrim
Bradshaw (H.)	Ireland [Cheshire and Derby]			
Bradshaw (W.)	Lancashire			
Bradwardine	Hereford (?)			
Broke	Suffolk			

	Paternal grandfather.	Paternal grandmother.	Maternal grandfather.	Maternal grandmother.
Brooke				
Breton	Essex	England [? Norfolk]		
Brewster	Warwick [Wilts]	Scotland		
Bright				
Brontë (C.)	Down			Cornwall
Brontë (E.)	Down			Cornwall
Brougham	Cumberland			
Brown	Berwick	Midlothian	Fife	Ayr
Browne (H.)	Norfolk			Kent
Browne (R.)	Lincs			Herts
Browne (T.)	Cheshire			Sussex
Browne (W.)	Devon			
Browning (E.)		Northumberland		
Browning (R.)	Dorset		Germany	Scotland
Bruce (H.)	Glamorgan [and Scotland] Stirling			
Bruce (J.)	Stirling	Kinross		Stirling
Bruce (M.)				Haddington
Buchanan		Somerset		Yorks
Buckle				
Bull				

	Paternal grand-father.	Paternal grand-mother.	Maternal grand-father.	Maternal grand-mother.
Bunyan				Bedford
Burbage	Bedford			Bedford
Burges	Herts			
Burke	Dublin	Somerset		Ireland / England
Burne-Jones	Wales			
Burnet	Aberdeen		Dumfries	Ayr
Burns	Kincardine		Herts	Ayr
Burton (Richard)	Westmoreland	Ireland [and Fr. Huguenot]		Scotland
Burton (Robert)	Leicester			
Butler (J.)		Berks		
Butler (S.)		Worcester England		
Butterfield				
Byng	Kent	Lincoln (?)		
Byrd		Cornwall		
Byron		Ireland (?)		Aberdeen
Cade		Yorks		
Cadogan	Ireland [Somerset]	Norfolk		
Caedmon				
Cairns	Down [Scotland]			
Caius	France			
Calamy		Suffolk		
Camden	Staffs		Lancs	Cumberland

	Paternal grandfather.	Paternal grandmother.	Maternal grandfather.	Maternal grandmother.
Campbell (C.)	Lanark			Argyle
Campbell (G.)	Fife			Fife
Campbell (J.)		Scotland		
Campbell (T.)	Argyle			Argyle
Campion (E.)	Essex	Essex		Essex
Campion (T.)	Ayr			Ayr
Candlish	Londonderry [Wilts]			
Canning (C.)	Wilts and Londonderry			
Canning (G.)	Wilts and Londonderry			
Canning (S.)	Bucks			
Cantelupe		Gloucester		
Canton		Northants		France
Carey				
Carleton	Tyrone [Londonderry]			Tyrone
Carlile	Devon			
Carlyle	Dumfries			
Carpenter (M.)	Worcester			Worcester
Carpenter (W.)	Worcester			Worcester
Carrington	Middlesex			
Carstares	Lanark			Ayr
Cartwright		Herts		
Case	Kent	Norfolk		
Cattermole				

	Paternal grand-father.	Paternal grand-mother.	Maternal grand-father.	Maternal grand-mother.
Cavendish (H.)				
Cavendish (M.)				
Cavendish (T.)	Essex		England	
Caxton	Yorks [Norfolk]			
Cayley			Suffolk	
Cecil		Northants	Kent	Lincoln
Centlivre		Lincoln		Norfolk
Challoner			Sussex	
Chalmers		Fife		
Chantrey			Yorks	
Chapman			Herts	
Chatterton		Gloucester		Gloucester
Chaucer	Suffolk [? Essex]			
Cheke	Hants			
Cheselden				Cambs
Chesney			Rutland	
Chichele	Antrim [Scotland]			
Chichester	Northants (?)			Devon
Childers	Devon		England [partly Jewish both sides]	
Chillingworth	Oxford			
Church	England			England
Churchill (C.)		Yorks	Germany	Scotland (?)

	Paternal grandfather.	Paternal grandmother.	Maternal grandfather.	Maternal grandmother.
Churchill (J.)				
Cibber (C.)	Dorset			
Cibber (S.)	Denmark			
Clapperton	Dumfries			
Clare	Northants		England	Devon
Clarke	Norfolk			Rutland
Clifford				
Clive (K.)	Kilkenny		Devon	England
Clive (R.)	Shropshire			Lancs
Clough	Denbigh			Yorks
Cobbett			Suffolk (?)	
Cobden			Sussex	France
Cockburn	Berwick			
Cockerell	Somerset			
Coke	Norfolk			
Colby	Wales			
Colebrooke	England			Gloucester
Colenso	Cornwall			
Coleridge (H.)	Devon			Norfolk
Coleridge (S.)	Devon			Cambs
Colet	Bucks			
Collier			Sussex	
Collins (W.)				Scotland
Collins (W. Wicklow W.)			England	
Colman	Ireland (Connaught)			
Columba				Ireland (Leinster)

	Paternal grandfather.	Paternal grandmother.	Maternal grandfather.	Maternal grandmother.
Columban		Ireland (Leinster)		
Congreve	Staffs			
Conington	Lincs			
Constable	Suffolk			Suffolk
Cook	[Yorks] Northumberland (?)			
Cooke (G.)	England (?)	England		Scotland (?) [Scotland]
Cooke (H.)	Down [England]			Dorset
Cooper (First Lord Shaftesbury)	Hants	England		
Cooper (Third Lord)				
Cooper (Astley)	Norfolk			
Cooper (S.)				
Copley (J. S.)	Yorks and Limerick	Clare		Lancs and Clare
Copley (Lord Lyndhurst)	Limerick			England (?)
Cosin	Norfolk		Norfolk	Norfolk
Cotes				Leicester
Cotman				
Cotton (A.)	Cheshire			Essex

	Paternal grand-father.	Paternal grand-mother.	Maternal grand-father.	Maternal grand-mother.
Cotton (C.)	Staffs [Cheshire]			
Cotton (R.)				
Coutances				
Coverdale				
Cowley (A.)				
Cowley (H.)	Devon	Cornwall		
Cowper	Herts	Yorks		Derby
Cox	Warwick	England		Leicester
Cozens	Russia	Kent		Norfolk
Crabbe	Suffolk			Warwick
Cranmer	Lincs and Notts			Suffolk
Crashaw	Yorks			Lincs
Creighton	Cumberland			Cumberland
Crichton	Dumfries			Fife
Croker	Devon			Galway
Crome		Norfolk		
Cromwell (O.)	Glamorgan and Hunts			Cambs (?)
Cromwell (T.)	Notts			
Cross	Flint	England		
Cruikshank	Midlothian			
Cudworth	Lanark			Derby (?)
Cullen	Cumberland and Cork			
Curran				

	Paternal grand-father.	Paternal grand-mother.	Maternal grand-father.	Maternal grand-mother.
Cuthbert				
Dalrymple		Ayr	Scotland (? Lothians)	
Dalton		Cumberland		Cumberland
Dampier				
Danby		Wexford	Somerset [? Huguenot]	
Daniel			Somerset	
Darwin (C.)	Lincoln	Lincoln [Norfolk and Notts]	Staffs	Cheshire
Darwin (E.)				
D'Avenant			Oxford	
Davies	Cornwall [Norfolk]	Wilts		Wilts
Davy				
Dawson		Notts		
Day				
Deane		Gloucester	England	Bucks (?)
Dee		Radnor		England (?)
Defoe		Flanders (?) and Northants		
Dekker		Aberdeen		
De Morgan		England	England	
Dempster			England	Scotland
Denham	Notts		England	Ireland
Denman				Scotland
Dunbar				

	Paternal grandfather.	Paternal grandmother.	Maternal grandfather.	Maternal grandmother.
Etty				
Faber	Yorks			Yorks
Falconer	[Huguenot]			Yorks
Fanshawe	Elgin		[?Ireland]	Kent
Faraday	Derby	Yorks		
Farquhar	England			
Faucit	Westmoreland	Ireland	France	Wilts (?)
Fawcett				
Ferguson	Aberdeen	Banff		Aberdeen
Fergusson				Cheshire
Ferrar	Renfrew			Forfar
Ferrier	Warwick			Somerset
Fielding		Somerset		Ireland
Fitzgerald	Ireland (?)	Derby		
Fitzgibbon	Limerick			
Flamstead				
Flaxman	Norfolk			
Fletcher (A.)	Haddington			
Fletcher (J.)	Norfolk			
Flinders	Lincoln	Ireland		
Flood				
Flower	Herts			
Foote	Cornwall			Warwick
Forbes (C.)	Isle of Man			Isle of Man
Forbes (J.)	Aberdeen			Perth

Name	Paternal grandfather.	Paternal grandmother.	Maternal grandfather.	Maternal grandmother.
Ford				
Forster				
Fortescue	Devon			Devon
Fox (C. J.)	Devon (?)			Norfolk
Fox (G.)	Wilts			
Foxe (J.)	Leicester	Lincoln		
Foxe (R.)			Lincoln	
Francis	Ireland			
Frankland	Lincoln [Norfolk]		Lincoln	
Franklin			Lancashire	
Franks	Warwick			Norfolk
Freeman	Norfolk [Suffolk]		Worcester	Warwick
Frere		Surrey		
Frobisher	Yorks [Wales]			
Froude	Devon			Cumberland
Fry	Norfolk		Essex [and Suffolk]	Surrey
Fuller	[? Berks]			Suffolk
Gainsboro'	Suffolk			
Galt			Ayr	
Gardiner			Suffolk	
Garnett			Derby	

	Paternal grandfather.	Paternal grandmother.	Maternal grandfather.	Maternal grandmother.
Hamilton (W.)	Ireland	Wigton		Lanark
Hamilton (W. R.)	[Scotland]			Ireland (?)
Hamilton (T.)	Lanark			
Hamley				
Hampden	Cornwall			Berwick
Hardinge	Bucks			Shetland
Harrington				Hunts
Hartley	Lines			Kent
Harvey	Kent			Northants
Hastings	Worcester			Yorks (?)
Havelock	Durham [Lincoln]			Kent
Hawke	Cornwall	Devon	Yorks	Durham
Hawkins	Essex			Yorks
Hawkwood	Devon			Cornwall
Haydon	Antrim		Italy	Cambs
Hazlitt	Sligo			Lancashire
Hemans		Fife		
Henderson	Montgomery			
Herbert (A.)	Montgomery [Monmouth]			England (?)
Herbert (E.)	Montgomery [Monmouth]			Shropshire
Herbert (G.)	Montgomery [Monmouth]			Shropshire
Herrick	Leicester			
Herschel	Germany			England

	Paternal grandfather.	Paternal grandmother.	Maternal grandfather.	Maternal grandmother.
Heylin				
Heywood (J.)				
Heywood (T.)	Montgomery			
Hickes	Yorks		England	Kent
Hill	Worcester		Lincoln	
Hinton	Oxford and Bucks [and Essex]			Yorks
Hoadley				
Hobbes	Wilts (?)		England	
Hodgson	Cheshire			Wilts
Hogarth	Westmoreland			Lancashire
Hogg				
Holcroft			Selkirk	
Holl	Germany		England	England
Hood (S.)	Somerset			Dorset
Hood (T.)	Scotland			
Hook (T.)	Norfolk			
Hook (W.)	Norfolk			Aberdeen
Hooke	Devon		England	
Hooker	Midlothian			
Horner	Lancashire			
Horrocks	Ireland [and Somerset and Hants]			
Hort				England [? Suffolk]

Name	Paternal grandfather.	Paternal grandmother.	Maternal grandfather.	Maternal grandmother.
Kemble (J.)	Hereford			
Kemble (J. P.)	Hereford	Ireland	France	Switzerland
Kemp	Hereford [? Wilts]			
Ken	Kent [Somerset ?]			Ireland
Kennett	Kent			Middlesex
Kenyon	Flint			Kent
Killigrew	Cornwall			Cheshire
King (T.)			England	Norfolk
King (W.)	Aberdeen			
Kingsley (C.)	Devon			
Kingsley (M.)	Devon			
Kirkcaldy	Fife		England	Fife
Knight			Cheshire	
Knollys				Cork
Knowles	Dublin			
Knox			Haddington	Middlesex
Lake				Herts
Lamb				
Lambert	Lincoln			
Lancaster	Yorks		England	
Lander			Cornwall	
Landon	Hereford			Wales
Landor	Staffs			Warwick
Landseer	Lincoln			
Lane	Hereford			Suffolk (?)

Name	Paternal grandfather.	Paternal grandmother.	Maternal grandfather.	Maternal grandmother.
Langland				
Langton (S.)				
Langton (W.)				
Lardner				
Latimer	Hants		Shropshire (?)	Cumberland
Law (E., Baron Ellenboro')	Leicester	Westmoreland	England	
Law (E., Earl of Ellenboro')	Westmoreland	Cumberland	Leicester	
Law (J.)	Edinburgh			
Law (W.)	Northampton			
Lawes (H.)	Wilts (?)			
Lawes (J. B.)	Herts			
Lawrence (H.)	Londonderry			
Lawrence (J.)	Londonderry			
Lawrence (S.)	Hereford			Oxford
Lawrence (T.)				Donegal [Scotland]
Layard	[Huguenot]			Donegal [Scotland]
Leake	Suffolk			Worcester
Lee			England [Herts or Leicester?]	Kent
Leech	Ireland			

	Paternal grand-father.	Paternal grand-mother.	Maternal grand-father.	Maternal grand-mother.
Mackintosh	Inverness			Nairn
Mackenzie	Midlothian			Westmeath (?)
Macklin	Down (?)			
Maclaurin	Argyll			
Maclise	Elgin			Cork [Scotland]
Macnaghten	Antrim			Tyrone
Macready	Dublin			Lincoln and Derby
Maginn	Cork			
Maine	Roxburgh			Berks
Malcolm	Fife and Dumfries			Dumfries
Malone	Westmeath			
Malthus	Surrey			Essex
Manning				
Map	Herts		Hereford and Wales	
Marlowe	Kent			Kent (?)
Marryat	England [Huguenot]		England	Germany
Marsh	Hunts			
Marshall	Shropshire			Italy
Marston	Berks			
Marten	Norfolk [Huguenot]			Northumberland
Martineau (H.)				

	Paternal grand-father.	Paternal grand-mother.	Maternal grand-father.	Maternal grand-mother.
Martineau (J.)	Norfolk [Huguenot]			
Marvell				Northumberland
Massinger	Wilts			Yorks
Mathews (C.)	Glamorgan	England		England (?)
Mathews (C. J.)	[Glamorgan]			
Maurice	Wales			Norfolk
Maxwell	Midlothian	Cornwall		Northumberland
Mayow				
Mead	Bucks			
Melville	Forfar		Norfolk	Forfar
Merivale	Devon [North-ants, Notts & France]	Germany		Devon
Middleton (C.)		Yorks (?)		
Middleton (T.)	Forfar	England		Forfar
Mill (J.)	Forfar	Jersey [France]		England
Mill (J. S.)		Cromarty (?)		England
Millais		Forfar		
Miller	Devon			
Milman	Lancashire	Devon		
Milner (I.)	Yorks			
Milner (J.)	Yorks			Ross
Milton	Oxford			Gloucester

	Paternal grandfather.	Paternal grandmother.	Maternal grandfather.	Maternal grandmother.
Mitchell				
Mitford	Stirling Northumberland			Hants
Moffat	Devon			
Monck	Lincs			
Monson	Northants			
Montagu (C.)	Yorks			Haddington
Montagu (E.)				Devon
Montagu (R.)	Stirling	England		Lincs
Moore (J.)	Kerry			Lincs
Moore (T.)	Norfolk and Suffolk			Cambs and Kent
Moore (H.)	Herts (?)			Lanark
More (T.)	Wales			Wexford
Morgan (G. O.)				Gloucester
Morgan (H.)	Glamorgan	England		[Beds ?]
Morgan (S.)	Mayo			Sweden (?)
Morland (G.)	Berks (?)			[Huguenot & England]
Morland (S.)				Shropshire
Morley				Worcester
Morris	Worcester [from Welsh Border]	Notts	England	Ireland

	Paternal grand-father.	Paternal grand-mother.	Maternal grand-father.	Maternal grand-mother.
Morton				
Mulready	Yorks			
Mun	Clare			
Munday			England	
Mundella	Italy		Staffs (?)	
Munden				Wales
Munro	Lanark		England	
Murchison	Ross			Ross
Murdock	Ayr			
Murray	[Edinburgh]			
Myers	[Perth]			Cumberland
Nairne	Yorks			Perth
Napier (C.)	Perth	Scotland		Lanark (?)
Napier (C. J.)	Stirling	Dublin		[France]
Napier (J.)	Midlothian			
Napier (Sir J.)	Antrim			Antrim
Napier (R. C.)	Scotland (?)	Scotland		
Napier (W. J. P.)				[France]
Nash	Hereford	Dublin		
Nasmyth (J.)	Midlothian			[? Suffolk]
Nasmyth (P.)	Midlothian			Midlothian
Naylor			Yorks	Midlothian

	Paternal grandfather.	Paternal grandmother.	Maternal grandfather	Maternal grandmother.
Neale (E. V.)	Berks			
Neale (J. M.)				
Needham	Staffs			Warwick
Neill	Derby			Essex
Neilson (J.)	Ayr			Oxford
Neilson (L. A.)	Lanark			England
Nelson	Spain (?)	Norfolk		Suffolk and Norfolk
Newcomen	Devon	[Lincs]		
Newman (F.)	Cambs	[Holland]		[Huguenot]
Newman (J.)	Cambs	[Holland]		[Huguenot]
Newton	Lincoln	[English family in Haddington]		Rutland
Nicholson	Down			Antrim
Northcote	Devon			Bucks
Norton	Hereford			Norfolk
Nott	Lancashire			Lancashire
Nowell	Lancashire			
Noye	Cornwall			
Ochterlony	Forfar			
Ockham			Surrey (?)	

	Paternal grandfather.	Paternal grandmother.	Maternal grandfather.	Maternal grandmother.
Ockley				
O'Connell	Norfolk			
Oglethorpe	Kerry			Cork
Oldcastle	Yorks			Tipperary
Oldfield	Hereford [and Wales]	England		
Oldys	Dorset and Gloucester			
O'Leary		Cork		
Oliphant (L.)	Perth			[Highlands]
Oliphant (M.)	Midlothian			Fife
O'Neill	Tyrone			
Opie (A.)	Suffolk			Norfolk
Opie (J.)	Cornwall			Cornwall
Orderious	France			England
Otway	[Yorks ?]			
Oughtred	Northumberland	England		
Outram	Derby			Aberdeen
Owen (J.)	Wales			Lancashire
Owen (Sir R.)	Bucks			[Huguenot]
Owen (R.)	Montgomery			Montgomery
Paget (J.)	Norfolk		Cheshire	
Paget (W.)	Staffs			

	Paternal grandfather.	Paternal grandmother.	Maternal grandfather.	Maternal grandmother.
Pitman				
Pitt (Earl of Chatham)	Dorset	Elgin		
Pitt (W.)	Dorset	Waterford		Waterford
Pococke		Wilts		Bucks
Pollock				
Pope		Hants		England
Popham		Berwick		Yorks
Porson		Hants (?)	England	Norfolk
Pott		[Devon ?]	England	
Powell		Norfolk	Cheshire [& Lincoln]	Montgomery
Pownall		Radnor		
Pratt		Oxford [Devon]		Carnarvon
Preston		Shropshire [Lancs. & Ireland]	Northants	
Prestwich		Glamorgan		Shropshire
Price		Yorks		Yorks
Priestley		Dorset		Somerset
Prior				
Prynne	Glo'ster and Somerset [Shropshire?]			

Name	Paternal grandfather	Paternal grandmother	Maternal grandfather	Maternal grandmother
Pugin	France			
Pulteney	Leicester			England
Purcell	Shropshire (?)			
Pusey	Norfolk [Walloon Huguenot]			
Pym	Somerset			Kent
Quarles	Essex			
Quin	Dublin			
Radcliffe	Rutland [Holland]			Nottingham [or Essex]
Raeburn	Yorks			Dumfries
Raffles	Devon [and Cornwall]			Devon
Raleigh	Sussex			
Randolph	Essex			Northants
Ray	Oxford			
Reade	Aberdeen			
Reid (T.)	Aberdeen			Banff
Reid (W.)	Devon [and Holland]			Devon
Reynolds	Surrey			
Richardson	Northumberland			
Ridley	Westmoreland			
Ritson				

	Paternal grandfather.	Paternal grandmother.	Maternal grandfather.	Maternal grandmother.
Sidney				Sussex [Huguenot]
Simpson	Linlithgow			
Sinclair	Caithness		Norfolk (?)	
Skelton				
Smart				
Smith (A.)	Durham			Radnor
Smith (H. G.)	Aberdeen			Fife
Smith (H. J. S.)	Cambs			Northampton
Smith (R. A.)	England (?)			Cork
Smith (S.)	Ayr			Lanark
Smith (T.)	England			France
Smith (W.)	Essex			Lancashire
Smith (W. R.)	Oxford			Gloucester
Smith (W. S.)				
Smollett	Dumbarton	Dumbarton		
Somers	Worcester		Aberdeen	Worcester
Somerville	Surrey [Yorks]		England	Scotland
South	Somerset			Kent
Southey	Norfolk [? Suffolk]			Hereford
Southwell	Somerset			Hereford
Speke	Norfolk			Norfolk
Spelman	Lancashire			Surrey
Spenser	Dorset			
Sprat	Derby			Dorset
Stanhope	Cheshire			Derby
Stanley				

	Paternal grandfather.	Paternal grandmother.	Maternal grandfather.	Maternal grandmother.
Steele	Dublin			Dublin [or Wexford]
Steevens				
Stephen		England		Dorset (?)
Stephenson	Scotland (?) and Northumberland	Aberdeen		Northumberland
Sterne	Notts [Suffolk] & Yorks			Ireland
Stevens				
Stevenson	Lanark	Dorset		Dorset
Stewart		Bute	Midlothian	Ayr
Stothard		Yorks		Shropshire
Stow		Worcester		
Street			England	
Stubbs			Lancs (?)	Lancs
Sturgeon		Dumfries		
Suckling		Norfolk		
Sullivan		Ireland		Italy
Swift	Yorks	Hereford		Leicester
Sydenham		Dorset [Somerset]		
Symonds	Shropshire	Oxford [Wales]		[Lancashire & Yorks]

	Paternal grand-father.	Paternal grand-mother.	Maternal grand-father.	Maternal grand-mother.
Tait	Aberdeen & Midlothian			
Tallis			England [? Essex]	
Tarleton	Lancs			
Taylor (H.)	Northumberland			Lancs
Taylor (J.)	Gloucester & Cambs			Durham
Taylor (W.)	Norfolk			Norfolk
Telford			Dumfries	
Temple	Warwick & Derby			Lancs (?) & Surrey
Tennyson	Lincoln			Lincoln
Thackeray	Yorks			
Thirlwall	Northumberland	Wilts		Radnor
Thomas			Radnor (?)	
Thompson	Roxburgh		Cork	Berwick
Thomson			Essex (?)	
Thurloe	Norfolk			
Thurlow	Cheshire			Suffolk, Yorks
Tillotson				
Toland			London-derry	
Tone	Kildare		England	
Tooke				

Surname	Paternal grandfather	Paternal grandmother	Maternal grandfather	Maternal grandmother
Trelawney	Cornwall			Cornwall
Trevithick	Cornwall			Cornwall
Trollope (A.)	Lincoln			
Trollope (H.)	Lincoln	Holland		
Tunstall	Lancs			
Turner	Devon			Yorks (?)
Tye				Notts (?)
Tyndale	Gloucester (?)	England		
Tyndall	Carlow [Glo'ster]			
Udall		Hants		
Urquhart	Cromarty			
Ussher		Ireland [England]		
Vanbrugh	Flanders [Huguenot]	Kent		England
Vane	Lincoln [or Notts]			Essex
Varley				Yorks
Vaughan	Brecknock			
Vere (F.)	Essex			Essex
Vere (H.)	Essex			Essex
Vernon	Cheshire & Staffs			
Wakley	Devon			

	Paternal grandfather.	Paternal grandmother.	Maternal grandfather.	Maternal grandmother.
Walker			England	
Wallace	Renfrew and Ayr [? Shropshire]			Ayr
Waller (E.)		Bucks		
Waller (W.)		Kent		
Wallis	Norfolk	Northants		
		Suffolk		
Walpole (H.)		Norfolk		Kent
Walpole (R.)		Kent [Norfolk]		Kent
Walsh			Kildare	Suffolk
Walsingham		Staffs	England	Herts
Walter		Cheshire		
Walton		Yorks		
Warburton		Herts	England	
Ward (M.)				
Ward (S.)				Yorks
Ward (W. G.)				
Warham		Hants		
Warton		Westmore-land		Surrey
Watson (R.)			England	
Watson (T.)		Aberdeen & Renfrew Lincoln [? & Essex]		Lanark
Watt				
Waynflete				

	Paternal grand-father.	Paternal grand-mother.	Maternal grand-father.	Maternal grand-mother.
Webster	Yorks			
Wedgwood	Staffs			Yorks
Wentworth	Armagh			Shropshire
Wesley (C.)	Devon [& Ireland]	Staffs		Warwick
Wesley (J.)	Devon [& Ireland]	Staffs		Warwick
Westmacott			England	
Whately	Surrey [and Oxford ?]			Herts
Wheatstone	Gloucester			
Whewell	Lancashire		England	
Whiston				
Whitbread	Beds			Bucks
White (G.)	Hants			Sussex
White (J. B.)	Waterford [Dublin]			Spain
Whitefield	Gloucester			
Whitehead			Westmoreland	
Whitelocke				Bucks
Whitgift	Lincoln			
Whittington	Glo'ster (?)			
Whitworth	Yorks and Lancashire			
Wilberforce (S.)	Yorks	Oxford		Warwick

	Paternal grand-father.	Paternal grand-mother.	Maternal grand-father.	Maternal grand-mother.
Wilberforce (W.)	Yorks			
Wilde	Ireland [Durham]	Galway		Oxford
Wilfrid	Beds			
Wilkes	Midlothian			
Wilkie	Oxford		England	Fife
Wilkins	Worcester & Dublin			Cheshire
Wilks				
Willet	France		England	Somerset (?)
William of Malmesbury				
William of Newburgh	Mon-mouth [Worcester]		Yorks	
Williams (C. H.)	Denbigh			Denbigh
Williams (D.)	Monmouth			
Williams (Sir R.)	Wales (?)			
Williams (R.)	Anglesey			Denbigh
Williams (W.)				

	Paternal grand-father.	Paternal grand-mother.	Maternal grand-father.	Maternal grand-mother.
Williamson (J.)	Yorks			Yorks
Williamson (W. C.)		Yorks	England	
Willoughby	Notts			
Wilson (J.)			Renfrew	Perth
Wilson (R.)				Flint
Wilson (Sir R.)	Yorks		Haddington	Cheshire
Wilson (T.)				Essex
Windham	Norfolk			Suffolk
Winthrop	Suffolk			
Winwood	Northants			
Wiseman	Waterford [settled in Spain]			Kilkenny
Wishart	Hants		Forfar	
Wilton	[Lancashire]			
Woffington			Ireland	
Wolcot	Ireland		Devon	
Wolfe	[Wales]			
Wollaston	Staffs			Yorks
Wolsey	[? & French Huguenot]		Suffolk	

	Paternal grandfather.	Paternal grandmother.	Maternal grandfather.	Maternal grandmother.
Woodward				
Woolner	Suffolk			
Wordsworth (Charles)	Yorks		Warwick [Montgomery]	Glo'ster
Wordsworth (Christopher)]	Yorks	England	Warwick [Montgomery]	Glo'ster
Wordsworth (W.)	Yorks			
Wotton (H.)	Kent			Kent
Wotton (N.)	Kent			Wilts
Wren	Warwick [Durham]			
Wright (J.)	Derby			
Wright (T.)	Yorks			
Wulfstan				
Wyatt	Kent (?)			
Wycherley	Shropshire	Warwick		Surrey
Wycliffe		Yorks		
Wykeham	Waterford	Hants		Waterford
Wyse				
Yates	Wilts			
Yorke	Suffolk	England (?)		Kent
Young (A.)				Holland
Young (E.)		England		
Young (T.)	Somerset			Somerset

APPENDIX C

OCCUPATION OR SOCIAL POSITION OF FATHERS

Abbot	. . .	clothworker
Abercromby	. .	upper class
Abington	soldier	cobbler
Adam	. .	architect
Adams	. .	farmer
Adamson	. .	baker
Addison	. .	Church
Airy	. . .	collector of excise
Alexander	. .	upper class
Allen	. .	upper class
Andrewes	. .	merchant and sea captain
Arblay, D'	.	musician and author
Arkwright	.	humble
Arne	. .	upholsterer
Armstrong	.	corn merchant
Arnold (M.)	.	schoolmaster
Arnold (T.)	.	collector of customs
Arthur	. .	official
Ascham	. .	yeoman
Atterbury	. .	Church
Austen	. .	Church
Bacon (A.)	.	upper class
Bacon (F.)	.	upper class
Bacon (N.)	.	sheepreeve
Bacon (R.)	.	upper class
Bagehot	. .	banker
Baillie	. .	minister *
Baily	. .	banker
Baker	. .	merchant
Balfour	. .	upper class
Bancroft	. .	upper class
Banim	farmer	trader
Banks (T.)	steward	surveyor
Bannister	. .	actor
Barbauld	. .	Church
Barclay (J.)	.	lawyer
Barclay (R.)	.	army

Barnes	. .	farmer
Barnfield	. .	upper class
Barrow (I.)	.	draper
Barrow (J.)	.	peasant
Barry (A.)	.	apothecary
Barry (C.)	.	stationer
Barry (E.)	.	lawyer
Barry (J.)	.	builder
Baskerville	.	humble
Bates	. .	manufacturer
Baxter	. .	yeoman
Beardsley	. .	brewery manager
Beaumont	upper class	lawyer
Beckford	upper class	commerce
Beddoes	. .	doctor
Bedell	. .	yeoman
Becher	. .	actor
Behn	. .	barber
Bell (A.)	. .	barber
Bell (C.)	. .	Church
Bennett	. .	musician
Benson	. .	manufacturer
Bentham (G.)	.	naval architect
Bentham (J.)	.	lawyer
Bentley	. .	yeoman
Bessemer	. .	engineer
Bethell	. .	doctor
Betterton	. .	cook
Bewick	. .	farmer
Birch	. .	Church
Bishop	. .	merchant
Black	. .	wine merchant
Blackmore	. .	Church
Blackstone	. .	silk mercer
Blake (R.)	.	merchant
Blake (W.)	.	hosier
Bonington	. .	governor of gaol
Bonner	. .	priest (?)
Booth	. .	upper class
Borrow	maltster	soldier

---

* 'Minister' is here throughout applied to all religious denominations except the Church of England. 'Priest' has reference to the Roman Catholic Church, whether before or since the Reformation.

Boscawen . . .	upper class
Boswel upper class	lawyer
Bowen . . .	Church
Bowring . . .	woollen trade
Boyce . . .	cabinet maker
Boyle (R.) . .	upper class
Bracegirdle . .	innkeeper
Bradford . .	yeoman
Bradlaugh . .	clerk
Bradley . . .	upper class
Bradshaw (H.) .	banker
Breton . . .	trade
Brewster . .	minister
Bright . . .	miller
Brontë (C.) . .	Church
Brontë (E.) . .	Church
Burke . . .	civil service
✦ Brown . . .	purser
Browne (R.) . .	upper class
Browne (T.) . .	mercer
Browning (R.) .	clerk
Bruce (H.) . .	upper class
Bruce (M.) . .	weaver
Buchanan . .	farmer
Buckle . . .	merchant
Bunyan . . .	whitesmith
Burke . . .	lawyer
Burne-Jones .	carver and gilder
Burnet upper class	lawyer
Burns . .	farmer
Burton (Sir Richard)	army
Butler (J.) . .	draper
Butler (S.) . .	farmer
Byng . . .	upper class
Byron . . .	upper class
Cadogan . .	lawyer
Cairns . . .	army
Calamy . .	minister
Camden . .	painter stainer
Campbell (C.) .	carpenter
Campbell (G.) .	upper class
Campbell (J.) .	minister
Campbell (T.) .	trade
Campion (E.) .	bookseller
Candlish . .	doctor
Canning (C.) .	upper class
Canning (G.) .	upper class
Canning (S.) .	banker
Cantelupe . .	upper class
Canton . .	business
Carey . .	schoolmaster
Carleton . .	peasant farmer
Carlile . .	shoemaker
Carlyle . . .	mason
Carpenter (M.) .	minister

Carpenter (W. B.)	minister
Carrington .	brewer
Carstares . .	minister
Case . . .	Church
Cattermole .	upper class
Cavendish (H.) .	upper class
Cavendish (M.)	upper class
Cavendish (T.) .	upper class
Cayley . . .	merchant
Cecil . . .	upper class
Challoner . .	wine cooper
Chalmers . .	merchant
Chantrey carpenter	farmer
Chatterton .	shoemaker
Chaucer . .	vintner
Chesney . .	army
Chichele yeoman	draper
Chichester .	upper class
Childers upper class	Church
Church . . .	merchant
Churchill (C.) .	Church
Churchill (J.) .	upper class
Cibber (C.) . .	sculptor
Cibber (S.) . .	upholsterer
Clapperton .	doctor
Clare . . .	labourer
Clive (R.) . .	upper class
Clough . .	cotton merchant
Cobbett . .	peasant
Cobden . .	yeoman
Cockburn . .	upper class
Cockerell . .	architect
Coke . . .	upper class
Colby . . .	army
Colebrooke .	banker
Colenso . .	mineral agent
Coleridge (H.) .	author
Coleridge (S.) .	Church
Colet . .	merchant
Collier . . .	Church
Collins (W.) .	hatter
Collins (W. W.) .	artist
Colman . .	upper class
Columba . .	upper class
Congreve . .	army
Conington . .	Church
Constable . .	miller
Cook . . .	agricultural labourer
Cooke (G.) . .	army
Cooke (H.) . .	farmer
Cooper (First Lord Shaftesbury) .	upper class
Cooper (Third Lord Shaftesbury) .	upper class
Cooper (A.) . .	Church

Copley (Lord Lynd- hurst)	. .	. artist	Drummond (T.)	.	lawyer
Cotes	. .	. Church	Drummond (W.)	.	upper class
Cotman	. .	. mercer	Dryden	. .	upper class
Cotton (A.)	. .	. upper class	Dudley	. .	upper class
Cotton (C.)	. .	. upper class	Du Mau-	upper class	glass mfr.
Cowley	. .	. trade	rier		
Cowper	upper class	Church	Dundas	upper class	lawyer
Cox	. . .	. blacksmith	Dunning	. .	lawyer
Cozens	. .	. artist	Dunstan	. .	upper class
Crabbe	. .	. collector of customs	Dyce	. .	. doctor
Crashaw	. .	. Church	Eastlake (C.)	.	admiralty agent
Crichton	. .	. upper class	Eastlake (Lady)	.	doctor
Croker	. .	. surveyor of customs	Edgeworth	.	upper class
			Edwardes	. .	Church
Crome	. .	. journeyman weaver	Edwards	. .	army
			Eliot	. .	upper class
Cromwell (O.)	.	. upper class	Elyot	. .	lawyer
Cromwell (T.)	blacksmith	innkeeper	Emlyn	. .	trade
Cross	. .	. carpenter	Erskine	. .	minister
Cruikshank	. .	. artist	Etherege	. .	army
Cudworth	. .	. Church	Etty	. . .	miller and baker
Cullen	. .	. lawyer			
Dalrymple	. .	. upper class	Fanshawe	. .	upper class
Dalton	. .	. weaver	Faraday	. .	smith
Dampier	. .	. farmer	Farquhar	. .	Church
Danby	. .	. farmer	Faucit	. .	actor
Daniel	. .	. music master	Fawcett	. .	draper
Darwin (C.)	. .	. doctor	Ferguson	. .	day labourer
D'Avenant	.	. vintner and innkeeper	Fergusson	. .	clerk
			Ferrar	. .	merchant
Davy	. .	. yeoman	Ferrier	. .	law
Dawson	. .	. cheesemonger	Fielding	upper class	army
Day	. . .	. collector of customs	Fitzgerald	.	upper class
			Fitzgibbon	. .	lawyer
Deane	. .	. upper class	Flamsteed	. .	maltster
De Foe	butcher	yeoman	Fletcher (A.)	.	upper class
De Morgan	. .	. army	Fletcher (J.)	.	Church
Dempster	. .	. upper class	Flinders	. .	doctor
Denham	. .	. upper class	Flood	. .	lawyer
Denman	. .	. doctor	Foote	. .	trade
De Quincey	.	. merchant	Forbes (E.)	.	banker
D'Ewes	. .	. upper class	Forbes (J.)	.	upper class
Dibdin	. .	. merchant	Ford	. . .	upper class
Dickens	. .	. clerk	Forster	. .	minister
Digby	. .	. upper class	Fox (C. J.)	.	upper class
Dobell	. .	. wine merchant	Fox (G.)	. .	weaver
Doddridge	. .	. oilman	Foxe (R.)	. .	yeoman
Dodgson	. .	. Church	Francis	. .	Church
Dodwell	. .	. army	Franklin	. .	trade
Dolben	. .	. Church	Franks	. .	navy
Donne	. .	. trade	Frere	. . .	ironmaster
Douglas	. .	. upper class	Froude	. .	Church
Doyle	. .	. artist	Fry	. . .	banker
Drake	. .	. upper class	Fuller	. . .	Church

Gainsborough .	. woollen manufacturer
Galt . . .	. sea captain
Gardiner .	. clothworker
Garrick .	. army
Gascoigne .	. upper class
Gaskell .	. minister
Gauntlett .	. Church
Geoffrey .	. priest
Gibbons .	. musician
Gibson .	. market gardener
Gifford .	. sailor
Gilbert (J.)	. estate agent
Gilbert (W.)	. recorder
Gillray .	. soldier
Giraldus .	. upper class
Girtin .	. rope-maker
Gladstone .	. merchant
Godwin (W.)	. minister
Goldsmith .	. Church
Gordon .	. army
Gower .	. upper class
Graham (G.)	. doctor
Graham (J.)	. upper class
Grattan .	. lawyer
Gray money scrivener lawyer	
Grenville (G.)	. upper class
Grenville (W.)	. upper class
Gresham .	. merchant
Grew .	. minister
Grey .	. army
Grote .	. banker
Hale . .	. lawyer
Hallam .	. Church
Halley .	. soap-boiler
Hamilton (A.)	. upper class
Hamilton (W.)	. doctor
Hamley .	. navy
Hampden .	. upper class
Hardinge .	. Church
Harrington .	. upper class
Hartley .	. Church
Harvey .	. yeoman
Havelock .	. shipbuilder
Hawke .	. lawyer
Hawkwood .	. tanner
Haydon .	. printer
Hazlitt .	. minister
Hemans .	. merchant
Henderson .	. farmer
Herbert (A.)	. lawyer
Herbert (E.)	. upper class
Herbert (G.)	. upper class
Herschel .	. man of science
Hickes .	. farmer

Hill . .	. schoolmaster
Hinton .	. minister
Hoadley Church	schoolmaster
Hobbes .	. Church
Hodgson .	. banker
Hogarth .	. yeoman
Hogg .	. farmer
Holcroft .	. shoemaker
Holl .	. engraver
Hood (S.) .	. Church
Hood (T.) .	. publisher
Hook (T.) .	. composer
Hook (W.) .	. Church
Hooke .	. Church
Horner .	. merchant
Horrocks .	. farmer
Hort .	. upper class
Howard .	. upholsterer
Howell .	. Church
Hughes .	. author
Hunter (J.)	. farmer
Hutcheson .	. minister
Hutton (J.)	. merchant
Hutton (R.)	. minister
Huxley .	. schoolmaster
Hyde .	. upper class
Inchbald .	. farmer
Irving .	. tanner
Jameson .	. artist
Jeffrey lawyer	(Clerk in court of sessions)
Jenner .	. Church
Jerrold .	. actor
Jervis upper class	lawyer
Jevons .	. nail maker
Johnson .	. trade
Johnston .	. trade
Jones (I.) .	. clothworker
Jones (W.)	. yeoman
Jonson .	. minister
Jordan .	. stage underling
Joule .	. brewer
Jowett .	. furrier
Keats .	. livery stableman
Keble .	. Church
Keene .	. law
Kemble (F.)	. actor
Kemble (J. M.)	. actor
Kemble (J. P.)	. actor
Kemp .	. upper class
Ken .	. lawyer
Kennett .	. Church

Kenyon	. .	. farmer	Lockhart	. .	. minister
Killigrew	.	. upper class	Lodge	. .	. grocer
King (T.)	. .	. trade	Lovelace	. .	. upper class
King (W.)	.	. miller	Lover	. .	. stockbroker
Kingsley (C.)	.	. Church	Lowe	. .	. Church
Kingsley (M.)	.	. doctor	Lowth	. .	. Church
Kirkcaldy	.	. upper class	Lucas	. .	. upper class
Knight	.	. Church	Ludlow	. .	. upper class
Knowles	.	. author	Lyell .	. .	. botanist
Knox	.	. peasant	Lytton (B.)	.	. army
			Lytton (Earl)	.	. upper class
Lancaster soldier		shopkeeper			
Lander	. .	. innkeeper	Macaulay	. .	. author
Landor	. .	. doctor	Macfarren	. .	. theatrical
Landseer	. .	. artist			manager
Lane	. .	. Church	Mackenzie	.	. doctor
Lardner	. .	. minister	Mackintosh	.	. army
Latimer	. .	. yeoman	Maclaurin	.	. minister
Laud .	. .	. clothier	Maclise soldier		shoemaker
Law (J.)	. .	. goldsmith	Macnaghten	.	. lawyer
Law (E., Baron .			Macready	.	. actor-manager
Ellenborough)		. Church	Maginn	. .	. schoolmaster
Law (E., Earl of			Maine	. .	. doctor
Ellenborough)		. upper class	Malthus	. .	. author
Law (W.)	. .	. grocer	Manning	. .	. merchant
Lawes (H.)	.	. musician	Marlowe	. .	. shoemaker
Lawes (J.)	.	. upper class	Marsh	. .	. Church
Lawrence (H.)	.	. army	Marshall	. .	. poor glover
Lawrence (J.)	.	. army	Marston	. .	. lawyer
Lawrence (S.)	.	. trade	Marten	. .	. lawyer
Lawrence (T.)	.	. innkeeper	Martineau (H.)	.	. manufacturer
Layard	. .	. civil service	Martineau (J.)	.	. manufacturer
Leake	. .	. naval gunner	Marvell	. .	. Church
Lee	. .	. Church	Mathews (C.) bookseller		minister
Leech.	.	. coffee house	Mathews (C. J.)		. actor
		keeper	Maurice	. .	. minister
Lefroy	. .	. Church	Mead	. .	. minister
Leighton (F.)	.	. doctor	Merivale	. .	. lawyer
Leighton (R.)	.	. doctor	Middleton (C.)	.	. Church
Leslie (A.) upper class		army	Mill (J.)	. .	. shoemaker
Leslie (C.)	.	. Church	Mill (J. S.)	.	. author
Leslie (J.) upper class		Church	Miller	. .	. captain of
L'Estrange	.	. upper class			sloop
Lever	. .	. builder	Milman	. .	. doctor
Lewis (G. C.)	.	. upper class	Milner (I.)	.	. business
Lewis (J. F.)	.	. engraver	Milner (J.)	.	. tailor
Lewis (W. T.)	.	. actor	Milton scrivener		yeoman (?)
Liddon	. .	. navy	Mitford	. .	. upper class
Lightfoot	.	. accountant	Moffat	. .	. custom house
Lillo .	. .	. jeweller	Monck	. .	. upper class
Lingard	. .	. carpenter	Monson	. .	. upper class
Linnell	. .	. wood carver	Montagu (E.)	.	. upper class
Linton (E.)	.	. Church	Montagu (R.)	.	. Church
Lister	. .	. wine merchant	Moore (J.) doctor		author
Livingstone	.	. small tea dealer	Moore (T.)	.	. provision
Lloyd	. .	. Church			dealer
Locke	. .	. lawyer	More (T.) .	.	. lawyer

Morgan (G. O.) .	. Church
Morgan (H.) .	. upper class
Morgan (S.) .	. actor
Morland (G.) .	. artist
Morland (S.) .	. Church
Morris .	. bill broker
Morley .	. upper class
Morton .	. mercer
Mulready .	. leather breeches maker
Mun .	. merchant
Munday .	. draper
Munden .	. poulterer
Munro .	. merchant
Murchison .	. doctor
Murdock .	. millwright
Murray .	. publisher
Myers .	. Church
Nairne .	. upper class
Napier (C.) .	. upper class
Napier (C. J.) upper class army
Napier (J.) .	. upper class
Napier (Sir J.) .	. merchant
Napier (R.) .	. army
Napier (W. J. P.) upper class army
Nash .	. Church
Nasmyth (J.) .	. artist
Nasmyth (P.) .	. artist
Naylor .	. yeoman
Neale (E.) .	. Church
Neale (J.) .	. Church
Neill .	. army
Neilson (J.) .	. millwright
Nelson .	. Church
Newman (F. W.)	. banker
Newman (J. H.)	. banker
Newton .	. yeoman farmer
Nicholson .	. doctor
Northcote .	. watchmaker
Norton .	. business
Nott .	. yeoman farmer
Oglethorpe .	. army
Oldcastle .	. upper class
Oldfield .	. army
Oldys .	. lawyer
Oliphant (L.) .	. lawyer
Oliphant (M.) .	. business
O'Neill .	. upper class
Opie (A.) .	. doctor
Opie (J.) .	. carpenter
Ordericus .	. priest (married)
Otway .	. Church
Oughtred .	. Church
Outram .	. civil engineer

Owen (J.) .	. Church
Owen (Sir R.) .	. merchant
Owen (R.) .	. saddler
Paget (J.) brewer	shipowner
Paine .	. farmer
Paley .	. Church
Palmer (E. H.) .	. schoolmaster
Palmer (J.) .	. soldier
Palmer (R.) .	. Church
Palmer (S.) .	. bookseller
Park .	. farmer
Parker (M.) .	calenderer of stuffs
Parker (T.) .	. lawyer
Parkes (H.) .	. farmer
Parkes (H. S.) .	. ironmaster
Parnell .	. upper class
Parr .	. doctor
Parsons (R.) yeoman	blacksmith
Parsons (W.) .	. carpenter
Pater .	. doctor
Patmore .	. author
Patrick .	. deacon (married)
Pattison .	. Church
Pearson (J.) .	. Church
Pearson (J. L.) .	. artist
Peel .	. manufacturer
Peele .	. business
Pellew .	. sea captain
Penn (Sir W.) merchant	sea captain
Penn (W.) .	. navy
Pepys .	. tailor
Perry .	. builder
Petty .	. clothier
Phelps .	. outfitter
Phillip .	. soldier
Pitman .	. factory over-seer
Pitt (W., Earl of Chatham) .	. upper class
Pitt (W.) .	. upper class
Pollock .	. saddler
Pope .	. merchant
Porson .	. weaver
Pott .	. lawyer (scrivener)
Powell .	. ale keeper
Pratt .	. lawyer
Preston .	. farmer
Prestwich .	. wine merchant
Price .	. minister
Priestley .	. cloth dresser
Prior .	. joiner
Pugin .	. architect
Pulteney .	. upper class
Purcell .	. music copyist

Pusey	. upper class	Simpson	. baker
		Sinclair	. upper class
Quarles	. upper class	Smart	. nobleman's steward
Quin .	. lawyer		
		Smith (A.)	. lawyer
Radcliffe	. trade	Smith (H. J. S.).	. lawyer
Raeburn	. mill owner	Smith (S.) .	. business
Raffles	. sea captain	Smith (T.)	. upper class
Raleigh	. upper class	Smith (W.)	. farmer
Randolph	. steward	Smith (W. R.) .	. minister
Ray .	. blacksmith	Smith (W. S.)	. army
Reid (T.)	. minister	Somers	. lawyer
Reid (W.)	. minister	Somerville .	. navy
Reynolds	. Church	South	. merchant
Richardson	. carpenter	Southey	. farmer
Ritson	. yeoman	Southwell .	. upper class
Robertson	. minister	Speke	. army
Robinson	. navy	Spelman	. upper class
Rogers	. merchant	Spenser	. cloth maker
Romney	. builder and cabinet maker	Sprat	. Church
		Stanhope	. upper class
Roscoe market gardener	tavern keeper	Stanley	. Church
		Steele	. lawyer
Rose .	. Church	Stephen	. official
Ross (H. D.)	. army	Stephenson	. fireman
Ross (R.) .	. army	Sterne	. army
Rossetti (C.).	. opera librettist, etc.	Steevens	. house painter
		Stevens	. sea captain
Rossetti (D. G.)	. opera librettist, etc.	Stevenson .	. engineer
		Stewart	. minister
Rowe	. lawyer	Stothard	. publican
Rowlandson	. merchant	Street	. lawyer
Ruskin	. wine merchant	Stubbs	. currier
		Sturgeon	. shoemaker
Sadler	. upper class	Suckling	. upper class
St. John	. upper class	Sullivan	. musician
St. Leger	. upper class	Sydenham .	. upper class
Sale .	. army	Symonds	. doctor
Sancroft	. yeoman		
Scott (D.)	. engraver	Tait .	. upper class
Scott (G. G.)	. Church	Tarleton	. merchant
Scott (J.)	. coal factor	Taylor (H.)	. upper class
Scott (Walter)	. lawyer	Taylor (J.)	. barber surgeon
Scott (William)	. coal factor	Taylor (W.)	. manufacturer
Sedgwick	. Church	Telford	. shepherd
Seeley	. publisher	Temple	. upper class
Selden	. yeoman	Tennyson .	. Church
Shakespeare yeoman	trade	Thirlwall .	. Church
Sharp	. salter	Thompson .	. upper class
Sheil	. upper class	Thomson .	. minister
Sheldon	. menial servant	Thurloe	. Church
		Thurlow	. Church
Shelley	. upper class	Tillotson .	. clothworker
Sheridan	. actor	Toland	. priest
Siddons	. actor	Tone .	. coach maker
Sidgwick	. Church	Tooke	. poulterer
Sidney	. upper class	Trelawney .	. army

Trevithick	. .	mine manager of humble origin
Trollope (A.)	. .	lawyer
Trollope (H.)	. .	Church
Tunstall	. .	upper class
Turner	. .	barber
Tyndall	. .	upper class
Urquhart	. .	upper class
Ussher	. .	lawyer
Vanburgh	. .	sugar baker
Vane	. .	upper class
Varley	. .	tutor
Vaughan	. .	upper class
Vere (F.)	. .	upper class
Vere (H.)	. .	upper class
Vernon	. .	upper class
Walker	. .	working jeweller
Wallace	. .	upper class
Waller (E.)	. .	upper class
Waller (W.)	. .	upper class
Wallis	. .	Church
Walpole (H.)	. .	upper class
Walpole (R.)	. .	upper class
Walsingham	. .	lawyer
Walter	. .	coal merchant
Walton	. .	yeoman
Warburton	. .	town clerk
Ward (M.).	. .	upper class
Ward (S.)	. .	lawyer
Ward (W. G.)	. .	financier
Warham	. .	upper class
Warton	. .	author
Watson (R.)	. .	Church
Watt	. .	carpenter
Webster	. .	actor and musical composer
Wedgwood	. .	potter
Wentworth	. .	doctor
Wesley (C.)	. .	Church
Wesley (J.)	. .	Church
Westmacott	. .	sculptor
Whately	. .	Church
Wheatstone	. .	music seller
Whewell	. .	carpenter
Whiston	. .	Church
Whitbread	. .	brewer

White (G.).	. .	lawyer
White (J. B.)	. .	merchant
Whitefield	. .	innkeeper
Whitelocke	. .	lawyer
Whitgift	. .	merchant
Whitworth	. .	minister
Wilberforce (W.)	.	upper class
Wilde	. .	doctor
Wilfrid	. .	upper class
Wilkes	. .	malt distiller
Wilkie	. .	minister
Wilkins	. .	goldsmith
Willett	. .	lawyer
Williams (C. H.)		manufacturer
Williams (Sir R.)		upper class
Williams (R.)	. .	tailor
Williams (W.)	. .	Church
Williamson (J.)	. .	Church
Williamson (W.)	.	gardener
Wilson (J.)	. .	manufacturer
Wilson (R.)	. .	Church
Wilson (R. T.)	. .	artist
Windham	. .	army
Winthrop	. .	lawyer
Wiseman	. .	merchant
Woffington	. .	bricklayer
Wolcot	. .	doctor
Wolfe	. .	army
Wollaston	. .	Church
Wolsey	. .	grazier
Woodward	. .	tallow chandler
Woolner	. .	post office official
Wordsworth (Chas.)	.	Church
Wordsworth (Christopher)	.	Church
Wordsworth (W.)	.	lawyer
Wotton (H.)	. .	upper class
Wotton (N.)	. .	upper class
Wren	. .	Church
Wright (J.)	. .	lawyer
Wright (T.)	. .	printer
Wulfstan	. .	upper class
Wyatt	. .	upper class
Wycherley	. .	lawyer
Yates	. .	ship's steward
Yorke	. .	lawyer
Young (A.)	. .	Church
Young (E.)	. .	Church

APPENDIX D

STATURE

5 ft. 0 in. . . . . { W. Blake / T. Moore

5 ft. 1 in. . . . . { Caius / H. Coleridge / Keats

5 ft. 2 in. . . . . Hunter

5 ft. 3 in. . . . . { De Quincey / G. White / S. Wilberforce

5 ft. 4 in. . . . . Nelson

5 ft. 5 in. . . . . { Linnell / Richardson

5 ft. 6 in. . . . . { Cockburn / R. Fergusson / Jeffrey* / B. Lytton / J. Wesley

5 ft. 7 in. . . . . { Bright / Madox Brown / Maurice / C. J. Napier / Otway

5 ft. 8 in. . . . { Byron / T. Lawrence / Macaulay / J. S. Mill / Rossetti / Swift † / Tooke

5 ft. 9 in. . . . . { Burns / S. Coleridge / Dickens / Gordon / Paine / Priestley / W. Wordsworth

5 ft. 10 in. . . . { Burke / O. Cromwell / Grote / Hogg / Huxley / Kenyon / Marryat / C. Mathews

5 ft. 10 in. . . . { Mulready / Prestwich / Ruskin / Stevenson / Street / A. Trollope / Wakley

5 ft. 11 in. . . . { Sir R. Burton / Carleton / Carlyle / Froude / Liston / O'Connell / Porson / Sedgwick / Southey / J. Wilson.

6 ft. 0 in. . . . . { R. Boyle / Clapperton / C. Darwin / Millais / W. J. Napier / Park / W. Scott / Selden / Tait

6 ft. 1 in. . . . . { Cobbett / J. Cook / Fielding / Galt / Hobbes / Leech / Petty / Reade / Tennyson

6 ft. 2 in. . . . . Trevithick

6 ft. 3 in. . . . . { Borrow / Fawcett / Irving ‡ / Thackeray

6 ft. 4 in. . . . . { J. Bruce / Duncan / Graham

---

* According to one description Jeffrey was 'scarcely five feet.'
† It is worth noting that Swift was considered tall by his contemporaries.
‡ The estimates of Irving's height vary between 6 ft. 2 in. and 6 ft. 4 in.

APPENDIX E

PIGMENTATION

THE individuals whose pigmentation I have been able to ascertain are here arranged alphabetically in their groups: Fair, Medium, Dark. To facilitate reference no note is here taken of the three sub-divisions of the medium group.

I. — FAIR

Addison, Amherst, Arkwright, Beaton, Berkeley, Blackmore, Bright, Brown, Buchanan, C. Campbell, J. Campbell, S. Canning, Cantelupe, Clifford, Congreve, Copley (Lord Lyndhurst), Cowper, Cullen, Dee, Denham, Etty, Fergusson, Fitzgerald, A. Fletcher, J. Fletcher, Freeman, Frobisher, Gordon, Gray, Hardinge, Hogarth, Hogg, Hort, Hutcheson, A. Leslie, B. Lytton, Earl Lytton, Munden, Newton, H. S. Parkes, Peel, Pellew, Sir W. Penn, Pusey, Randolph, Richardson, Ruskin, Sabine, Shelley, A. Smith, Smollett, Street, Thackeray, Tooke, Trevithick, Turner, Tyndall, Vane, Wakley, Walker, W. Waller, Wallis, Westmacott, Whitefield, Whitgift, J. Wilson, Wolfe.

II. — MEDIUM

Anson, M. Arnold, Austen, Austin, F. Bacon, N. Bacon, Baillie, Bancroft, J. Banks, Barnes, I. Barrow, J. Barrow, E. Barry, J. Barry,* Becher, C. Brontë, Bennett, J. Bentham, Bentley, Bewick, Blackstone, W. Blake, Bonington, Boscawen, Boswell, Bowring, R. Boyle, Bradley, H. Bradshaw, Brewster, Brougham, E. Browning, R. Browning, Burbage, Burke, Burns, S. Butler, Byng, Byron, Cadogan, T. Campbell, Canton, Carlyle, M. Carpenter, Cayley, Cecil, Chalmers, Chantrey, Chatterton, Chaucer, Chillingworth, C. Churchill, C. Cibber, Clark, R. Clive, Cobbett, Cockburn, Coke, S. Coleridge, William Collins, Colman, Cooper (First Lord Shaftesbury), R. Cotton, A. Cowley, Crabbe, Cranmer, Crichton, Croker, O. Cromwell, Cross, Cruikshank, C. Darwin, E. Darwin, Davy, Defoe, Denman, De Quincey, Dickens, Dobson, Dryden, Flaxman, Flowers, C. J. Fox, Francis, Fry, Gainsborough, Gifford, Girtin, Gladstone, Goldsmith, G. Graham, Grattan, Grote, Harrington, Harvey, Hastings, Haydon, Hazlitt, Hill, Hoadley, Hobbes, Holcroft, T. Hood, Hooke, Horner, J. Hunter, Huxley, Hyde, Inchbald, Jenner, Jerrold, Jervis, Johnson, I. Jones, Jonson, Jowett, Keats, F. Kemble, Kenyon, Knox, Lambert, Lander, Landon, Landor, Landseer, E. Law (Baron Ellenborough), J. Law, W. Law, Latimer, H. Lawrence, J. Lawrence, S. Lawrence, Leech, J. Leslie, Lever, G. H. Lewes, Livingstone, Locke, Macaulay, Mackenzie, Mackintosh, Maclise, Macready, Maginn, Malone, Manning, Marryat, H. Martineau, J. Martineau, Mead, C. Middleton, J. S. Mill, Millais, Miller, Milton, Mitford, C. Montagu, T. More, G. Morland, Morris, Murchison, C. Napier, C. J. Napier, Nelson, J. H. Newman, O'Connell, Oldfield, A. Opie, J. Opie, Sir R. Owen, R. Owen, W. Paget,

---

* I have since noted that in his own portrait of himself Barry's eyes are blue and hair light.

Paine, Park, Patmore, Pepys, Petty, Perkins, Pitt (Lord Chatham), Pitt, Pococke, Pope, Popham, Pratt, Priestley, Prior, Pulteney, Raffles, Reynolds, Rogers, Roscoe, Rose, C. Rossetti, D. G. Rossetti, Sancroft, J. Scott, Walter Scott, William Scott, Selden, Shakespeare, Sidgwick, Sidney, Sinclair, Smart, W. S. Smith, Somers, Somerville, Spelman, Spenser, Stanley, Stephenson, Stewart, Stothard, Suckling, Swift, Sydenham, Tait, H. Taylor, Thomson, Thurloe, H. Vere, E. Waller, R. Walpole, Warburton, Warham, Watt, J. Wesley, Whiston, G. White, S. Wilberforce, W. Wilberforce, Wilde, Wilkie, C. H. Williams, W. Williamson, Wolcot, W. Wordsworth, Wren, Wyatt, Wycherley.

III. — DARK

Abercromby, Babbage, Bagehot, Baxter, Betterton, Bishop, Black, Borrow, Bracegirdle, J. Bruce, Burnet, Burton (Sir R.), Camden, J. Churchill, S. Cibber, Cobden, H. Coleridge, J. Cook, Crome, T. Cromwell, Curran, Dampier, Day, Dempster, Dibdin, Digby, Dolben, W. Drummond, Faraday, Ferrier, Fielding, J. Foxe, Froude, Galt, Garrick, Gay, Gibson, M. Godwin, Grenville (Baron), Gresham, Hale, Henderson, E. Herbert, T. Hook, Hooker, Howard, Hunt, Ireton, Irving, Jeffrey, Jewel, Juxon, Kean, Keble, Keene, J. M. Kemble, J. P. Kemble, Ken, Lamb, Lancaster, Laud, T. Lawrence, A. Leslie, Lovelace, Marvell, Melville, J. Milner, J. Moore, T. Moore, H. More, L. A. Neilson, Nicholson, Northcote, M. Oliphant, Otway, Oughtred, Outram, J. Owen, Paley, Parr, R. Parsons, Phillip, Picton, Prestwich, Quarles, Raleigh, Raeburn, Ray, Reade, R. Reid, Ridley, Romney, Sedgwick, Sheridan, Siddons, S. Smith, Southey, Steele, Steevens, Stevenson, Symonds, J. Taylor, Temple, Tennyson, Thurlow, Tillotson, Ussher, H. Walpole, Whitelocke, J. Williamson, Windham, Winwood, Wishart, Woffington, Wolsey, J. Wright, Yates.

INDEX